WRITER: **JONATHAN HICKMAN**

PENCILER: **LEINIL FRANCIS YU**

INKERS: **GERRY ALANGUILAN** [#18-22] & **LEINIL FRANCIS YU** [#23]

COLORIST, #18-19 & #21-23: **SUNNY GHO** WITH **DAVID CURIEL** [#22] & **PAUL MOUNTS** [#23]

COLORIST, #20: **DAVID CURIEL**

LETTERER: **VC'S CORY PETIT**

COVER ART: **LEINIL FRANCIS YU & LAURA MARTIN**

ASSISTANT EDITOR: **JAKE THOMAS**

EDITORS: **TOM BREVOORT WITH LAUREN SANKOVITCH**

COLLECTION EDITOR: **JENNIFER GRÜNWALD**
ASSISTANT EDITOR: **SARAH BRUNSTAD**
ASSOCIATE MANAGING EDITOR: **ALEX STARBUCK**
EDITOR, SPECIAL PROJECTS: **MARK D. BEAZLEY**
SENIOR EDITOR, SPECIAL PROJECTS: **JEFF YOUNGQUIST**
SVP PRINT, SALES & MARKETING: **DAVID GABRIEL**

EDITOR IN CHIEF: **AXEL ALONSO**
CHIEF CREATIVE OFFICER: **JOE QUESADA**
PUBLISHER: **DAN BUCKLEY**
EXECUTIVE PRODUCER: **ALAN FINE**

AVENGERS VOL. 4: INFINITY. Contains material originally published in magazine form as AVENGERS #18-23. First printing 2014. ISBN# 978-0-7851-8415-7. Published by MARVEL WORLDWIDE, INC., a subsidiary of MARVEL ENTERTAINMENT, LLC. OFFICE OF PUBLICATION: 135 West 50th Street, New York, NY 10020. Copyright © 2013 and 2014 Marvel Characters, Inc. All rights reserved. All characters featured in this issue and the distinctive names and likenesses thereof, and all related indicia are trademarks of Marvel Characters, Inc. No similarity between any of the names, characters, persons, and/or institutions in this magazine with those of any living or dead person or institution is intended, and any such similarity which may exist is purely coincidental. **Printed in the U.S.A.** ALAN FINE, EVP - Office of the President, Marvel Worldwide, Inc. and EVP & CMO Marvel Characters B.V.; DAN BUCKLEY, Publisher & President - Print, Animation & Digital Divisions; JOE QUESADA, Chief Creative Officer; TOM BREVOORT, SVP of Publishing; DAVID BOGART, SVP of Operations & Procurement, Publishing; C.B. CEBULSKI, SVP of Creator & Content Development; DAVID GABRIEL, SVP Print, Sales & Marketing; JIM O'KEEFE, VP of Operations & Logistics; DAN CARR, Executive Director of Publishing Technology; SUSAN CRESPI, Editorial Operations Manager; ALEX MORALES, Publishing Operations Manager; STAN LEE, Chairman Emeritus. For information regarding advertising in Marvel Comics or on Marvel.com, please contact Niza Disla, Director of Marvel Partnerships, at ndisla@marvel.com. For Marvel subscription inquiries, please call 800-217-9158. **Manufactured between 7/25/2014 and 9/1/2014** by R.R. DONNELLEY, INC., SALEM, VA, USA.

10 9 8 7 6 5 4 3 2 1

"AVENGERS UNIVERSE 1"

PREVIOUSLY IN INFINITY

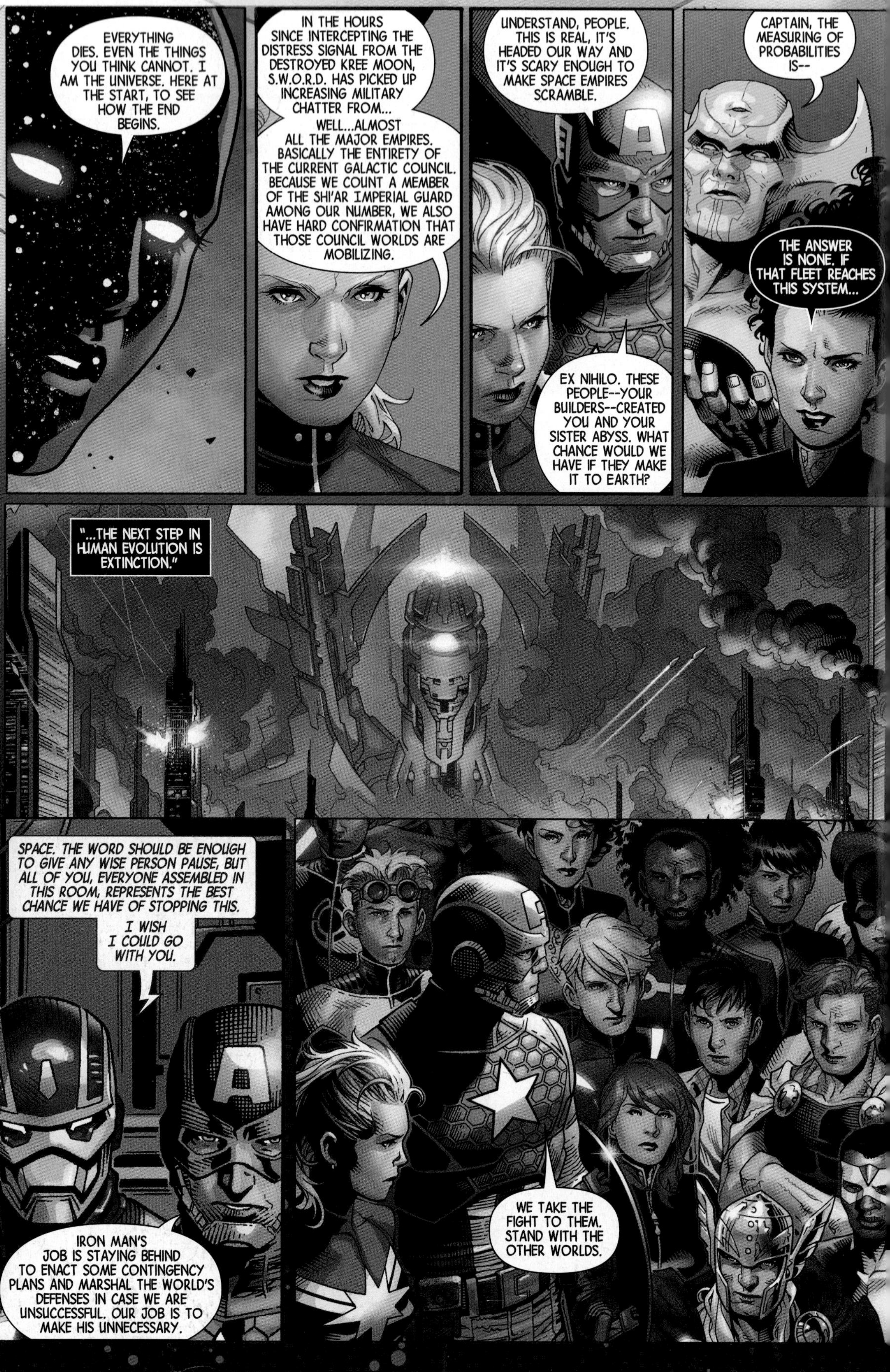
EVERYTHING DIES. EVEN THE THINGS YOU THINK CANNOT. I AM THE UNIVERSE. HERE AT THE START, TO SEE HOW THE END BEGINS.
IN THE HOURS SINCE INTERCEPTING THE DISTRESS SIGNAL FROM THE DESTROYED KREE MOON, S.W.O.R.D. HAS PICKED UP INCREASING MILITARY CHATTER FROM...
WELL...ALMOST ALL THE MAJOR EMPIRES. BASICALLY THE ENTIRETY OF THE CURRENT GALACTIC COUNCIL. BECAUSE WE COUNT A MEMBER OF THE SHI'AR IMPERIAL GUARD AMONG OUR NUMBER, WE ALSO HAVE HARD CONFIRMATION THAT THOSE COUNCIL WORLDS ARE MOBILIZING.
UNDERSTAND, PEOPLE. THIS IS REAL, IT'S HEADED OUR WAY AND IT'S SCARY ENOUGH TO MAKE SPACE EMPIRES SCRAMBLE.
EX NIHILO. THESE PEOPLE--YOUR BUILDERS--CREATED YOU AND YOUR SISTER ABYSS. WHAT CHANCE WOULD WE HAVE IF THEY MAKE IT TO EARTH?
CAPTAIN, THE MEASURING OF PROBABILITIES IS--
THE ANSWER IS NONE. IF THAT FLEET REACHES THIS SYSTEM...
"...THE NEXT STEP IN HUMAN EVOLUTION IS EXTINCTION."
SPACE. THE WORD SHOULD BE ENOUGH TO GIVE ANY WISE PERSON PAUSE, BUT ALL OF YOU, EVERYONE ASSEMBLED IN THIS ROOM, REPRESENTS THE BEST CHANCE WE HAVE OF STOPPING THIS.
I WISH I COULD GO WITH YOU.
IRON MAN'S JOB IS STAYING BEHIND TO ENACT SOME CONTINGENCY PLANS AND MARSHAL THE WORLD'S DEFENSES IN CASE WE ARE UNSUCCESSFUL. OUR JOB IS TO MAKE HIS UNNECESSARY.
WE TAKE THE FIGHT TO THEM. STAND WITH THE OTHER WORLDS.

CAST

THE AVENGERS

QUINCRUISER 1

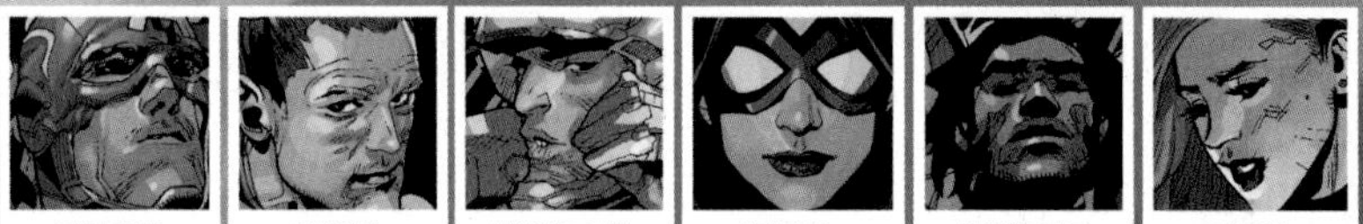

CAPTAIN AMERICA · BRUCE BANNER (HULK) · SHANG-CHI · SPIDER-WOMAN · MANIFOLD · BLACK WIDOW

QUINCRUISER 2

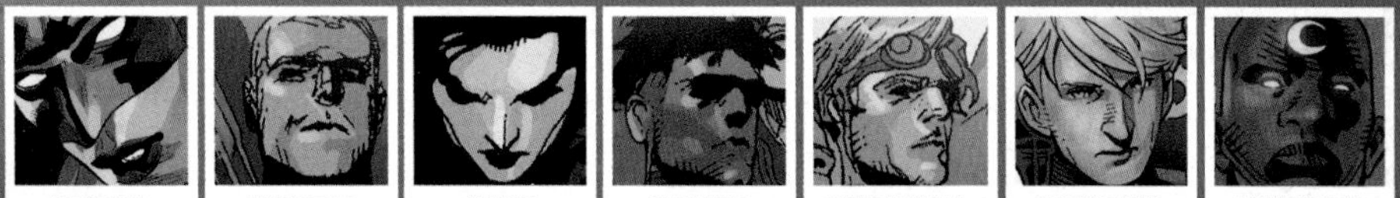

CAPTAIN MARVEL · HAWKEYE · ABYSS · SUNSPOT · CANNONBALL · STARBRAND · NIGHTMASK

FREE-FLYING

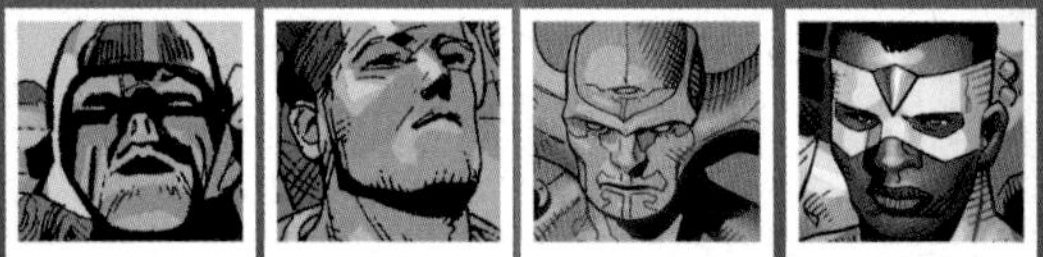

THOR · HYPERION · EX NIHILO · FALCON

THE BUILDERS

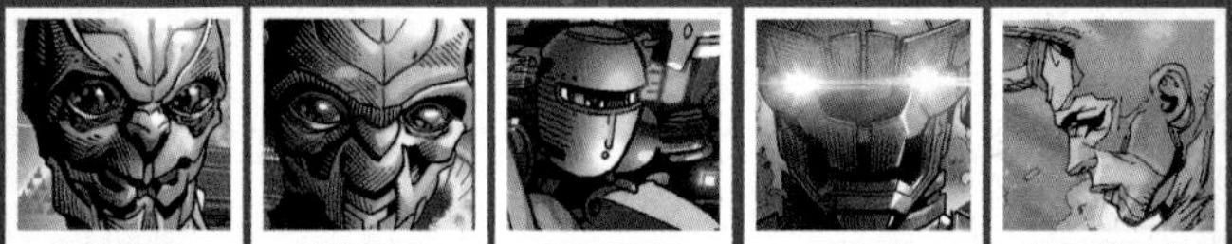

BUILDERS-CREATORS · BUILDERS-ENGINEERS · CURATORS · ALEPHS · GARDENERS

THE GALACTIC COUNCIL

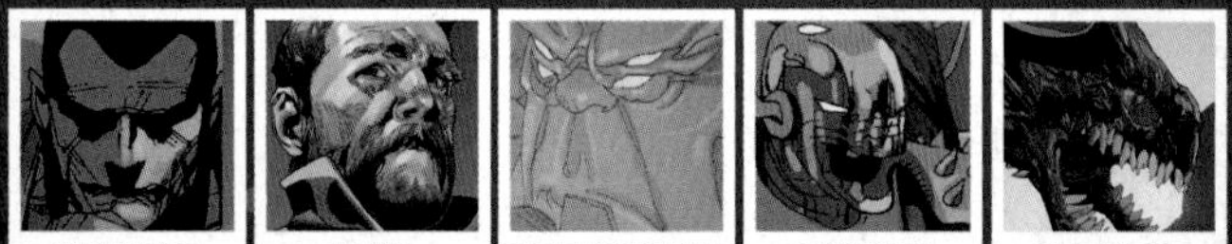

GLADIATOR · J-SON OF SPARTAX · KREE SUPREME INTELLIGENCE · ANNIHILUS · QUEEN OF THE BROOD

SHI'AR IMPERIAL GUARD

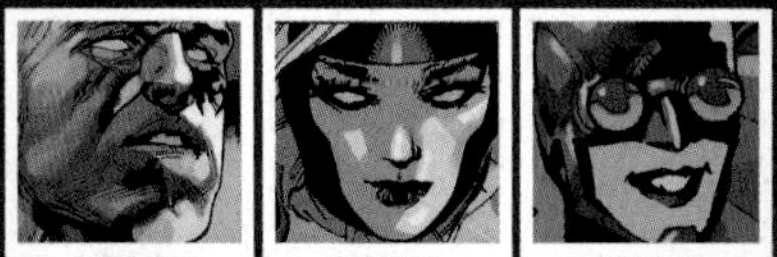

MENTOR · ORACLE · SMASHER

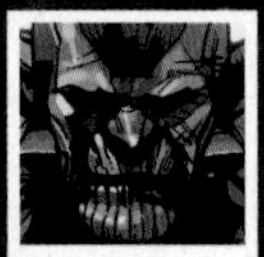

KL'RT, SUPER-SKRULL

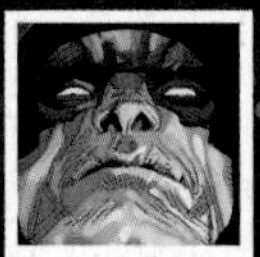

RONAN THE ACCUSER

WORLDS RISE

◆

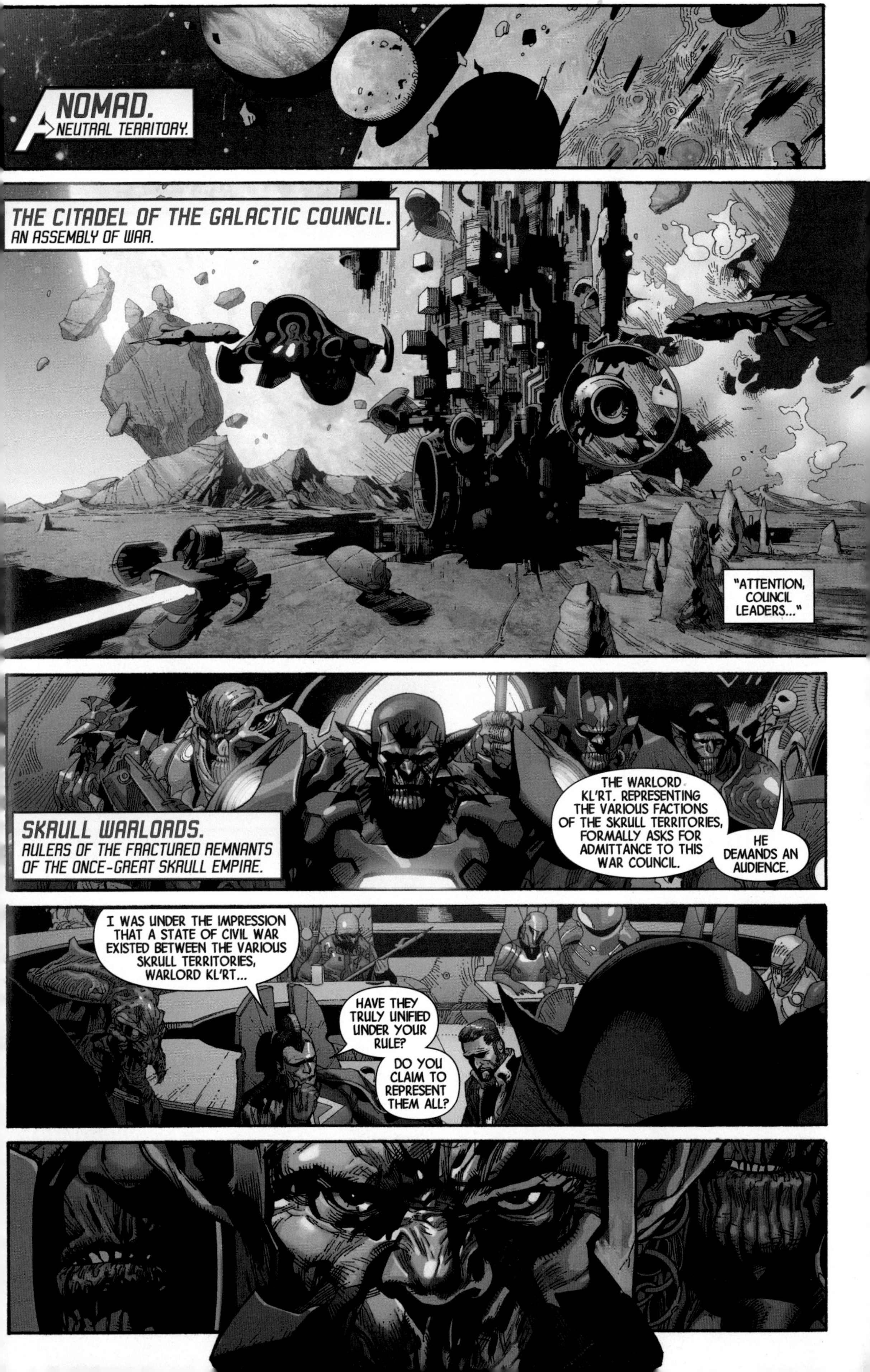
NOMAD.
NEUTRAL TERRITORY.
THE CITADEL OF THE GALACTIC COUNCIL.
AN ASSEMBLY OF WAR.
"ATTENTION, COUNCIL LEADERS..."
SKRULL WARLORDS.
RULERS OF THE FRACTURED REMNANTS OF THE ONCE-GREAT SKRULL EMPIRE.
THE WARLORD KL'RT, REPRESENTING THE VARIOUS FACTIONS OF THE SKRULL TERRITORIES, FORMALLY ASKS FOR ADMITTANCE TO THIS WAR COUNCIL.
HE DEMANDS AN AUDIENCE.
I WAS UNDER THE IMPRESSION THAT A STATE OF CIVIL WAR EXISTED BETWEEN THE VARIOUS SKRULL TERRITORIES, WARLORD KL'RT...
HAVE THEY TRULY UNIFIED UNDER YOUR RULE?
DO YOU CLAIM TO REPRESENT THEM ALL?

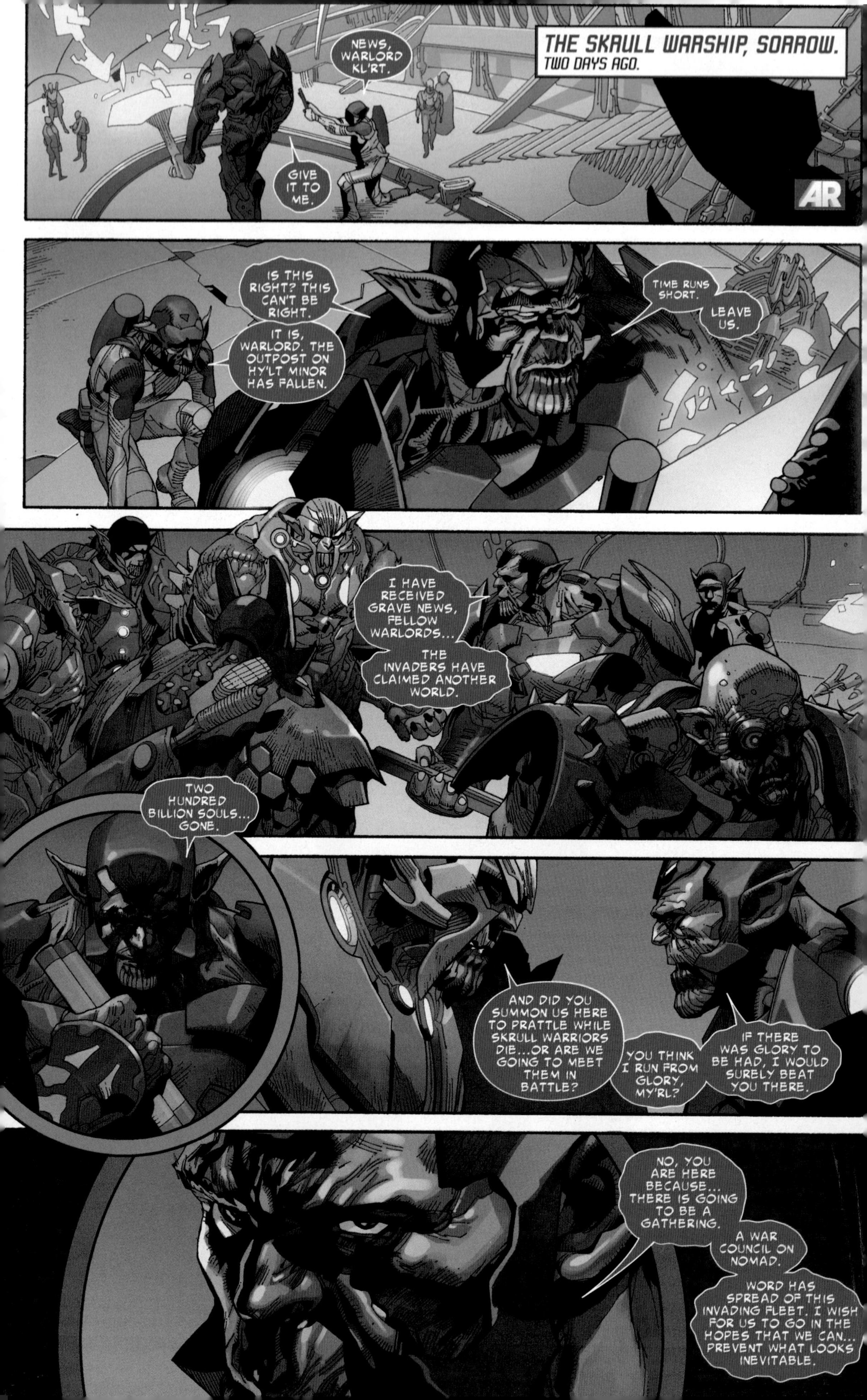
THE SKRULL WARSHIP, SORROW.
TWO DAYS AGO.
NEWS, WARLORD KL'RT.
GIVE IT TO ME.
AR
IS THIS RIGHT? THIS CAN'T BE RIGHT.
IT IS, WARLORD. THE OUTPOST ON HY'LT MINOR HAS FALLEN.
TIME RUNS SHORT.
LEAVE US.
I HAVE RECEIVED GRAVE NEWS, FELLOW WARLORDS...
THE INVADERS HAVE CLAIMED ANOTHER WORLD.
TWO HUNDRED BILLION SOULS... GONE.
AND DID YOU SUMMON US HERE TO PRATTLE WHILE SKRULL WARRIORS DIE...OR ARE WE GOING TO MEET THEM IN BATTLE?
YOU THINK I RUN FROM GLORY, MY'RL?
IF THERE WAS GLORY TO BE HAD, I WOULD SURELY BEAT YOU THERE.
NO, YOU ARE HERE BECAUSE... THERE IS GOING TO BE A GATHERING.
A WAR COUNCIL ON NOMAD.
WORD HAS SPREAD OF THIS INVADING FLEET. I WISH FOR US TO GO IN THE HOPES THAT WE CAN... PREVENT WHAT LOOKS INEVITABLE.

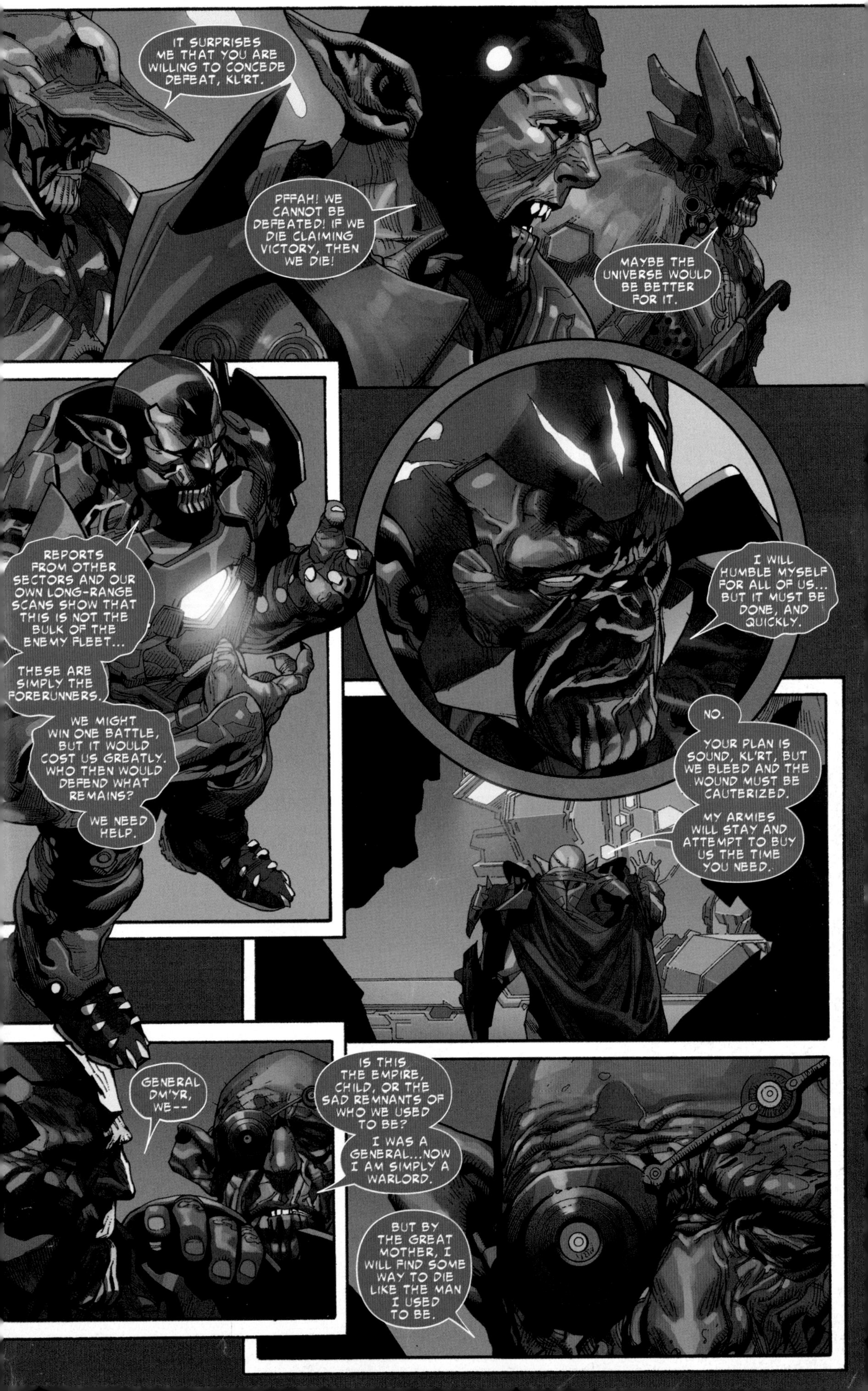
IT SURPRISES ME THAT YOU ARE WILLING TO CONCEDE DEFEAT, KL'RT.
PFFAH! WE CANNOT BE DEFEATED! IF WE DIE CLAIMING VICTORY, THEN WE DIE!
MAYBE THE UNIVERSE WOULD BE BETTER FOR IT.
REPORTS FROM OTHER SECTORS AND OUR OWN LONG-RANGE SCANS SHOW THAT THIS IS NOT THE BULK OF THE ENEMY FLEET...
THESE ARE SIMPLY THE FORERUNNERS.
WE MIGHT WIN ONE BATTLE, BUT IT WOULD COST US GREATLY. WHO THEN WOULD DEFEND WHAT REMAINS?
WE NEED HELP.
I WILL HUMBLE MYSELF FOR ALL OF US... BUT IT MUST BE DONE, AND QUICKLY.
NO.
YOUR PLAN IS SOUND, KL'RT, BUT WE BLEED AND THE WOUND MUST BE CAUTERIZED.
MY ARMIES WILL STAY AND ATTEMPT TO BUY US THE TIME YOU NEED.
GENERAL DM'YR, WE--
IS THIS THE EMPIRE, CHILD, OR THE SAD REMNANTS OF WHO WE USED TO BE?
I WAS A GENERAL...NOW I AM SIMPLY A WARLORD.
BUT BY THE GREAT MOTHER, I WILL FIND SOME WAY TO DIE LIKE THE MAN I USED TO BE.

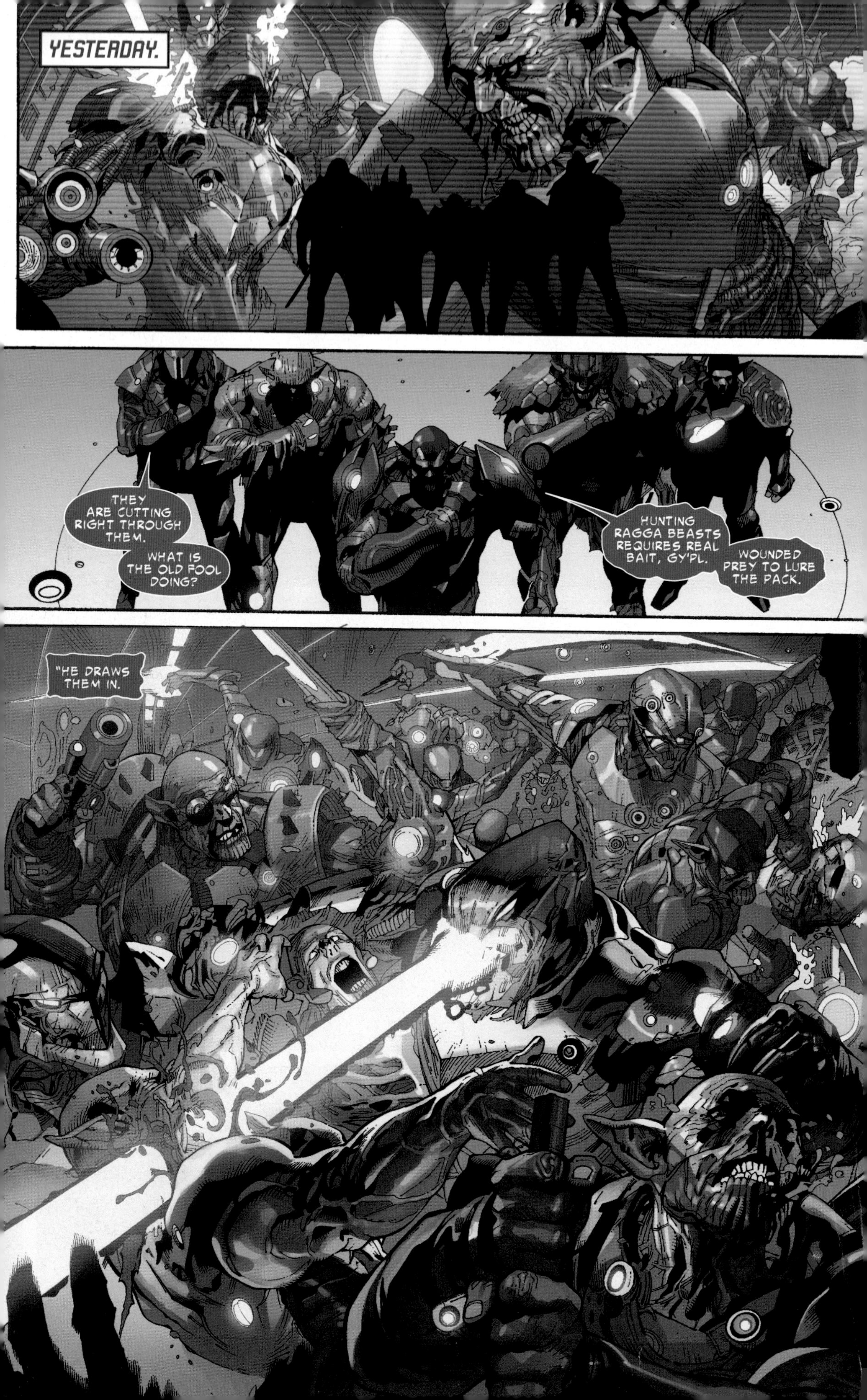
YESTERDAY.
THEY ARE CUTTING RIGHT THROUGH THEM.
WHAT IS THE OLD FOOL DOING?
HUNTING RAGGA BEASTS REQUIRES REAL BAIT, GY'PL.
WOUNDED PREY TO LURE THE PACK.
"HE DRAWS THEM IN.

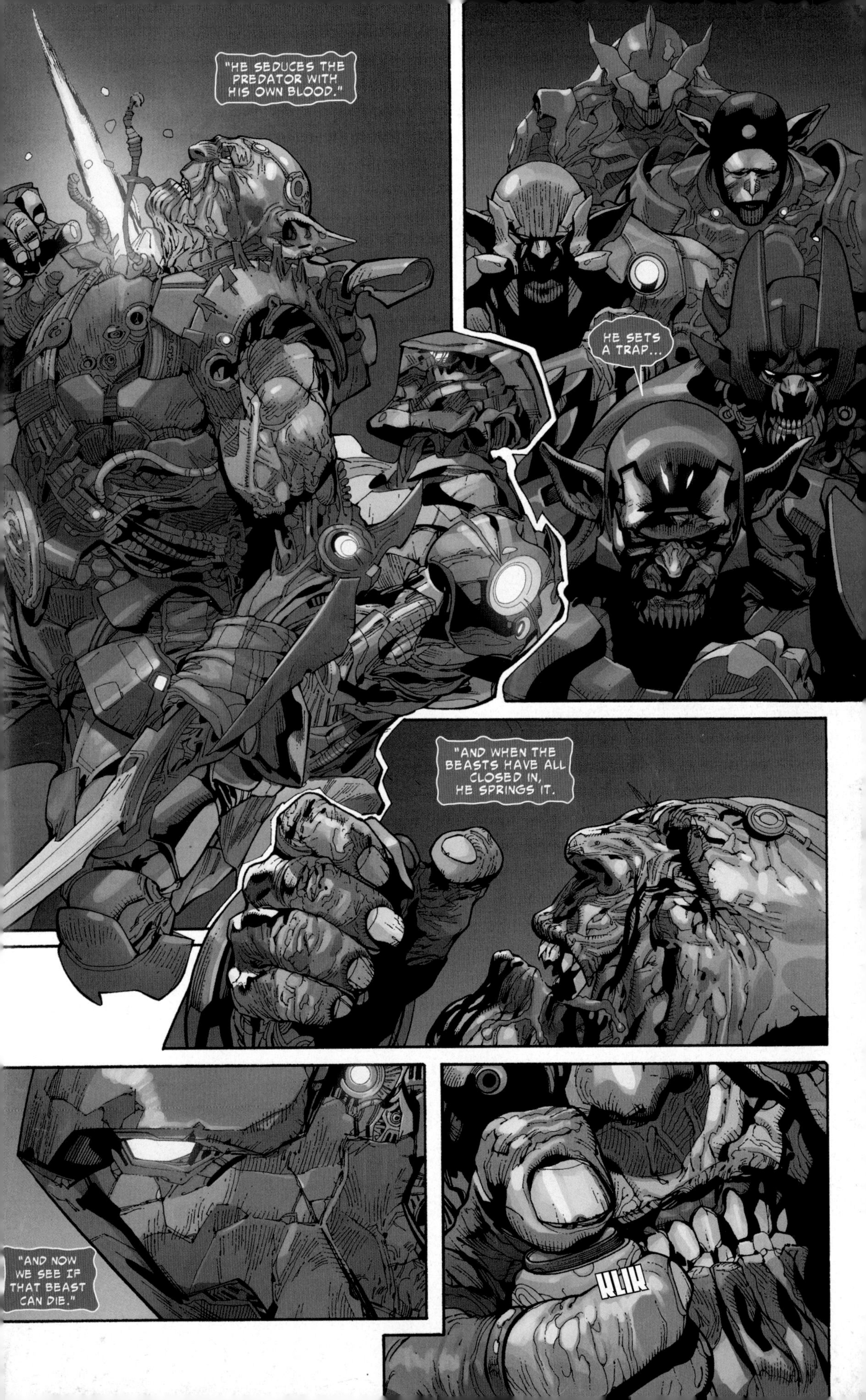
"HE SEDUCES THE PREDATOR WITH HIS OWN BLOOD."
HE SETS A TRAP...
"AND WHEN THE BEASTS HAVE ALL CLOSED IN, HE SPRINGS IT.
"AND NOW WE SEE IF THAT BEAST CAN DIE."
KLIK

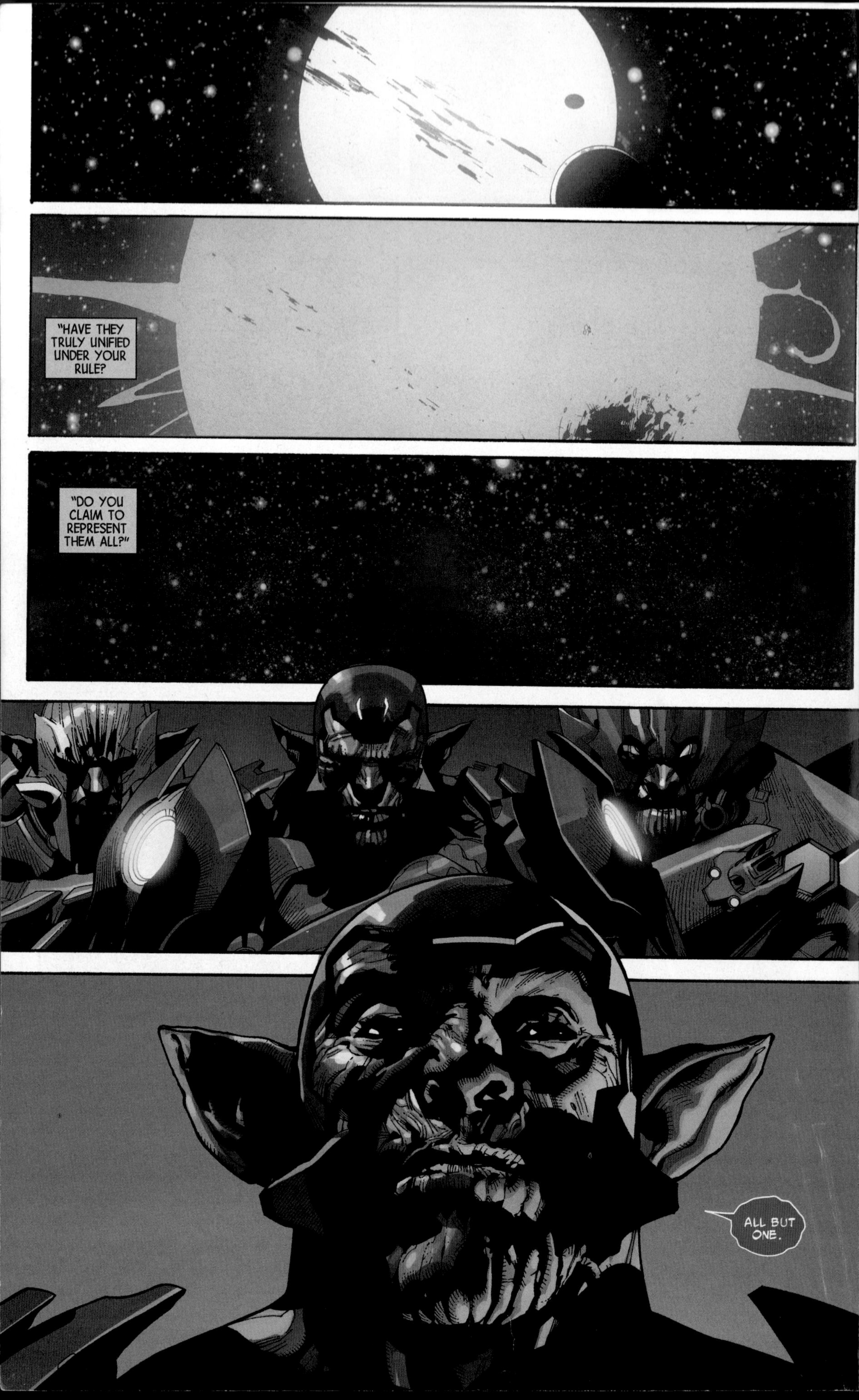
"HAVE THEY TRULY UNIFIED UNDER YOUR RULE?
"DO YOU CLAIM TO REPRESENT THEM ALL?"
ALL BUT ONE.

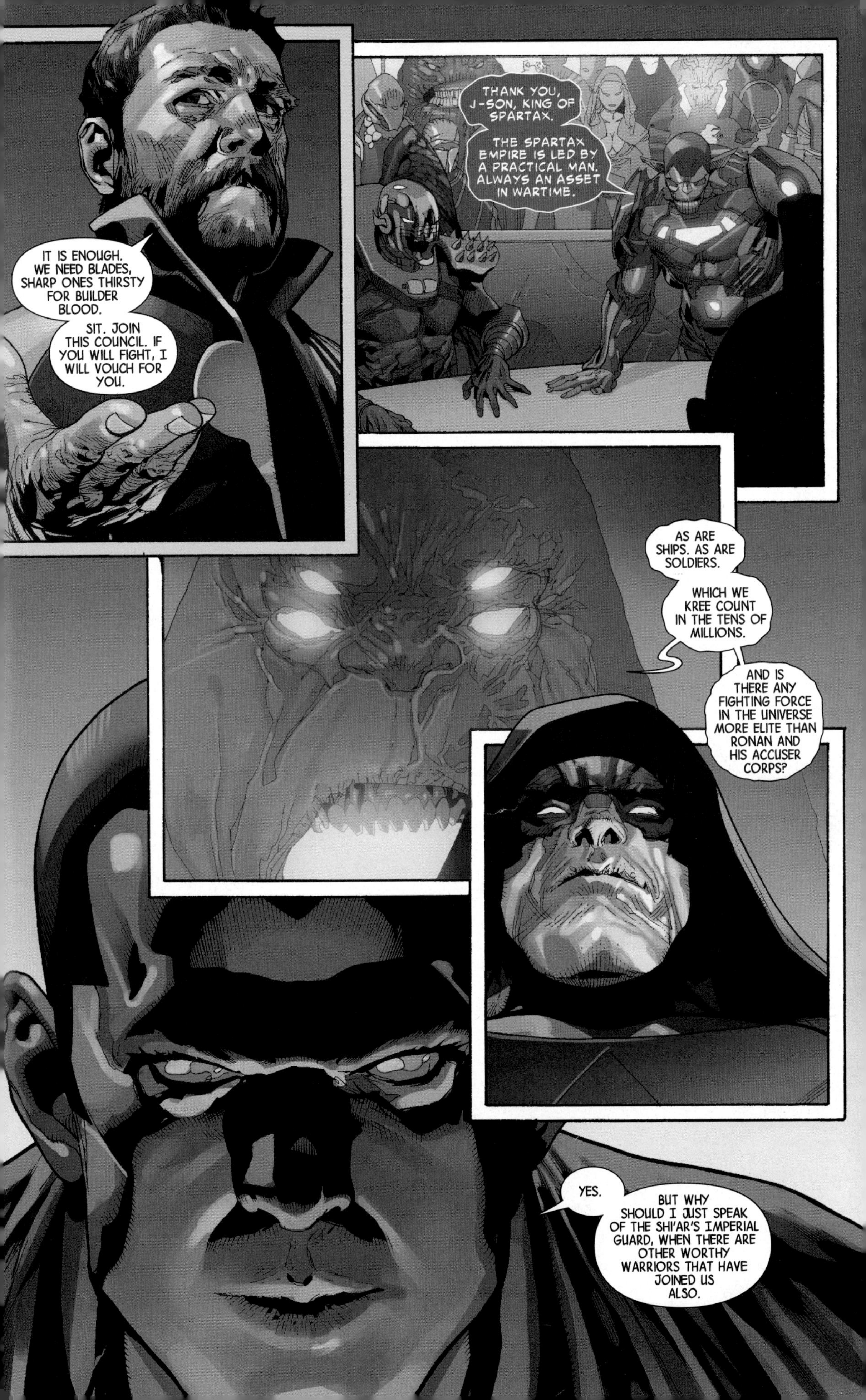
IT IS ENOUGH. WE NEED BLADES, SHARP ONES THIRSTY FOR BUILDER BLOOD.
SIT. JOIN THIS COUNCIL. IF YOU WILL FIGHT, I WILL VOUCH FOR YOU.
THANK YOU, J-SON, KING OF SPARTAX.
THE SPARTAX EMPIRE IS LED BY A PRACTICAL MAN. ALWAYS AN ASSET IN WARTIME.
AS ARE SHIPS. AS ARE SOLDIERS.
WHICH WE KREE COUNT IN THE TENS OF MILLIONS.
AND IS THERE ANY FIGHTING FORCE IN THE UNIVERSE MORE ELITE THAN RONAN AND HIS ACCUSER CORPS?
YES.
BUT WHY SHOULD I JUST SPEAK OF THE SHI'AR'S IMPERIAL GUARD, WHEN THERE ARE OTHER WORTHY WARRIORS THAT HAVE JOINED US ALSO.

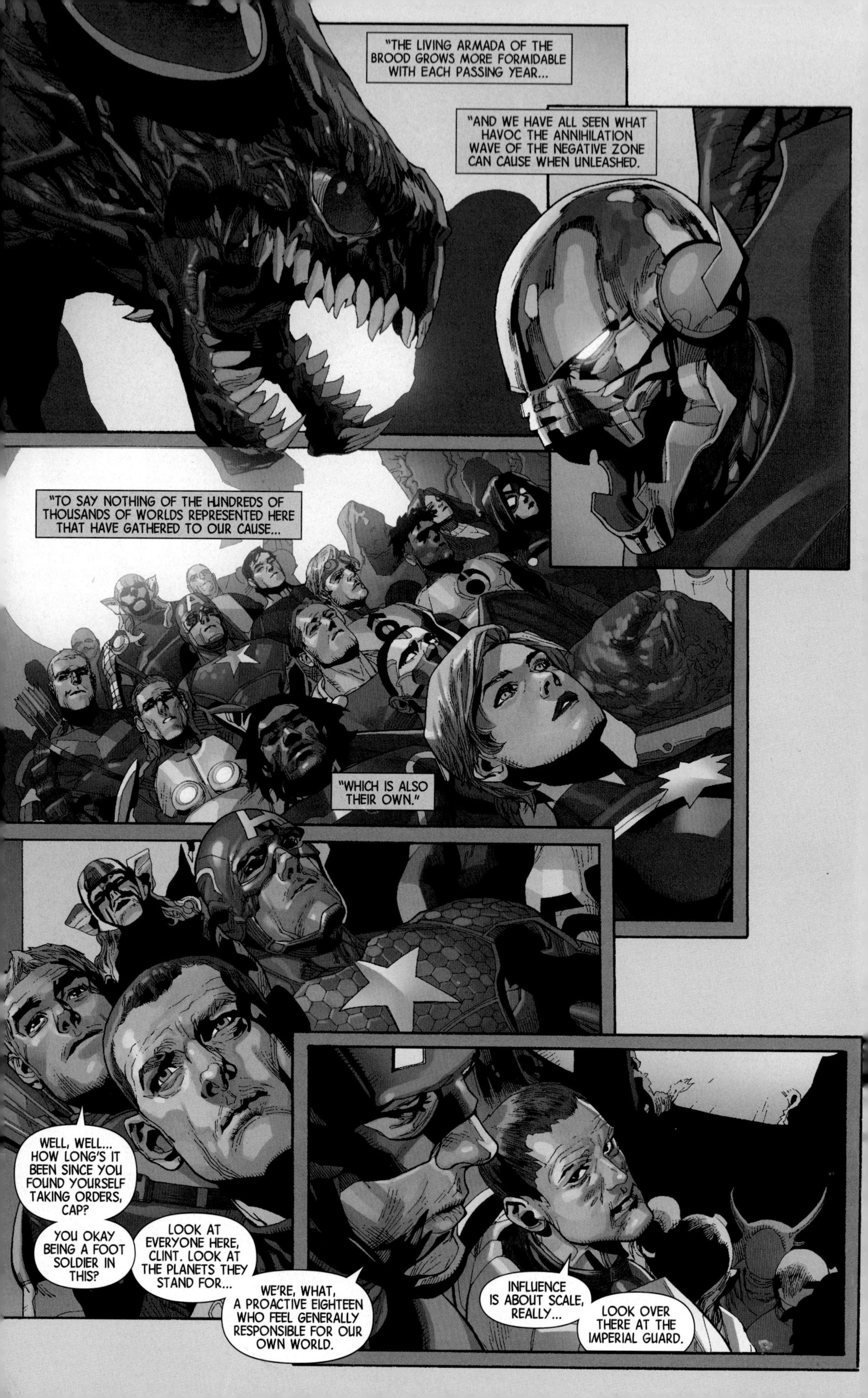
"THE LIVING ARMADA OF THE BROOD GROWS MORE FORMIDABLE WITH EACH PASSING YEAR...
"AND WE HAVE ALL SEEN WHAT HAVOC THE ANNIHILATION WAVE OF THE NEGATIVE ZONE CAN CAUSE WHEN UNLEASHED.
"TO SAY NOTHING OF THE HUNDREDS OF THOUSANDS OF WORLDS REPRESENTED HERE THAT HAVE GATHERED TO OUR CAUSE...
"WHICH IS ALSO THEIR OWN."
WELL, WELL... HOW LONG'S IT BEEN SINCE YOU FOUND YOURSELF TAKING ORDERS, CAP?
YOU OKAY BEING A FOOT SOLDIER IN THIS?
LOOK AT EVERYONE HERE, CLINT. LOOK AT THE PLANETS THEY STAND FOR...
WE'RE, WHAT, A PROACTIVE EIGHTEEN WHO FEEL GENERALLY RESPONSIBLE FOR OUR OWN WORLD.
INFLUENCE IS ABOUT SCALE, REALLY...
LOOK OVER THERE AT THE IMPERIAL GUARD.

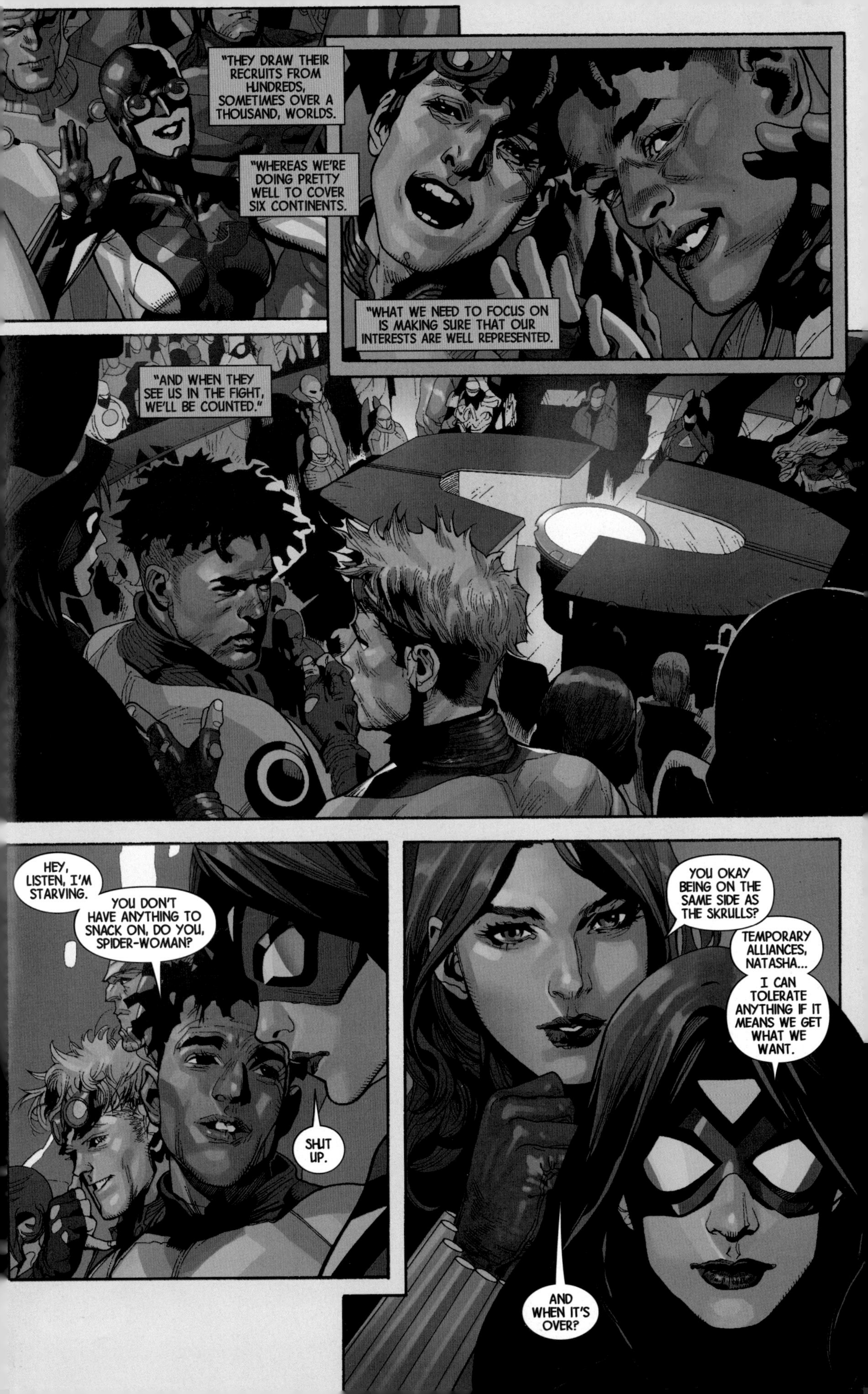
"THEY DRAW THEIR RECRUITS FROM HUNDREDS, SOMETIMES OVER A THOUSAND, WORLDS.
"WHEREAS WE'RE DOING PRETTY WELL TO COVER SIX CONTINENTS.
"WHAT WE NEED TO FOCUS ON IS MAKING SURE THAT OUR INTERESTS ARE WELL REPRESENTED.
"AND WHEN THEY SEE US IN THE FIGHT, WE'LL BE COUNTED."
HEY, LISTEN, I'M STARVING.
YOU DON'T HAVE ANYTHING TO SNACK ON, DO YOU, SPIDER-WOMAN?
SHUT UP.
YOU OKAY BEING ON THE SAME SIDE AS THE SKRULLS?
TEMPORARY ALLIANCES, NATASHA...
I CAN TOLERATE ANYTHING IF IT MEANS WE GET WHAT WE WANT.
AND WHEN IT'S OVER?

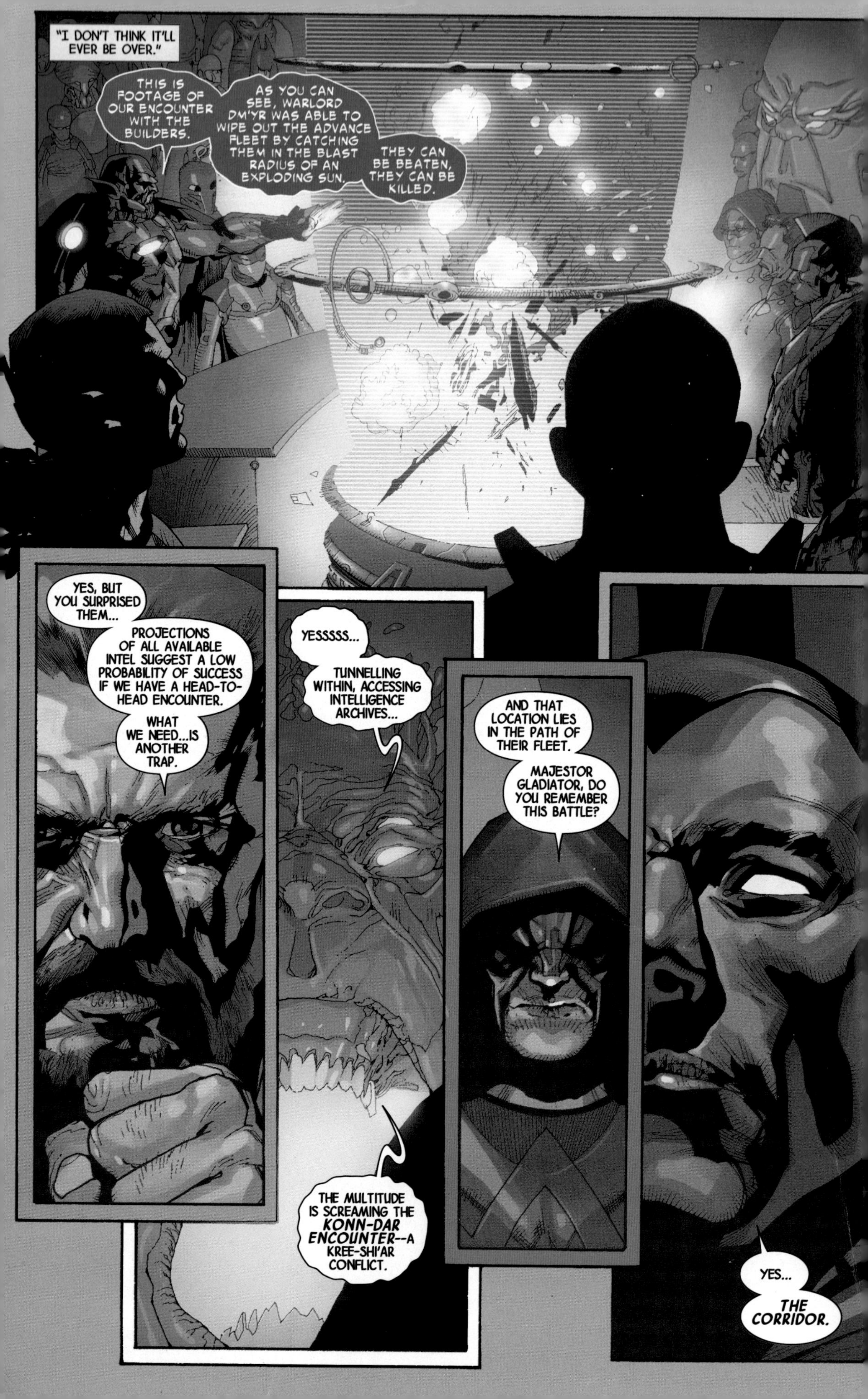
"I DON'T THINK IT'LL EVER BE OVER."
THIS IS FOOTAGE OF OUR ENCOUNTER WITH THE BUILDERS.
AS YOU CAN SEE, WARLORD DM'YR WAS ABLE TO WIPE OUT THE ADVANCE FLEET BY CATCHING THEM IN THE BLAST RADIUS OF AN EXPLODING SUN.
THEY CAN BE BEATEN, THEY CAN BE KILLED.
YES, BUT YOU SURPRISED THEM...
PROJECTIONS OF ALL AVAILABLE INTEL SUGGEST A LOW PROBABILITY OF SUCCESS IF WE HAVE A HEAD-TO-HEAD ENCOUNTER.
WHAT WE NEED...IS ANOTHER TRAP.
YESSSSS...
TUNNELLING WITHIN, ACCESSING INTELLIGENCE ARCHIVES...
THE MULTITUDE IS SCREAMING THE *KONN-DAR ENCOUNTER*--A KREE-SHI'AR CONFLICT.
AND THAT LOCATION LIES IN THE PATH OF THEIR FLEET.
MAJESTOR GLADIATOR, DO YOU REMEMBER THIS BATTLE?
YES...
THE CORRIDOR.

FALL INTO
SINGULARITY

◆

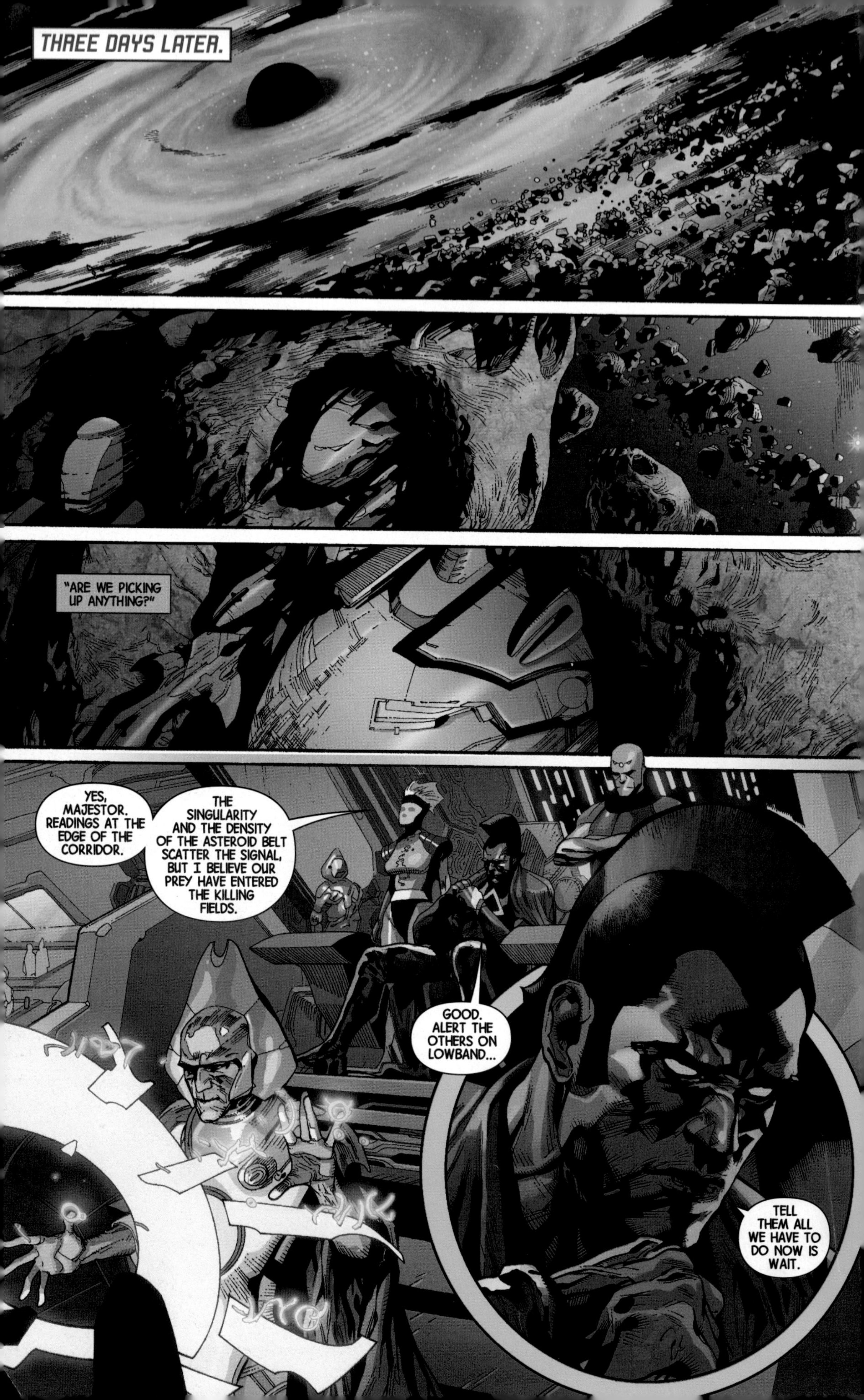
THREE DAYS LATER.
"ARE WE PICKING UP ANYTHING?"
YES, MAJESTOR. READINGS AT THE EDGE OF THE CORRIDOR.
THE SINGULARITY AND THE DENSITY OF THE ASTEROID BELT SCATTER THE SIGNAL, BUT I BELIEVE OUR PREY HAVE ENTERED THE KILLING FIELDS.
GOOD. ALERT THE OTHERS ON LOWBAND...
TELL THEM ALL WE HAVE TO DO NOW IS WAIT.

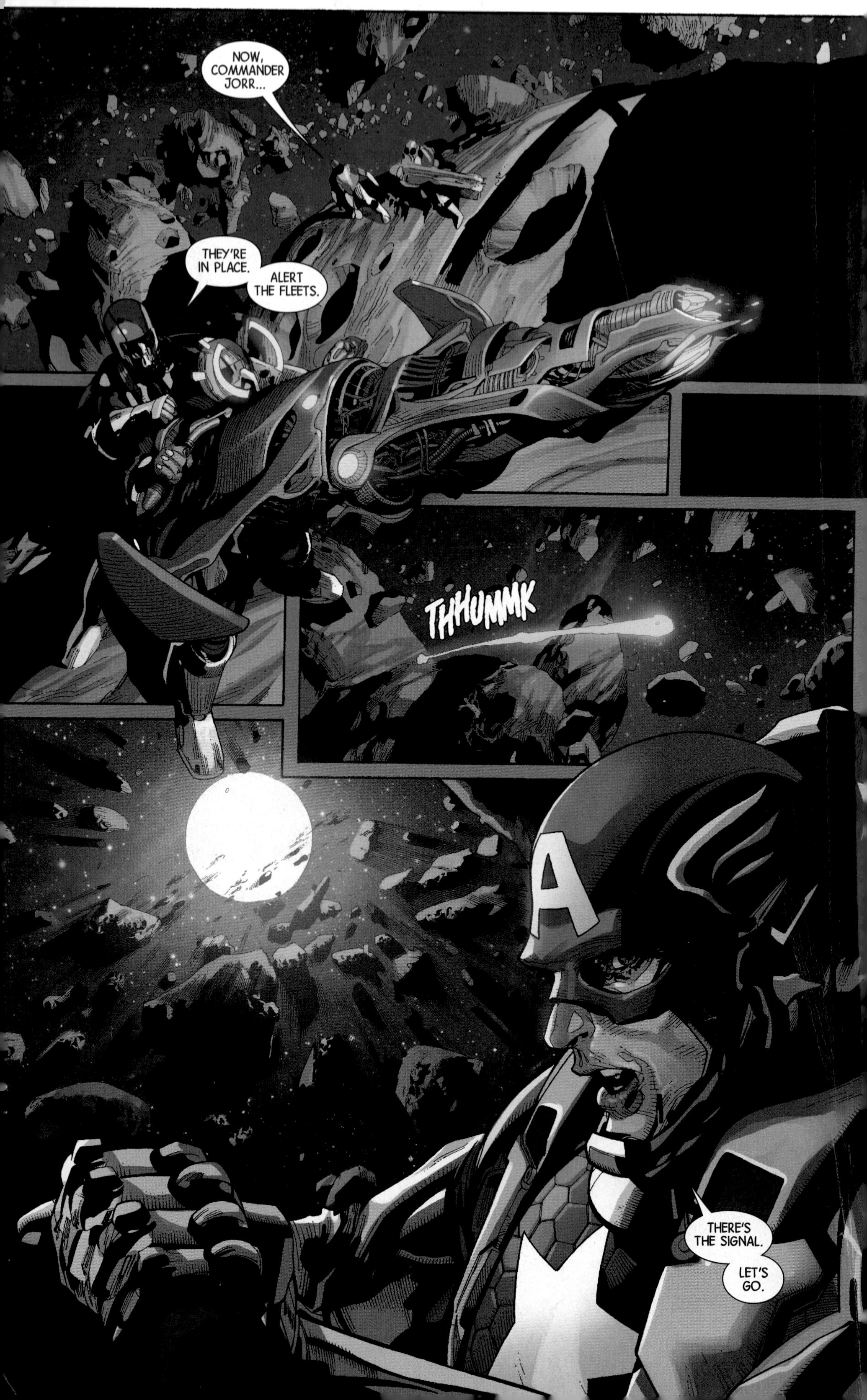

NOW, COMMANDER JORR...
THEY'RE IN PLACE.
ALERT THE FLEETS.
THHUMMK
THERE'S THE SIGNAL.
LET'S GO.

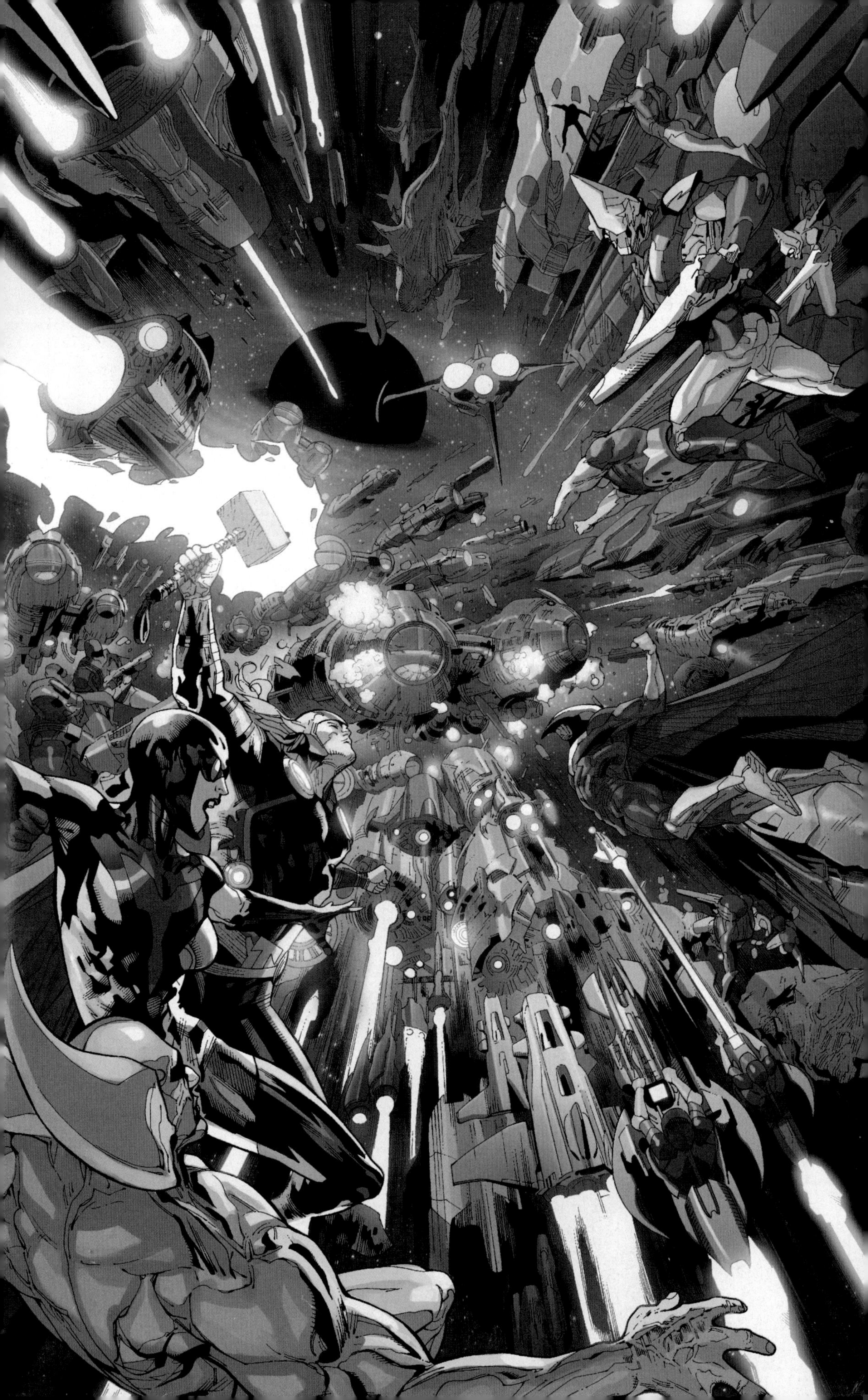

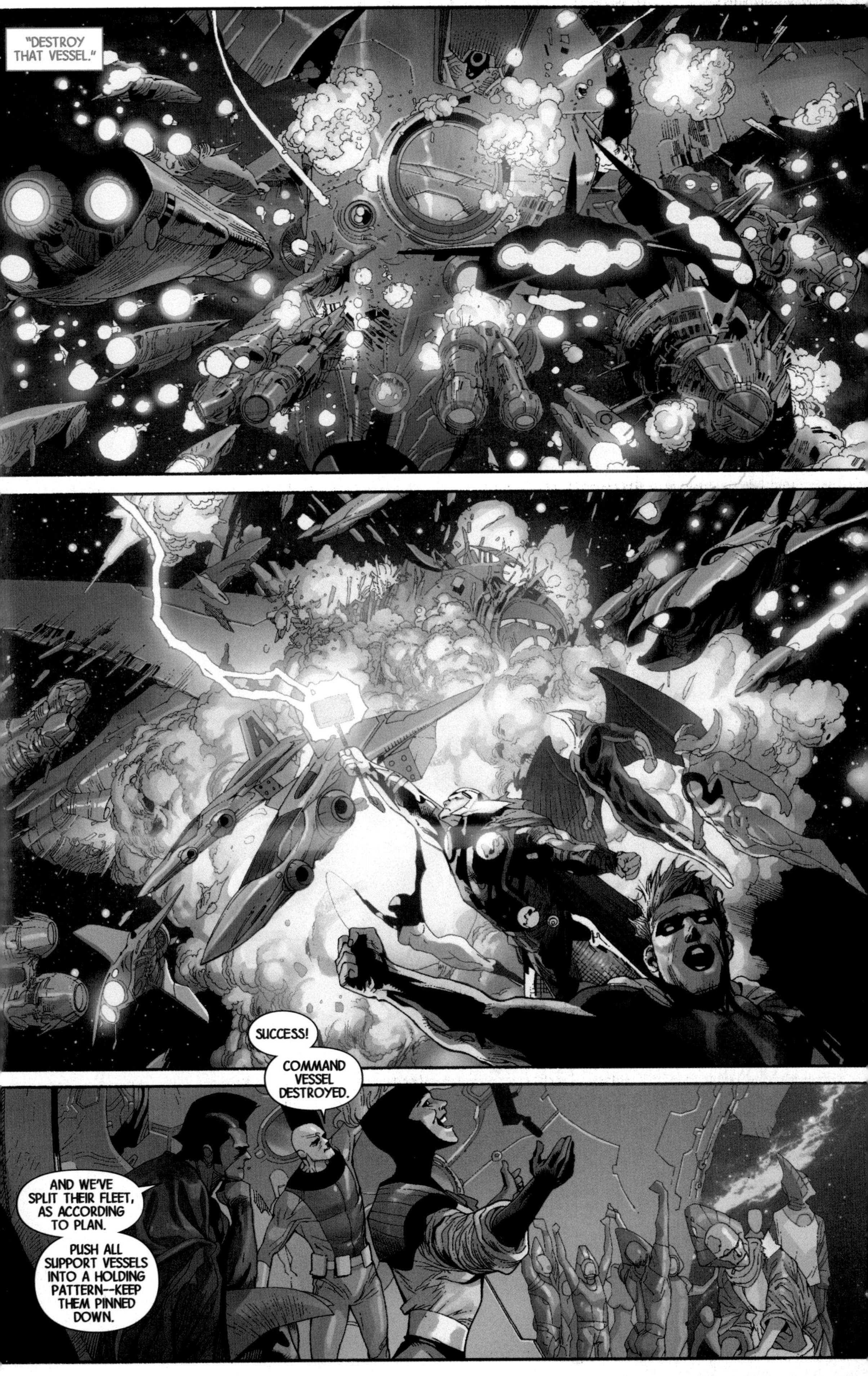
"DESTROY THAT VESSEL."
SUCCESS!
COMMAND VESSEL DESTROYED.
AND WE'VE SPLIT THEIR FLEET, AS ACCORDING TO PLAN.
PUSH ALL SUPPORT VESSELS INTO A HOLDING PATTERN--KEEP THEM PINNED DOWN.

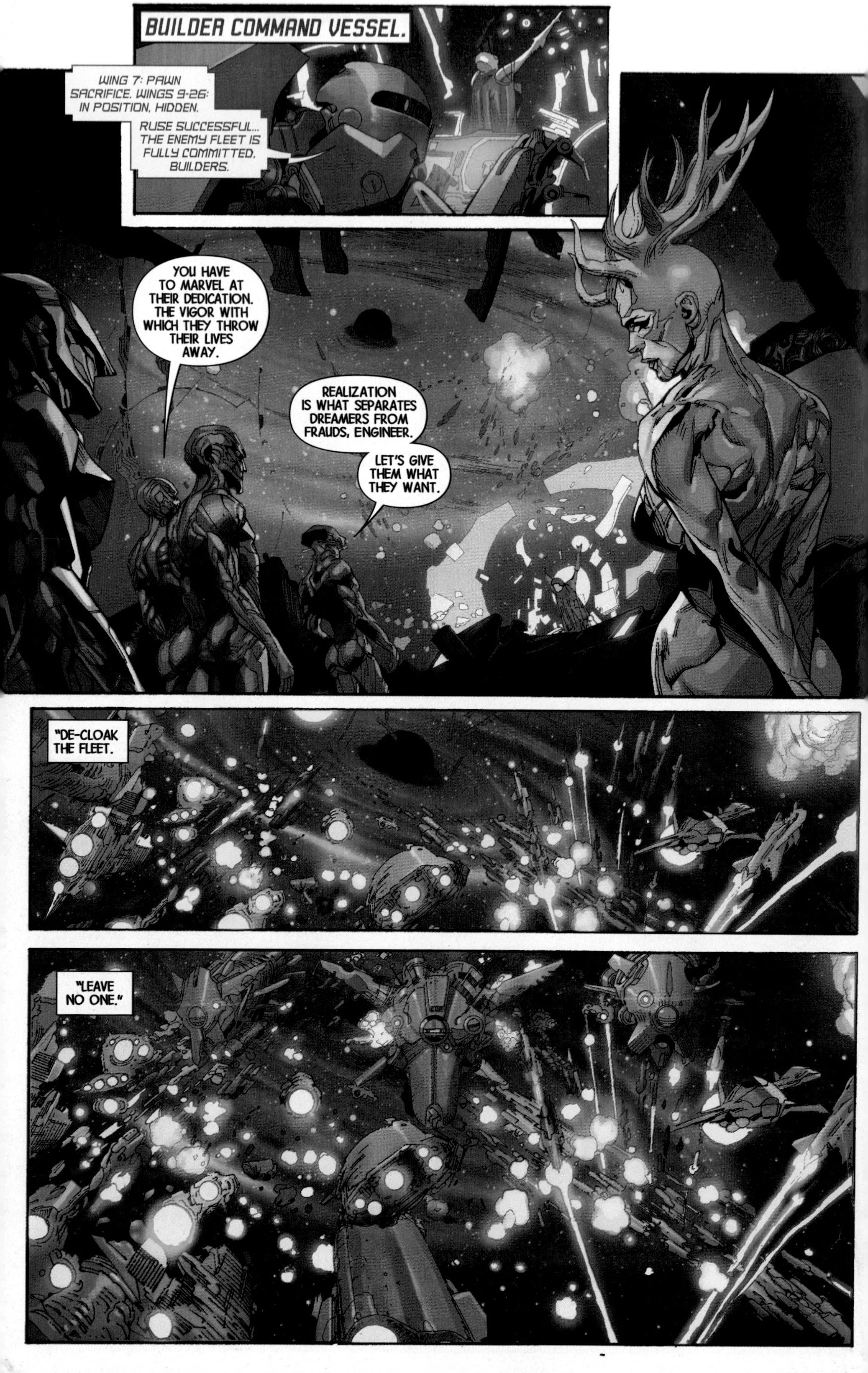
BUILDER COMMAND VESSEL.
WING 7: PAWN SACRIFICE. WINGS 9-26: IN POSITION, HIDDEN.
RUSE SUCCESSFUL... THE ENEMY FLEET IS FULLY COMMITTED, BUILDERS.
YOU HAVE TO MARVEL AT THEIR DEDICATION. THE VIGOR WITH WHICH THEY THROW THEIR LIVES AWAY.
REALIZATION IS WHAT SEPARATES DREAMERS FROM FRAUDS, ENGINEER.
LET'S GIVE THEM WHAT THEY WANT.
"DE-CLOAK THE FLEET.
"LEAVE NO ONE."

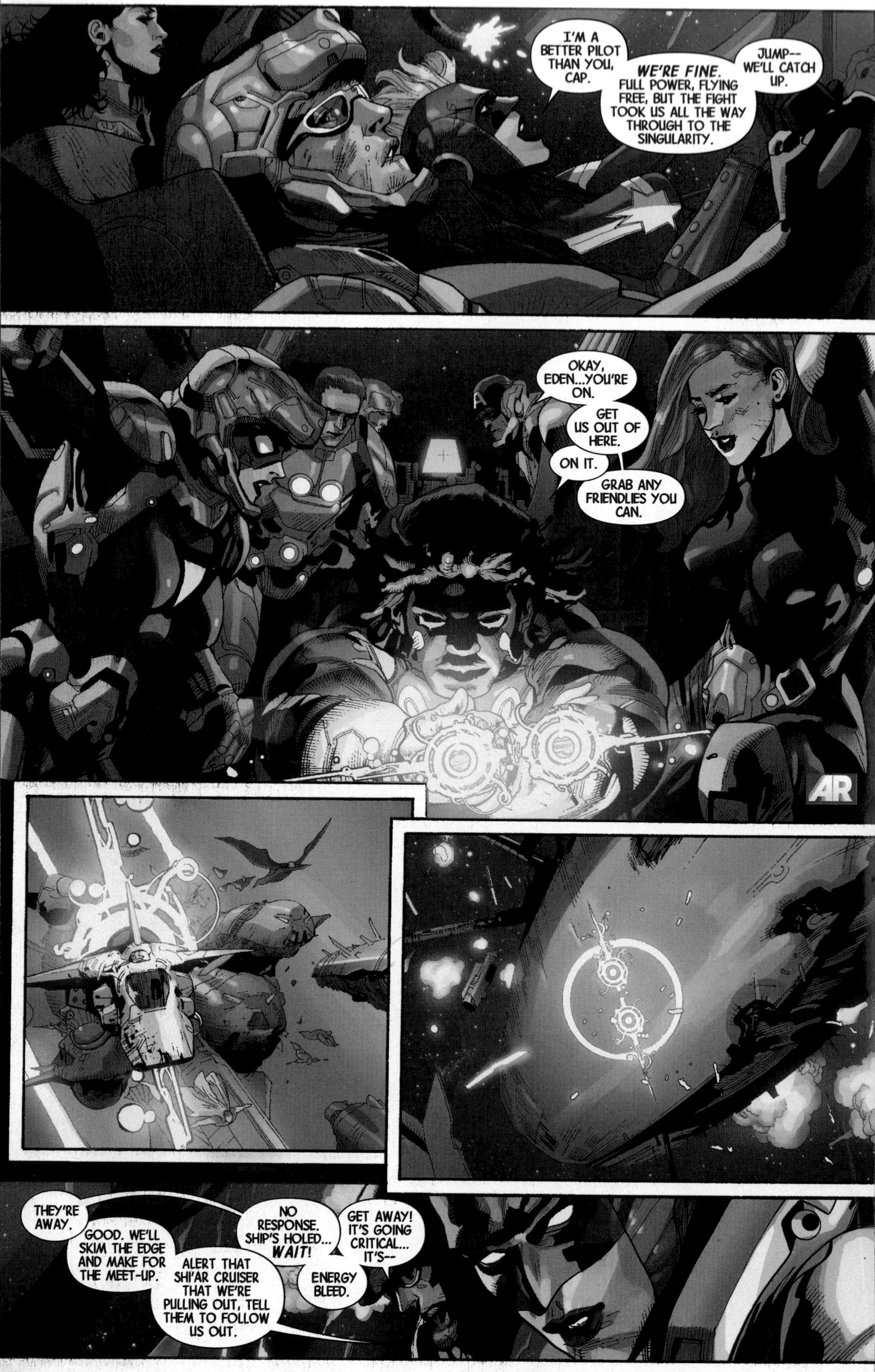
I'M A BETTER PILOT THAN YOU, CAP.
WE'RE FINE. FULL POWER, FLYING FREE, BUT THE FIGHT TOOK US ALL THE WAY THROUGH TO THE SINGULARITY.
JUMP-- WE'LL CATCH UP.
OKAY, EDEN...YOU'RE ON.
GET US OUT OF HERE.
ON IT.
GRAB ANY FRIENDLIES YOU CAN.
THEY'RE AWAY.
GOOD. WE'LL SKIM THE EDGE AND MAKE FOR THE MEET-UP.
ALERT THAT SHI'AR CRUISER THAT WE'RE PULLING OUT, TELL THEM TO FOLLOW US OUT.
NO RESPONSE. SHIP'S HOLED... WAIT!
ENERGY BLEED.
GET AWAY! IT'S GOING CRITICAL... IT'S--

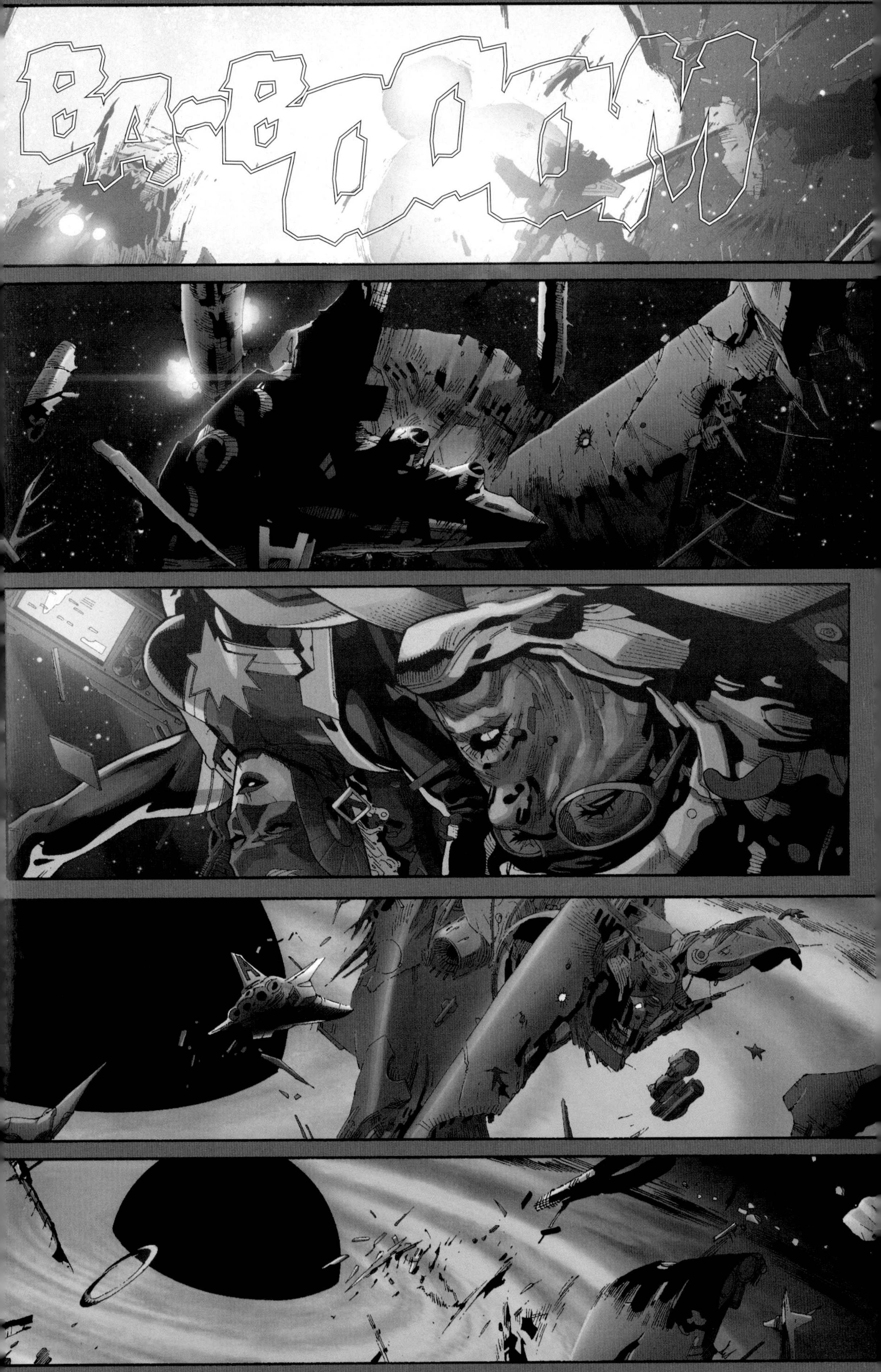
BA-BOOOM

"BUILDING TOWARDS COLLAPSE"

EVERYTHING DIES. EVEN THE THINGS YOU THINK CANNOT. I AM THE UNIVERSE. HERE AT THE START, TO SEE HOW THE END BEGINS.

IN THE HOURS SINCE INTERCEPTING THE DISTRESS SIGNAL FROM THE DESTROYED KREE MOON, S.W.O.R.D. HAS PICKED UP INCREASING MILITARY CHATTER FROM...

WELL...ALMOST ALL THE MAJOR EMPIRES. BASICALLY THE ENTIRETY OF THE CURRENT GALACTIC COUNCIL. BECAUSE WE COUNT A MEMBER OF THE SHI'AR IMPERIAL GUARD AMONG OUR NUMBER, WE ALSO HAVE HARD CONFIRMATION THAT THOSE COUNCIL WORLDS ARE MOBILIZING.

UNDERSTAND, PEOPLE. THIS IS REAL, IT'S HEADED OUR WAY AND IT'S SCARY ENOUGH TO MAKE SPACE EMPIRES SCRAMBLE.

CAPTAIN, THE MEASURING OF PROBABILITIES IS--

THE ANSWER IS NONE.

EX NIHILO. THESE PEOPLE--YOUR BUILDERS--CREATED YOU AND YOUR SISTER ABYSS. WHAT CHANCE WOULD WE HAVE IF THEY MAKE IT TO EARTH?

SUCCESS, MY FELLOW BUILDERS. OUR RUSE WORKED...WE PRESENTED WHAT THEY WANTED TO SEE, AND NOW THEY ARE COMPLETELY COMMITTED. YOU HAVE TO MARVEL AT THEIR DEDICATION. THE VIGOR WITH WHICH THEY THROW THEIR LIVES AWAY.

REALIZATION IS WHAT SEPARATES DREAMERS FROM FRAUDS, ENGINEER. LET'S GIVE THEM WHAT THEY WANT.

"DECLOAK THE FLEET.

"LEAVE NO ONE."

WE BARELY MADE IT TO THE RENDEZVOUS POINT. SMASHER, ANY WORD ON THE SECOND QUINCARRIER?

NO, BUT MAYBE THEY VECTORED OUT WITH THE SPARTAX OR THE BROOD. TRUTH IS...

"...IF CAPTAIN MARVEL'S CARRIER DIDN'T SHOW UP HERE, WE WOULDN'T KNOW EITHER WAY."

CAST

THE AVENGERS

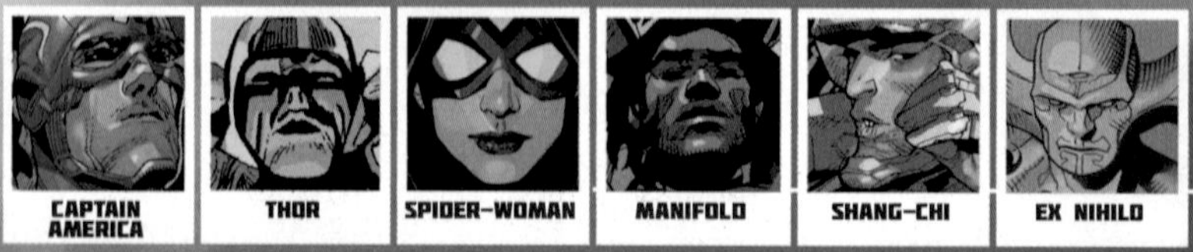

CAPTAIN AMERICA · THOR · SPIDER-WOMAN · MANIFOLD · SHANG-CHI · EX NIHILO

CAPTURED

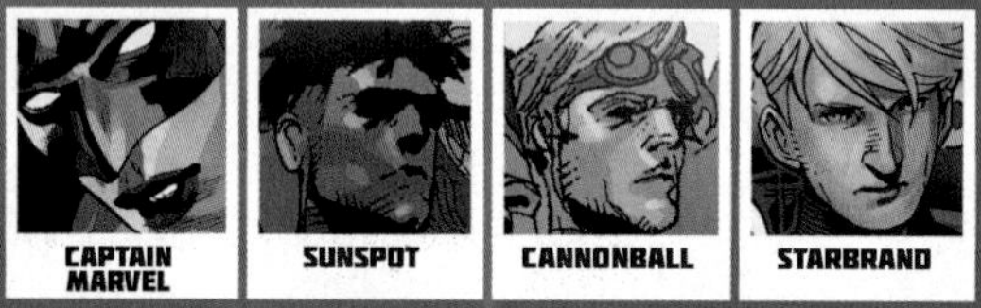

CAPTAIN MARVEL · SUNSPOT · CANNONBALL · STARBRAND

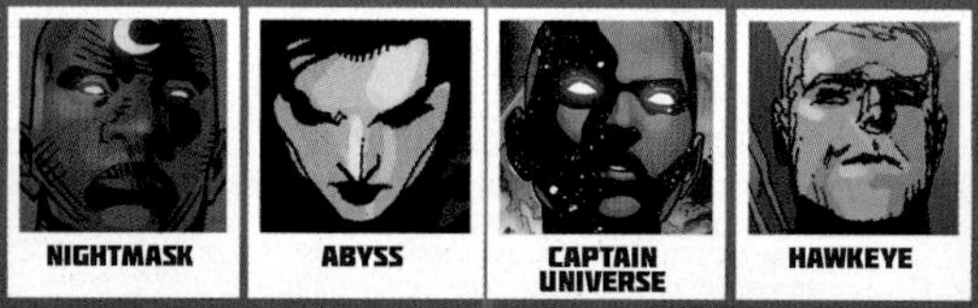

NIGHTMASK · ABYSS · CAPTAIN UNIVERSE · HAWKEYE

THE BUILDERS

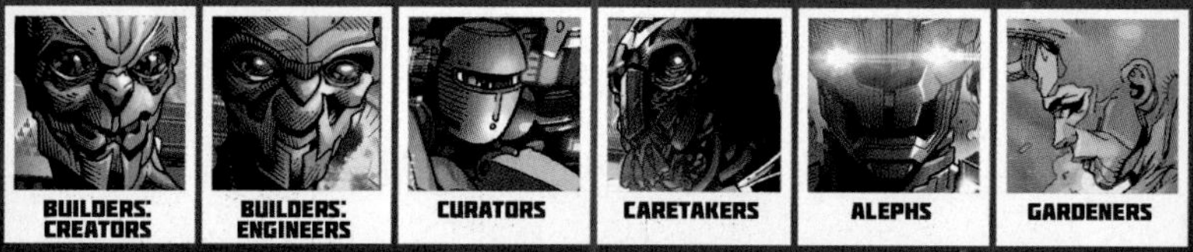

BUILDERS: CREATORS · BUILDERS: ENGINEERS · CURATORS · CARETAKERS · ALEPHS · GARDENERS

THE GALACTIC COUNCIL

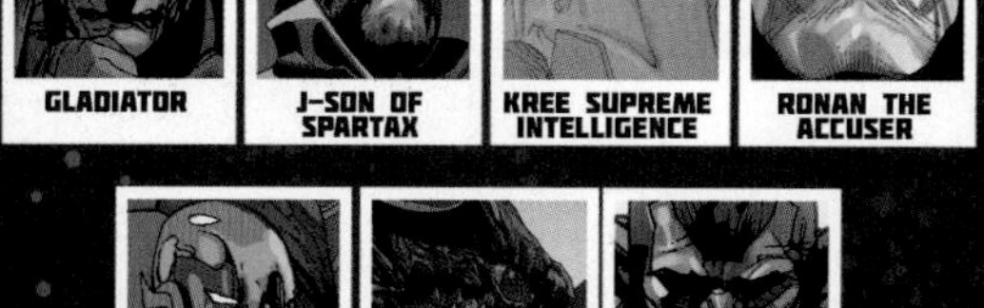

GLADIATOR · J-SON OF SPARTAX · KREE SUPREME INTELLIGENCE · RONAN THE ACCUSER

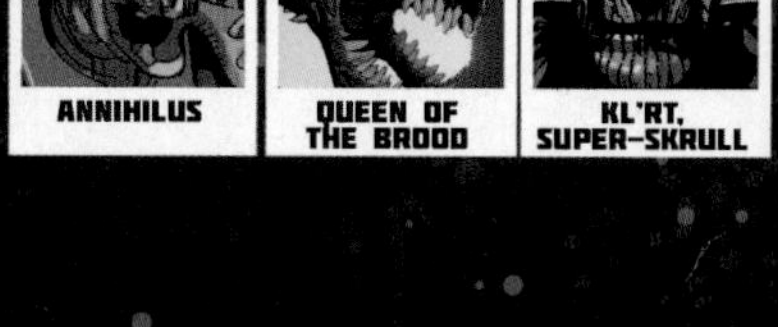

ANNIHILUS · QUEEN OF THE BROOD · KL'RT, SUPER-SKRULL

BINARY COLLAPSE

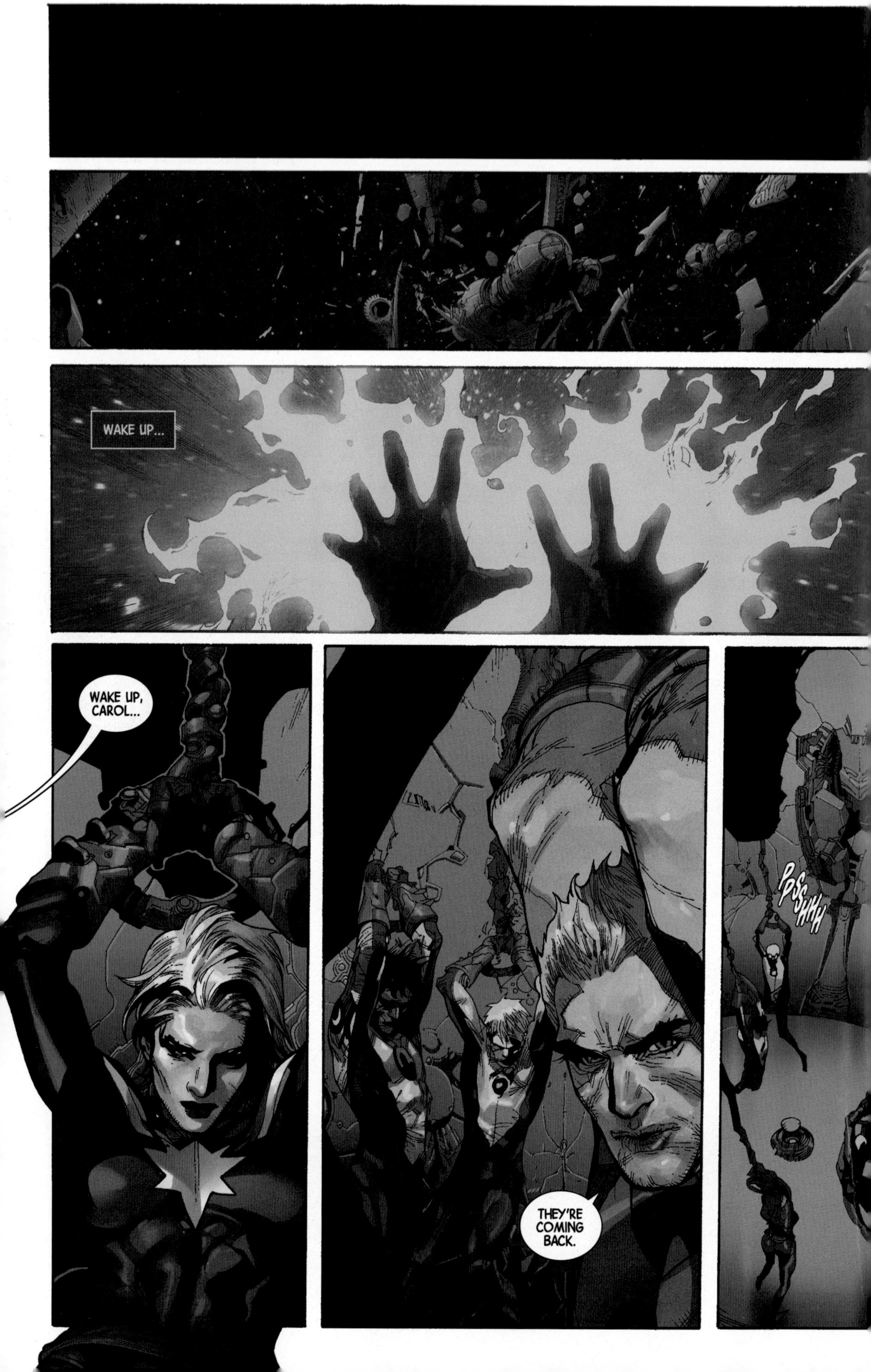
WAKE UP...
WAKE UP, CAROL...
THEY'RE COMING BACK.
PSSHHH

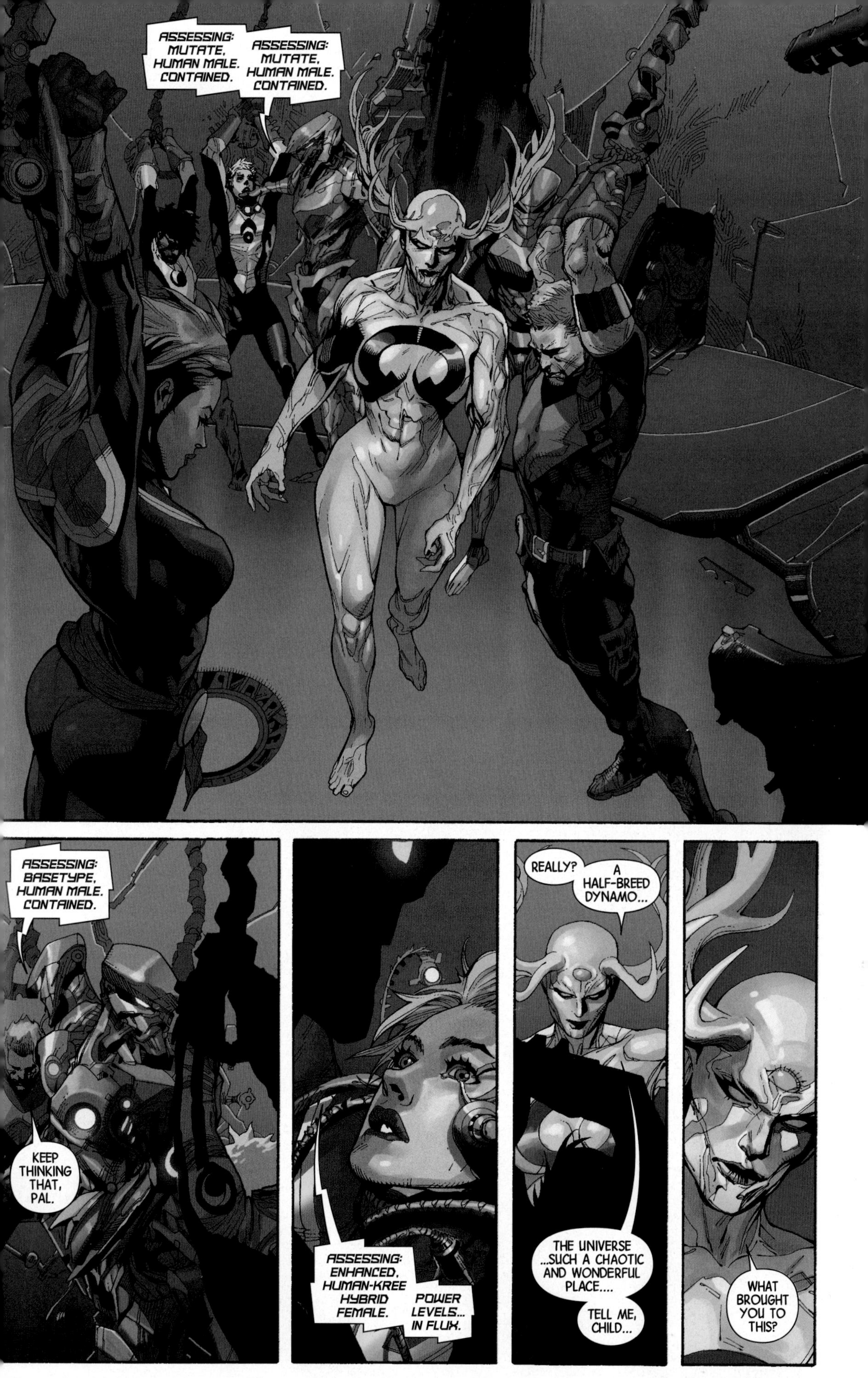
ASSESSING: MUTATE, HUMAN MALE. CONTAINED.
ASSESSING: MUTATE, HUMAN MALE. CONTAINED.
ASSESSING: BASETYPE, HUMAN MALE. CONTAINED.
KEEP THINKING THAT, PAL.
ASSESSING: ENHANCED, HUMAN-KREE HYBRID FEMALE.
POWER LEVELS... IN FLUX.
REALLY?
A HALF-BREED DYNAMO...
THE UNIVERSE ...SUCH A CHAOTIC AND WONDERFUL PLACE....
TELL ME, CHILD...
WHAT BROUGHT YOU TO THIS?

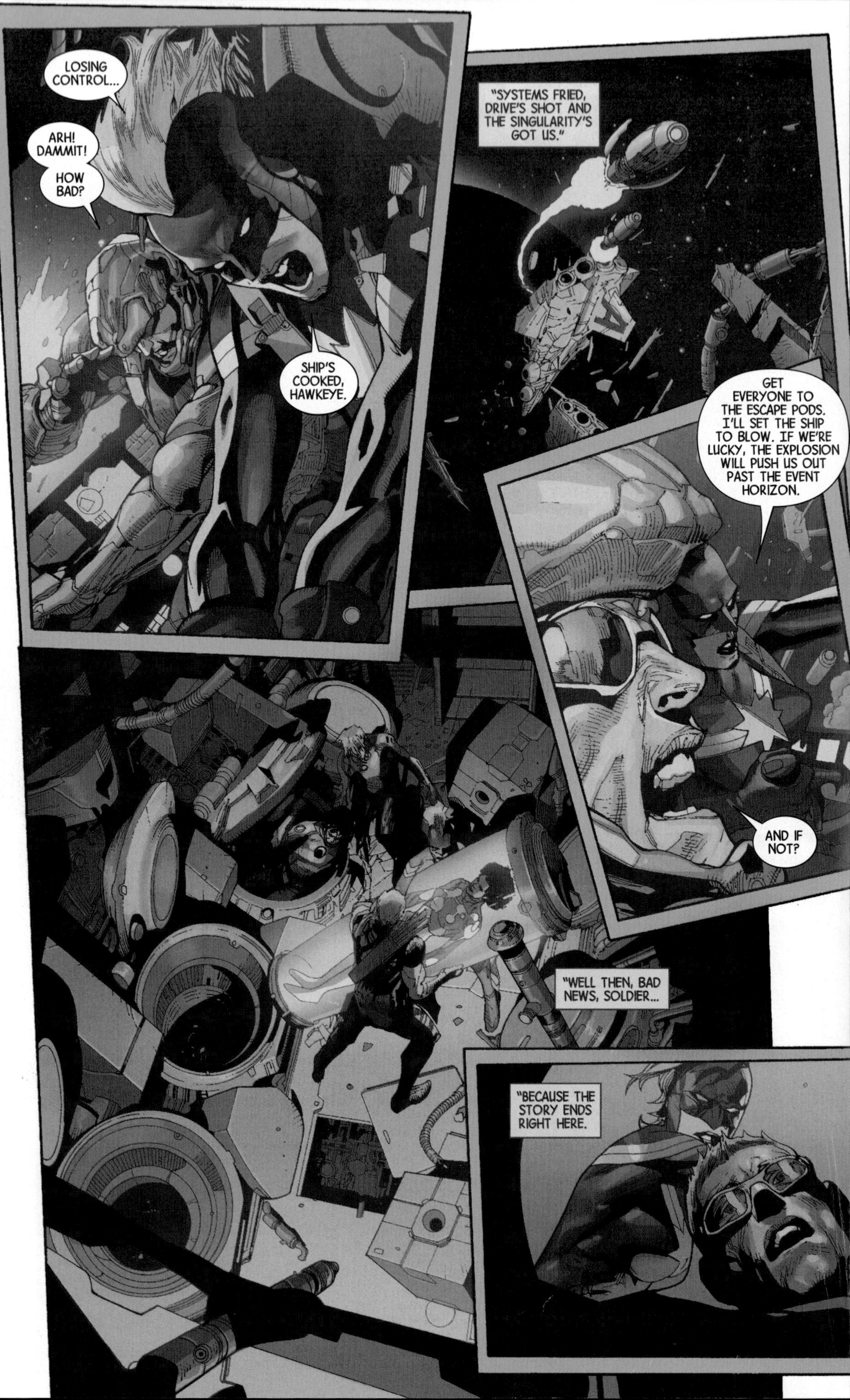
LOSING CONTROL...
ARH! DAMMIT!
HOW BAD?
SHIP'S COOKED, HAWKEYE.
"SYSTEMS FRIED, DRIVE'S SHOT AND THE SINGULARITY'S GOT US."
GET EVERYONE TO THE ESCAPE PODS. I'LL SET THE SHIP TO BLOW. IF WE'RE LUCKY, THE EXPLOSION WILL PUSH US OUT PAST THE EVENT HORIZON.
AND IF NOT?
"WELL THEN, BAD NEWS, SOLDIER...
"BECAUSE THE STORY ENDS RIGHT HERE.

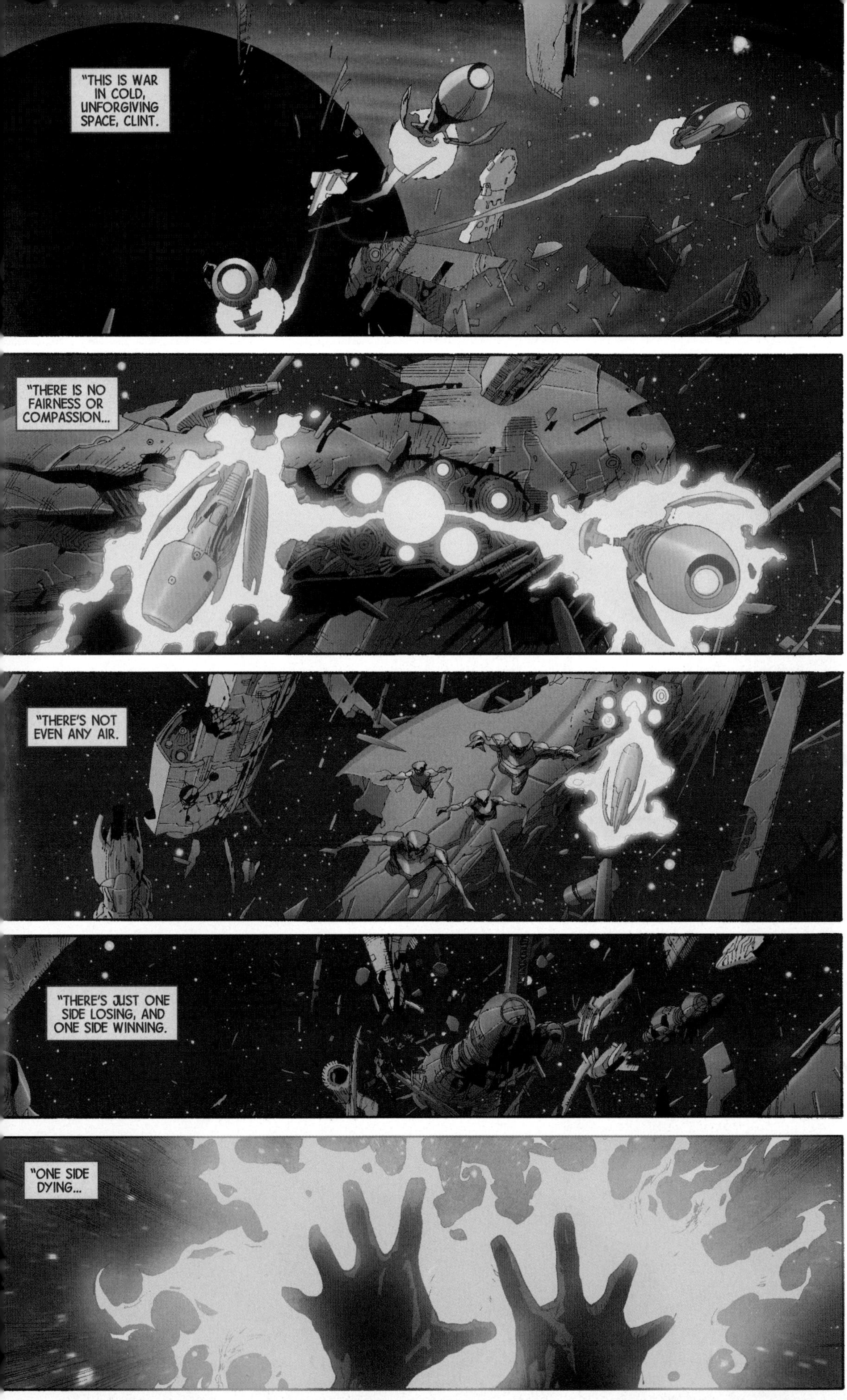
"THIS IS WAR IN COLD, UNFORGIVING SPACE, CLINT.
"THERE IS NO FAIRNESS OR COMPASSION...
"THERE'S NOT EVEN ANY AIR.
"THERE'S JUST ONE SIDE LOSING, AND ONE SIDE WINNING.
"ONE SIDE DYING...

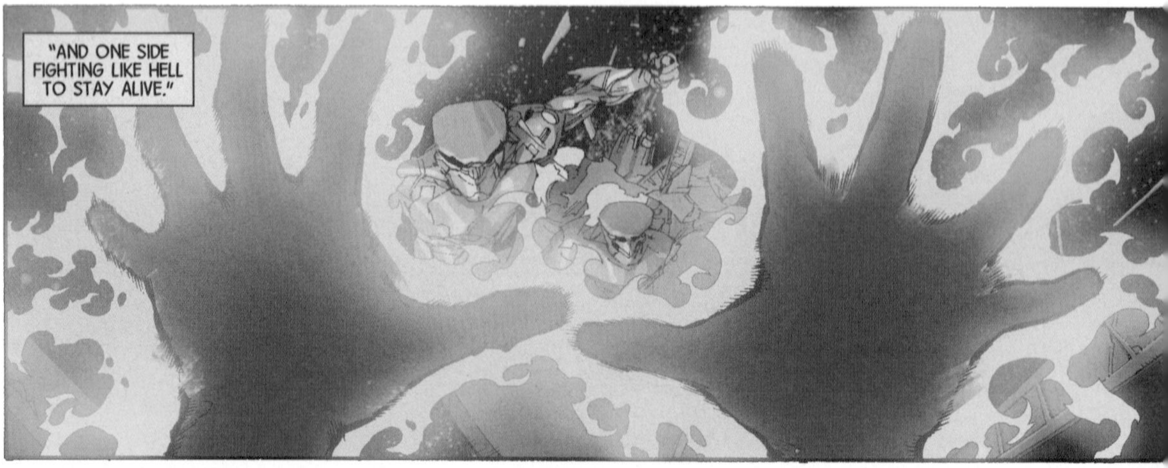
"AND ONE SIDE FIGHTING LIKE HELL TO STAY ALIVE."

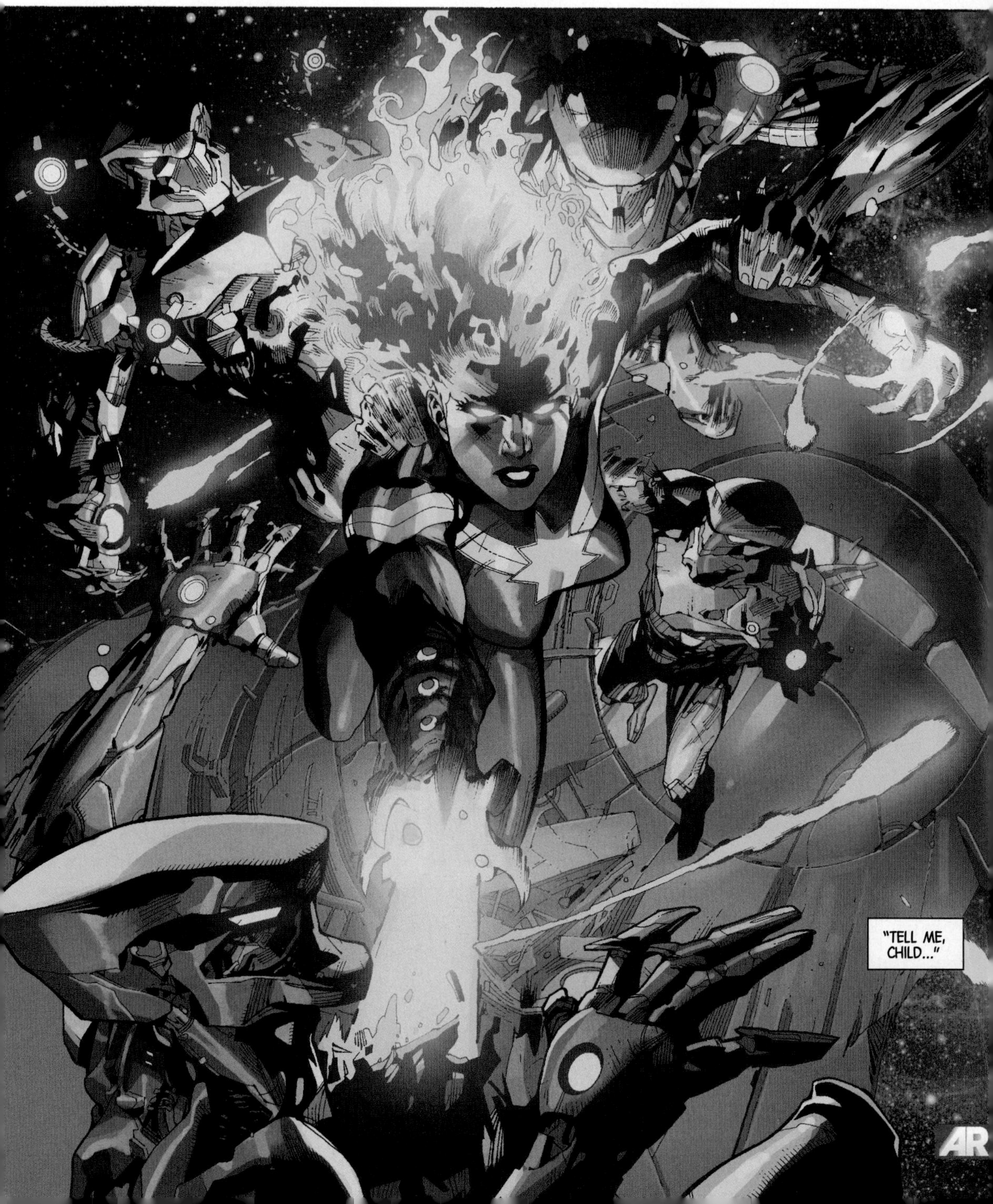
"TELL ME, CHILD..."

BEHEMOTH

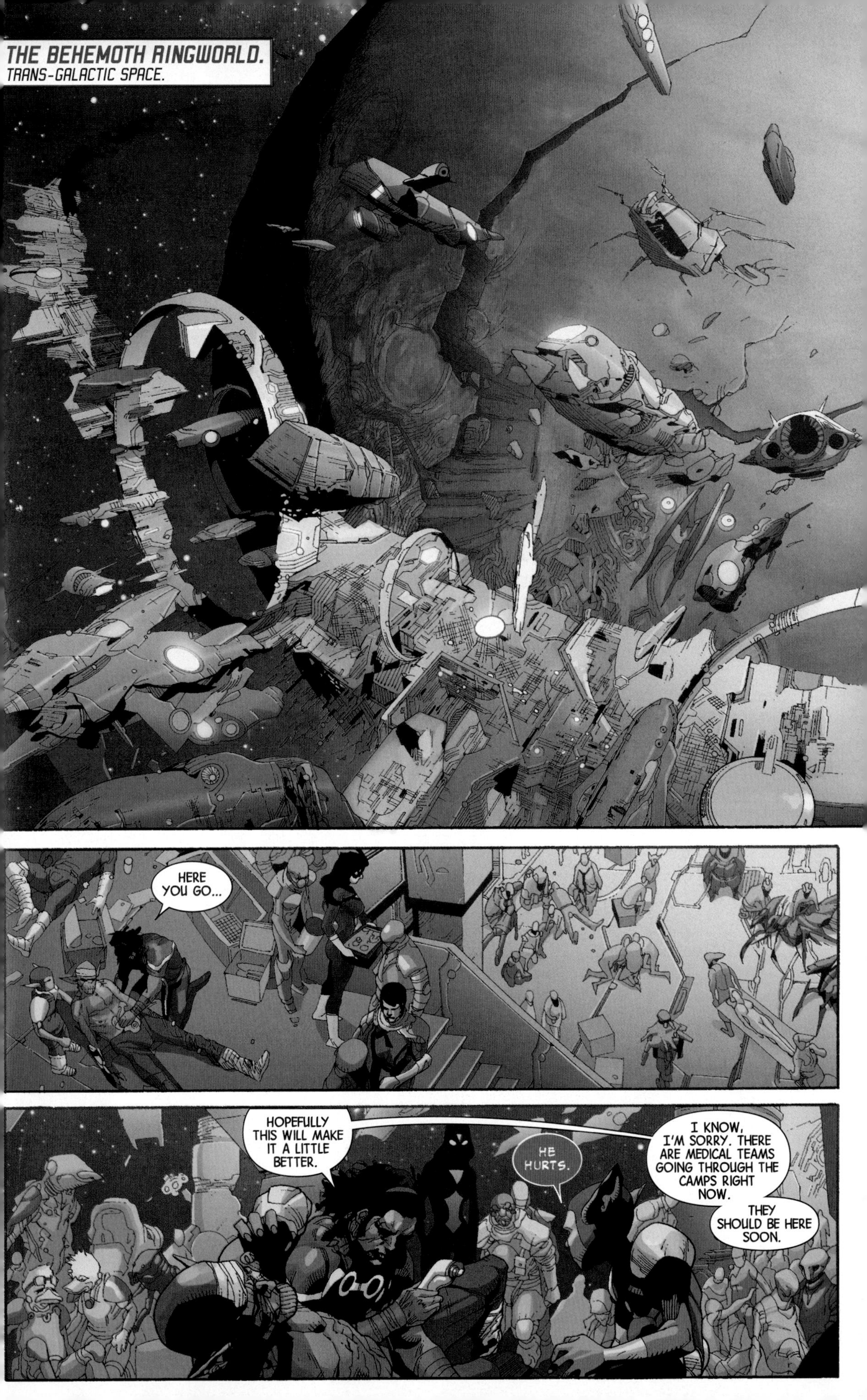
THE BEHEMOTH RINGWORLD.
TRANS-GALACTIC SPACE.
HERE YOU GO...
HOPEFULLY THIS WILL MAKE IT A LITTLE BETTER.
HE HURTS.
I KNOW, I'M SORRY. THERE ARE MEDICAL TEAMS GOING THROUGH THE CAMPS RIGHT NOW.
THEY SHOULD BE HERE SOON.

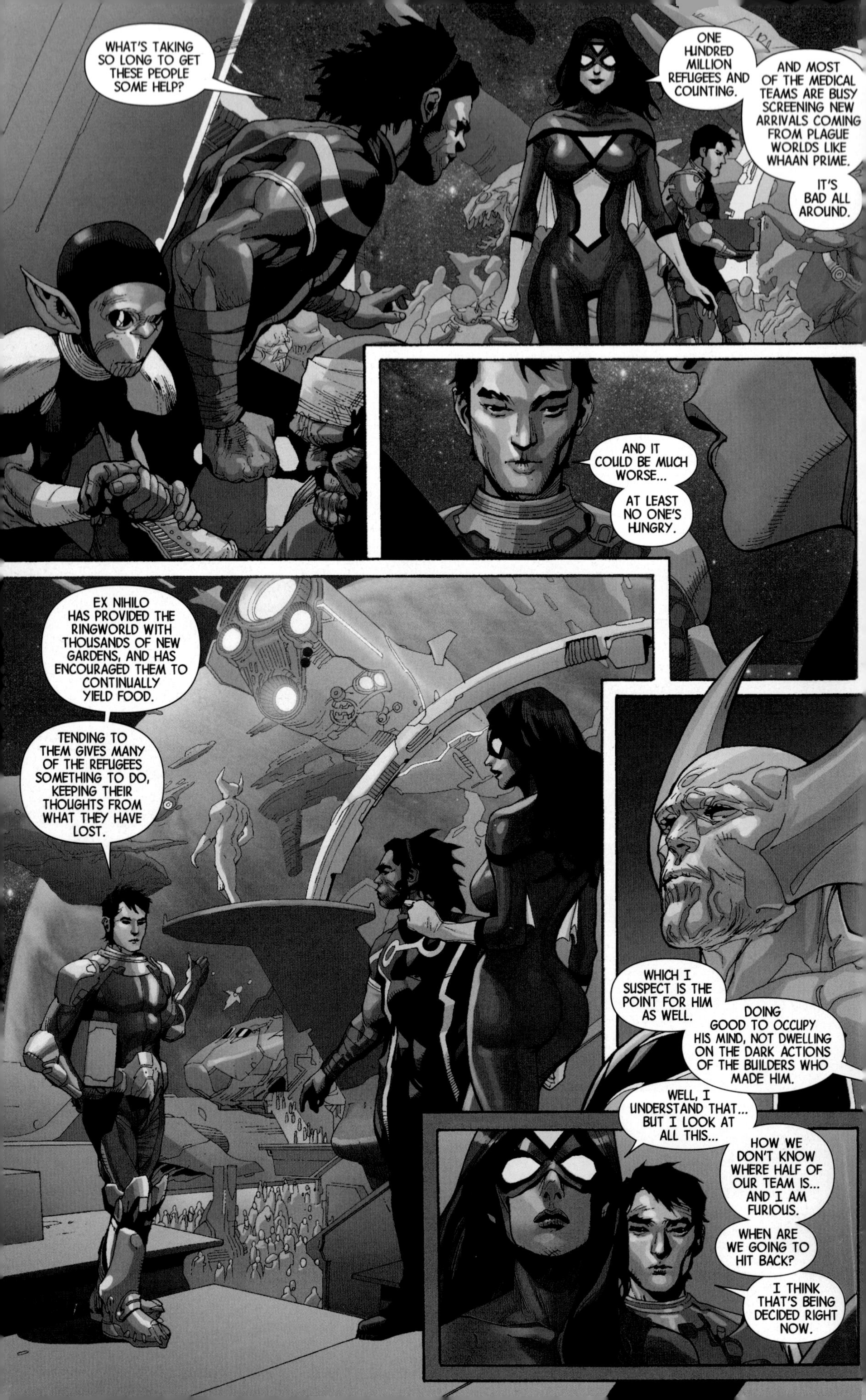
WHAT'S TAKING SO LONG TO GET THESE PEOPLE SOME HELP?
ONE HUNDRED MILLION REFUGEES AND COUNTING.
AND MOST OF THE MEDICAL TEAMS ARE BUSY SCREENING NEW ARRIVALS COMING FROM PLAGUE WORLDS LIKE WHAAN PRIME.
IT'S BAD ALL AROUND.
AND IT COULD BE MUCH WORSE...
AT LEAST NO ONE'S HUNGRY.
EX NIHILO HAS PROVIDED THE RINGWORLD WITH THOUSANDS OF NEW GARDENS, AND HAS ENCOURAGED THEM TO CONTINUALLY YIELD FOOD.
TENDING TO THEM GIVES MANY OF THE REFUGEES SOMETHING TO DO, KEEPING THEIR THOUGHTS FROM WHAT THEY HAVE LOST.
WHICH I SUSPECT IS THE POINT FOR HIM AS WELL.
DOING GOOD TO OCCUPY HIS MIND, NOT DWELLING ON THE DARK ACTIONS OF THE BUILDERS WHO MADE HIM.
WELL, I UNDERSTAND THAT... BUT I LOOK AT ALL THIS...
HOW WE DON'T KNOW WHERE HALF OF OUR TEAM IS... AND I AM FURIOUS.
WHEN ARE WE GOING TO HIT BACK?
I THINK THAT'S BEING DECIDED RIGHT NOW.

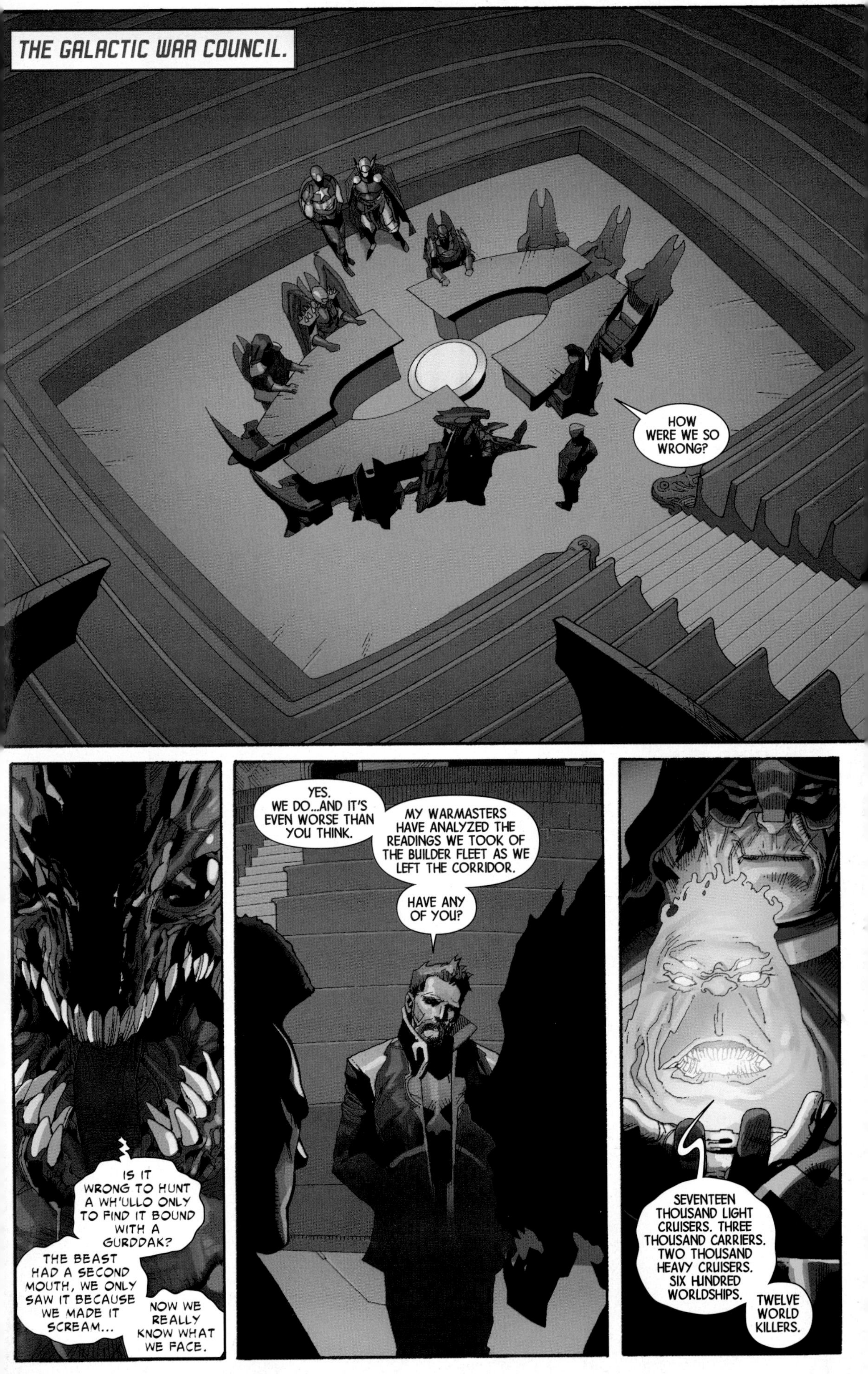
THE GALACTIC WAR COUNCIL.
HOW WERE WE SO WRONG?
IS IT WRONG TO HUNT A WH'ULLO ONLY TO FIND IT BOUND WITH A GURDDAK?
THE BEAST HAD A SECOND MOUTH, WE ONLY SAW IT BECAUSE WE MADE IT SCREAM...
NOW WE REALLY KNOW WHAT WE FACE.
YES. WE DO...AND IT'S EVEN WORSE THAN YOU THINK.
MY WARMASTERS HAVE ANALYZED THE READINGS WE TOOK OF THE BUILDER FLEET AS WE LEFT THE CORRIDOR.
HAVE ANY OF YOU?
SEVENTEEN THOUSAND LIGHT CRUISERS. THREE THOUSAND CARRIERS. TWO THOUSAND HEAVY CRUISERS. SIX HUNDRED WORLDSHIPS.
TWELVE WORLD KILLERS.

ALL THESE THINGS WE'VE MADE

◆

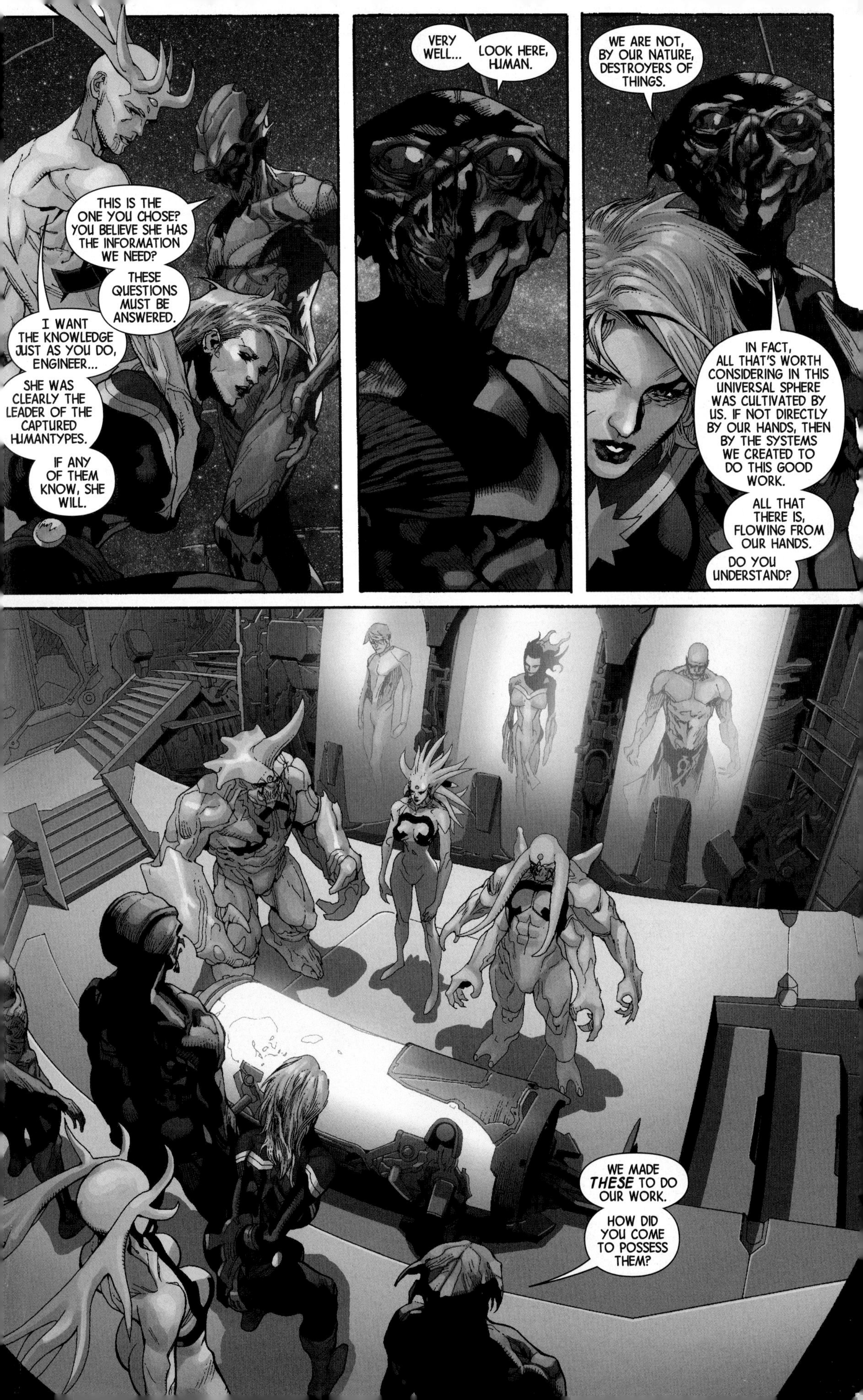
THIS IS THE ONE YOU CHOSE? YOU BELIEVE SHE HAS THE INFORMATION WE NEED?
THESE QUESTIONS MUST BE ANSWERED.
I WANT THE KNOWLEDGE JUST AS YOU DO, ENGINEER...
SHE WAS CLEARLY THE LEADER OF THE CAPTURED HUMANTYPES.
IF ANY OF THEM KNOW, SHE WILL.
VERY WELL...
LOOK HERE, HUMAN.
WE ARE NOT, BY OUR NATURE, DESTROYERS OF THINGS.
IN FACT, ALL THAT'S WORTH CONSIDERING IN THIS UNIVERSAL SPHERE WAS CULTIVATED BY US. IF NOT DIRECTLY BY OUR HANDS, THEN BY THE SYSTEMS WE CREATED TO DO THIS GOOD WORK.
ALL THAT THERE IS, FLOWING FROM OUR HANDS.
DO YOU UNDERSTAND?
WE MADE *THESE* TO DO OUR WORK.
HOW DID YOU COME TO POSSESS THEM?

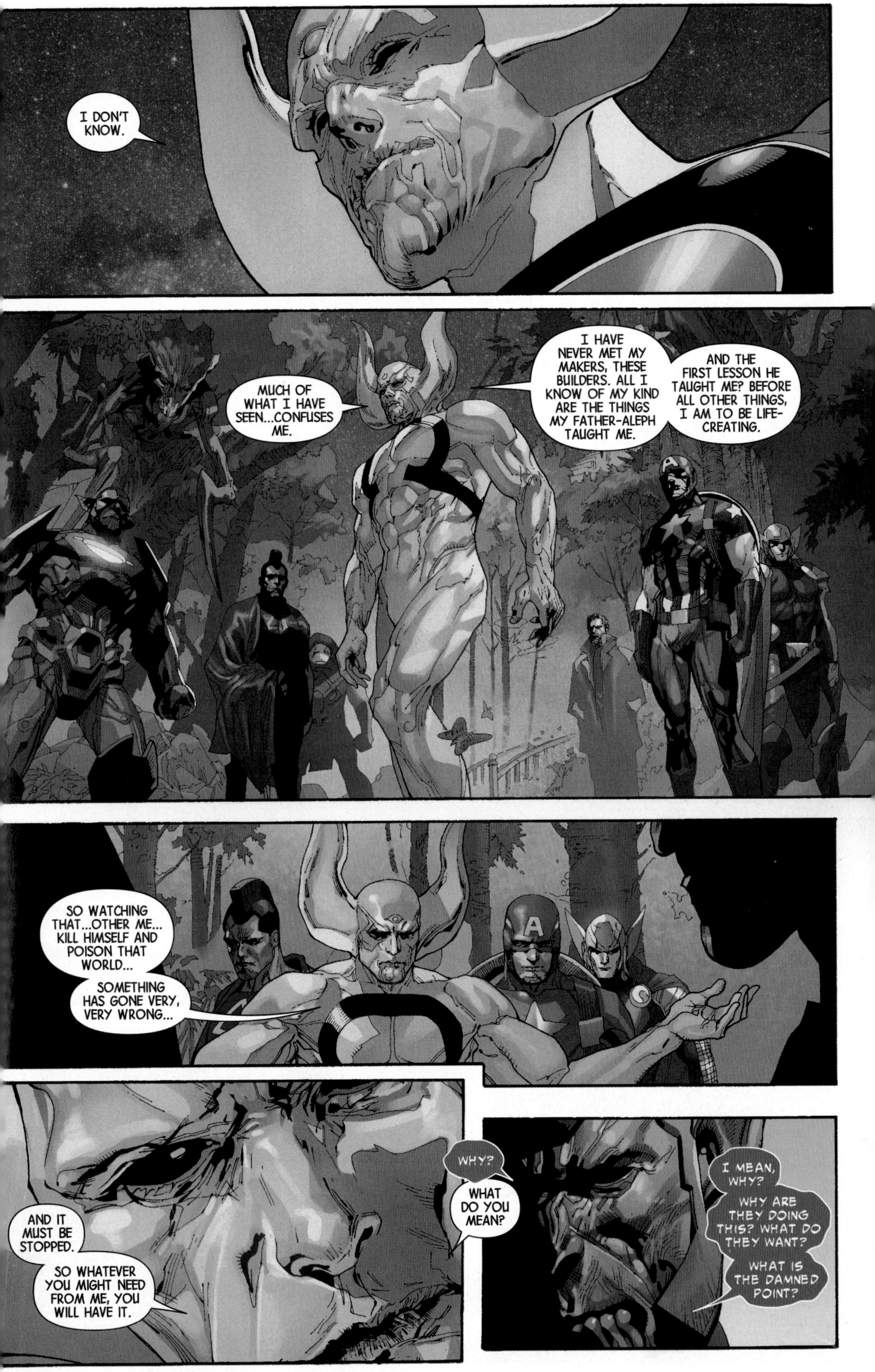
I DON'T KNOW.
MUCH OF WHAT I HAVE SEEN...CONFUSES ME.
I HAVE NEVER MET MY MAKERS, THESE BUILDERS. ALL I KNOW OF MY KIND ARE THE THINGS MY FATHER-ALEPH TAUGHT ME.
AND THE FIRST LESSON HE TAUGHT ME? BEFORE ALL OTHER THINGS, I AM TO BE LIFE-CREATING.
SO WATCHING THAT...OTHER ME... KILL HIMSELF AND POISON THAT WORLD...
SOMETHING HAS GONE VERY, VERY WRONG...
AND IT MUST BE STOPPED.
SO WHATEVER YOU MIGHT NEED FROM ME, YOU WILL HAVE IT.
WHY?
WHAT DO YOU MEAN?
I MEAN, WHY?
WHY ARE THEY DOING THIS? WHAT DO THEY WANT?
WHAT IS THE DAMNED POINT?

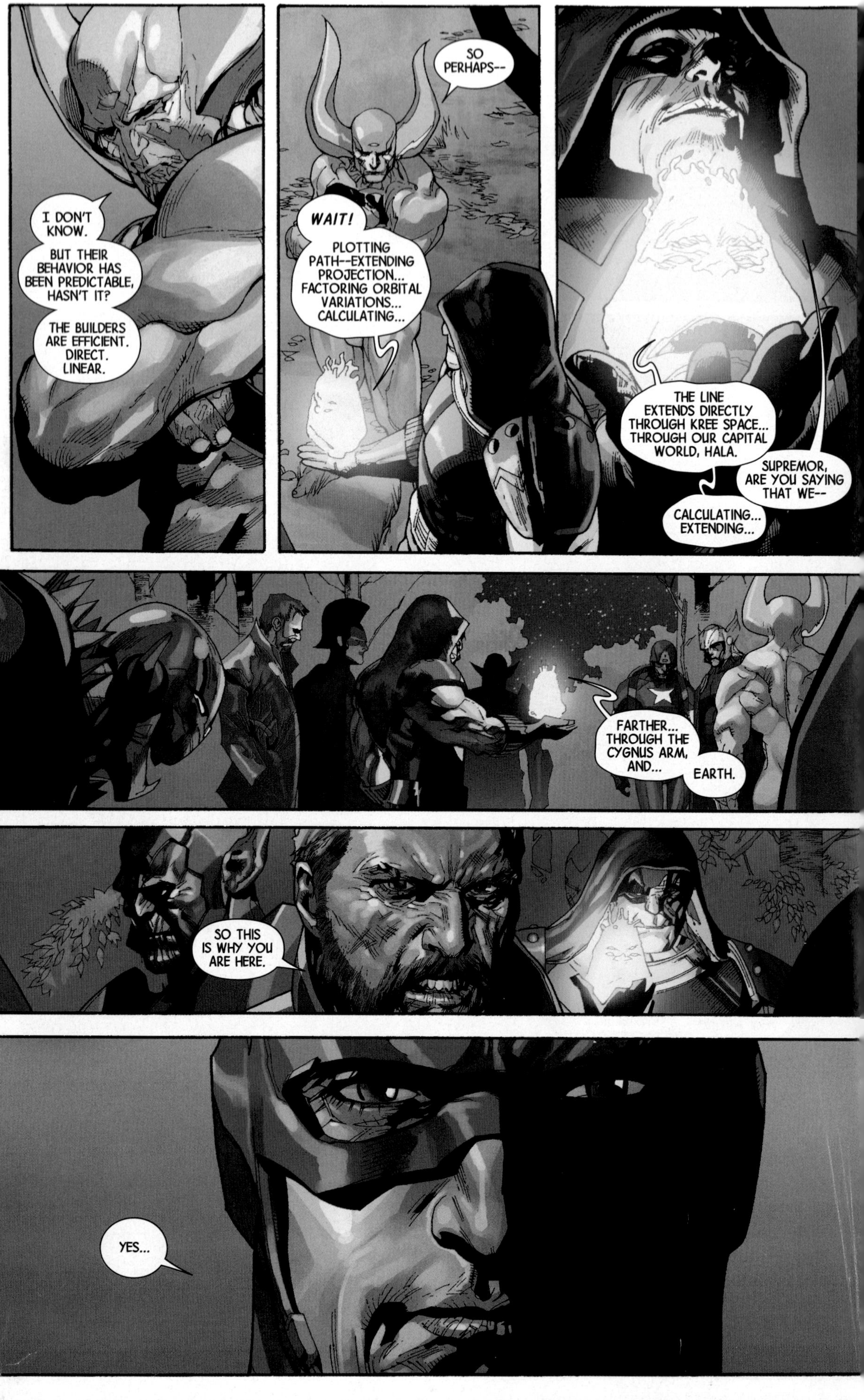
I DON'T KNOW.
BUT THEIR BEHAVIOR HAS BEEN PREDICTABLE, HASN'T IT?
THE BUILDERS ARE EFFICIENT. DIRECT. LINEAR.
SO PERHAPS--
WAIT!
PLOTTING PATH--EXTENDING PROJECTION... FACTORING ORBITAL VARIATIONS... CALCULATING...
THE LINE EXTENDS DIRECTLY THROUGH KREE SPACE... THROUGH OUR CAPITAL WORLD, HALA.
SUPREMOR, ARE YOU SAYING THAT WE--
CALCULATING... EXTENDING...
FARTHER... THROUGH THE CYGNUS ARM, AND...
EARTH.
SO THIS IS WHY YOU ARE HERE.
YES...

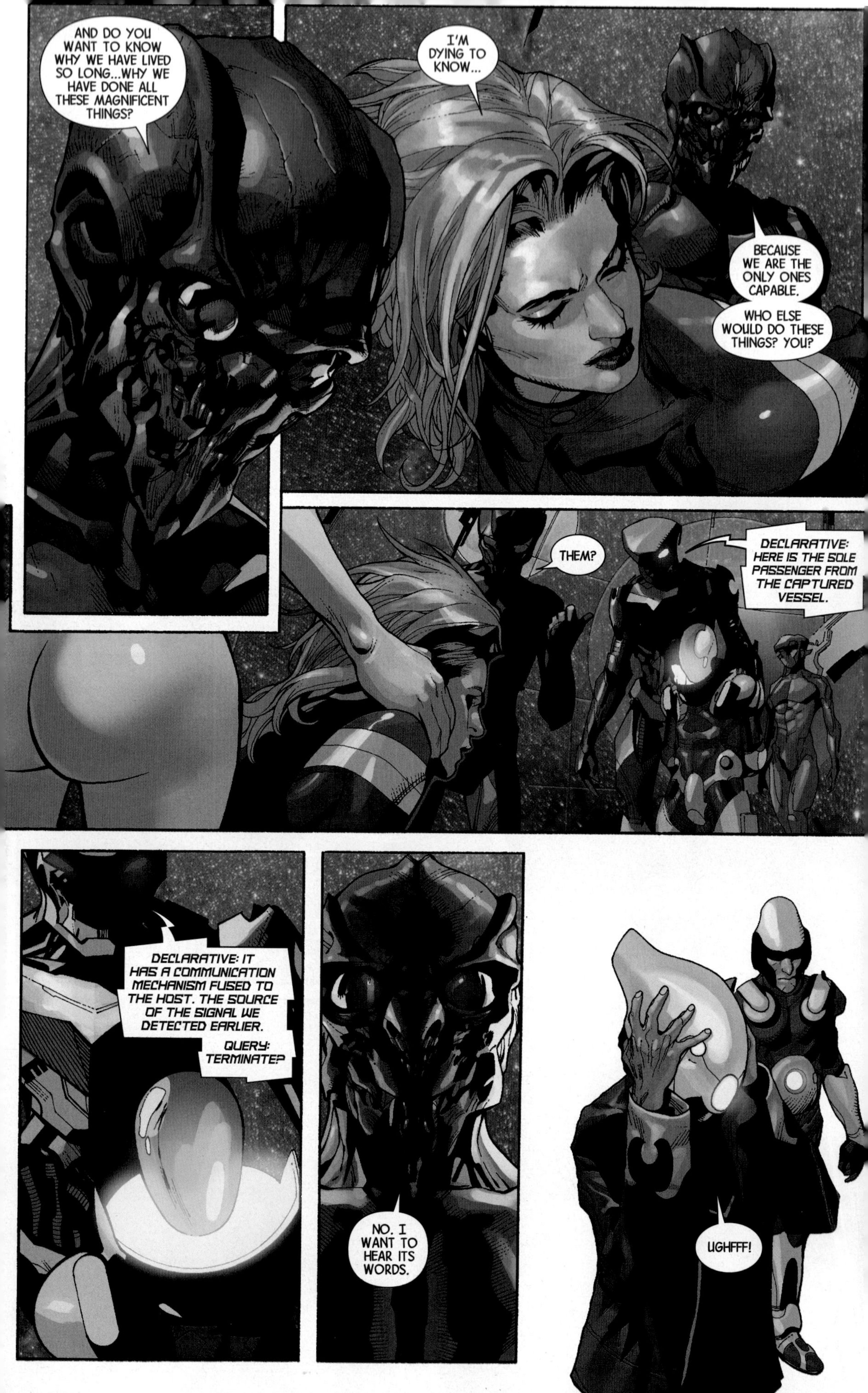
AND DO YOU WANT TO KNOW WHY WE HAVE LIVED SO LONG...WHY WE HAVE DONE ALL THESE MAGNIFICENT THINGS?
I'M DYING TO KNOW...
BECAUSE WE ARE THE ONLY ONES CAPABLE.
WHO ELSE WOULD DO THESE THINGS? YOU?
THEM?
DECLARATIVE: HERE IS THE SOLE PASSENGER FROM THE CAPTURED VESSEL.
DECLARATIVE: IT HAS A COMMUNICATION MECHANISM FUSED TO THE HOST. THE SOURCE OF THE SIGNAL WE DETECTED EARLIER.
QUERY: TERMINATE?
NO. I WANT TO HEAR ITS WORDS.
UGHFFF!

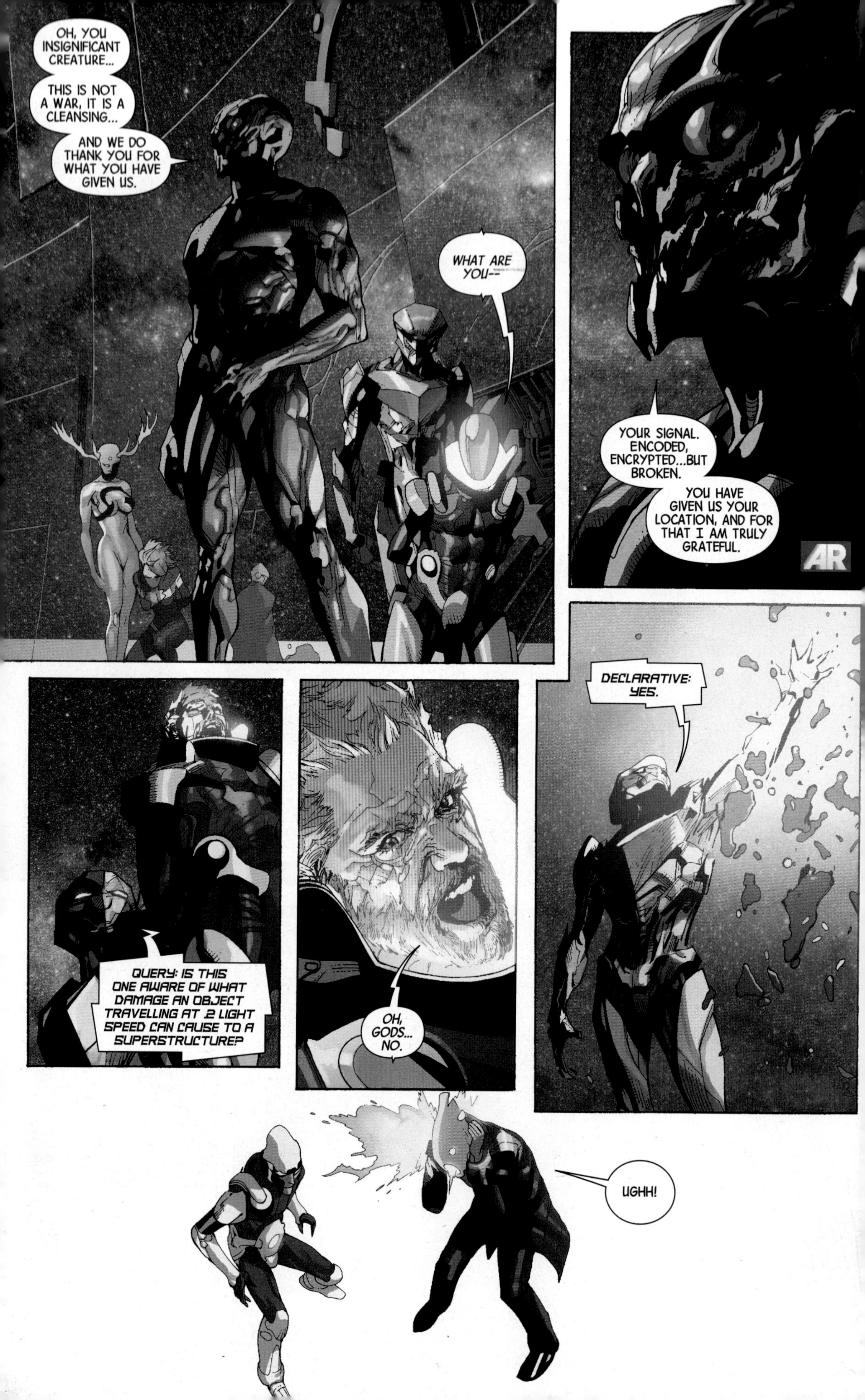
OH, YOU INSIGNIFICANT CREATURE...
THIS IS NOT A WAR, IT IS A CLEANSING...
AND WE DO THANK YOU FOR WHAT YOU HAVE GIVEN US.
WHAT ARE YOU--
YOUR SIGNAL. ENCODED, ENCRYPTED...BUT BROKEN.
YOU HAVE GIVEN US YOUR LOCATION, AND FOR THAT I AM TRULY GRATEFUL.
AR
QUERY: IS THIS ONE AWARE OF WHAT DAMAGE AN OBJECT TRAVELLING AT .2 LIGHT SPEED CAN CAUSE TO A SUPERSTRUCTURE?
OH, GODS... NO.
DECLARATIVE: YES.
UGHH!

IT IS A GOOD PLAN, BUT THERE IS A PROBLEM...

IT WILL NOT WORK WITHOUT A BELIEVABLE FORWARD ACTION. THE PRICE WILL BE HIGH.

YOU HAVE TO... TO... LISTEN...

CAN WE PLEDGE THE FULL MIGHT OF THE ACCUSERS, RONAN?

IF YOU CALL FOR IT, SUPREMOR, THE CORPS WILL ANSWER.

THEN IT IS SETTLED. WE WILL--

NO! SOMETHING'S WRONG... SOMETHING'S...

WRONG.

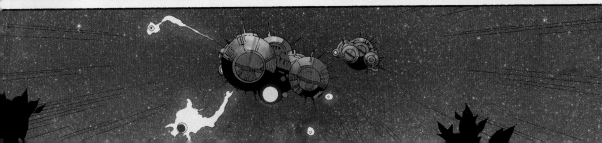

THEY'VE FOUND US.

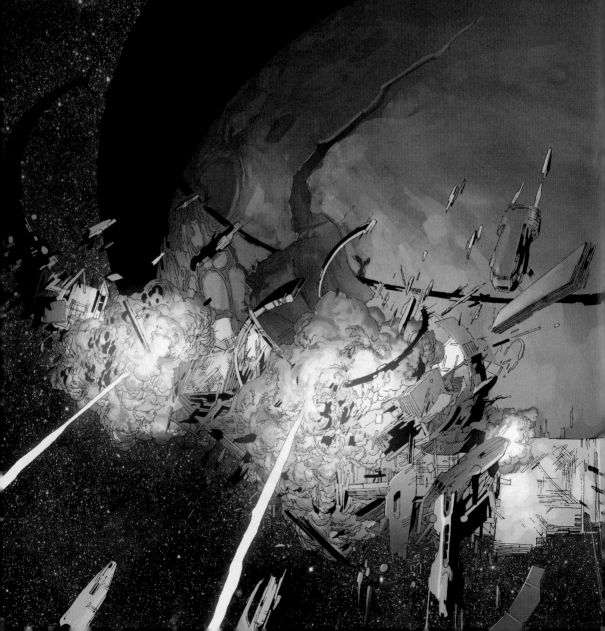

"THE OFFER"

PREVIOUSLY IN INFINITY

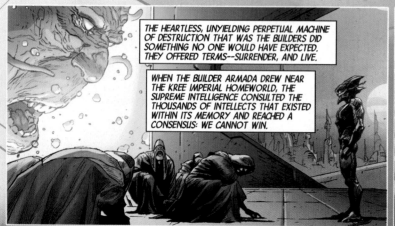

THE HEARTLESS, UNYIELDING PERPETUAL MACHINE OF DESTRUCTION THAT WAS THE BUILDERS DID SOMETHING NO ONE WOULD HAVE EXPECTED. THEY OFFERED TERMS--SURRENDER, AND LIVE.
WHEN THE BUILDER ARMADA DREW NEAR THE KREE IMPERIAL HOMEWORLD, THE SUPREME INTELLIGENCE CONSULTED THE THOUSANDS OF INTELLECTS THAT EXISTED WITHIN ITS MEMORY AND REACHED A CONSENSUS: WE CANNOT WIN.
IT HAS BEEN SO LONG...ARE WE SURE? HOW IS IT POSSIBLE?
I DON'T KNOW...BUT IT IS WONDERFUL, ISN'T IT? AN ABYSS... ALIVE.
MUCH OF WHAT I HAVE SEEN...CONFUSES ME. I HAVE NEVER MET MY MAKERS, THESE BUILDERS. ALL I KNOW IS WHAT MY FATHER-ALEPH TAUGHT ME, FIRST AND FOREMOST BEING I WAS MADE TO BE LIFE-CREATING. SO WATCHING THAT...OTHER ME...KILL HIMSELF AND POISON THAT WORLD...
SOMETHING HAS GONE VERY, VERY WRONG...
AND IT MUST BE STOPPED.
POWER IS FAILING. WE NEED TO RETREAT. WE NEED TO--
NO. THERE IS NOWHERE LEFT TO RUN, SOLDIER.
WE WIN HERE NOW... OR WE LOSE IT ALL. GIVE THE ORDER...
FIRE EVERYTHING WE'VE GOT.
WE HAVE LOST EIGHT OF THE GREAT WEAPONS, BUILDERS--AND OUR COMMAND SHIP IS SHIELDLESS AND INCAPABLE OF ESCAPING. THE ROGUE PLANET KILLERS HAVE TURNED TO FIRING AT THE FLEET.
GIVE THE ORDER FOR THE BULK OF THE VESSELS TO LEAVE.
YOU MUST LEAVE AS WELL, CREATOR.
WE HAVE BEEN STUNG TODAY. IT IS AN INSULT I WILL NOT FORGET. SCUTTLE THE SHIP, THEN JOIN IN THE BATTLE. MAKE YOUR END MEAN SOMETHING, EX NIHILA.

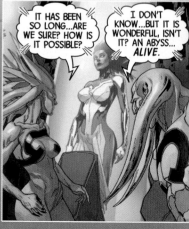

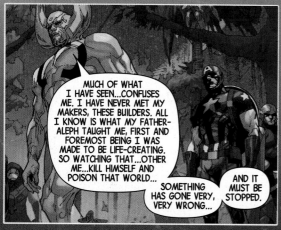

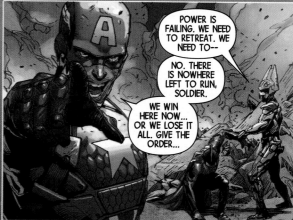

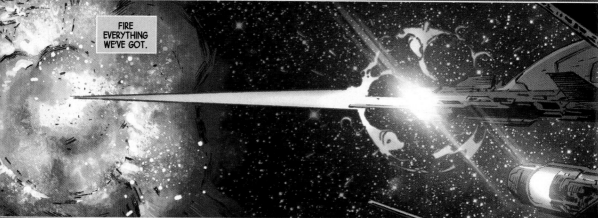

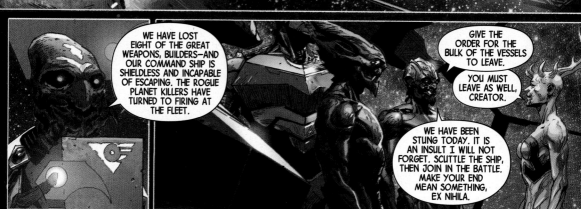

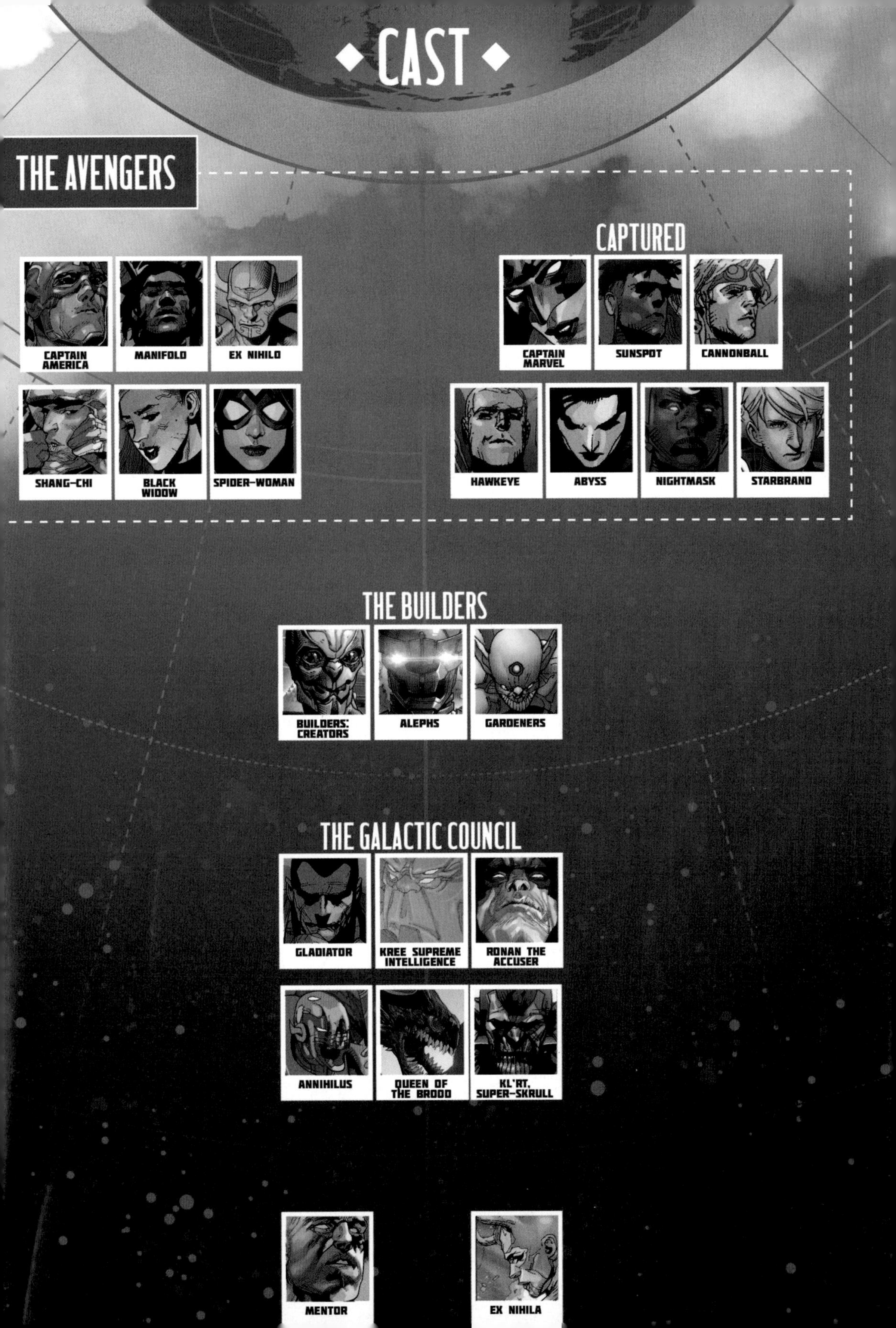
CAST
THE AVENGERS
CAPTAIN AMERICA
MANIFOLD
EX NIHILO
SHANG-CHI
BLACK WIDOW
SPIDER-WOMAN
CAPTURED
CAPTAIN MARVEL
SUNSPOT
CANNONBALL
HAWKEYE
ABYSS
NIGHTMASK
STARBRAND
THE BUILDERS
BUILDERS: CREATORS
ALEPHS
GARDENERS
THE GALACTIC COUNCIL
GLADIATOR
KREE SUPREME INTELLIGENCE
RONAN THE ACCUSER
ANNIHILUS
QUEEN OF THE BROOD
KL'RT, SUPER-SKRULL
MENTOR
EX NIHILA

THE WORDS OF A
GARDENER

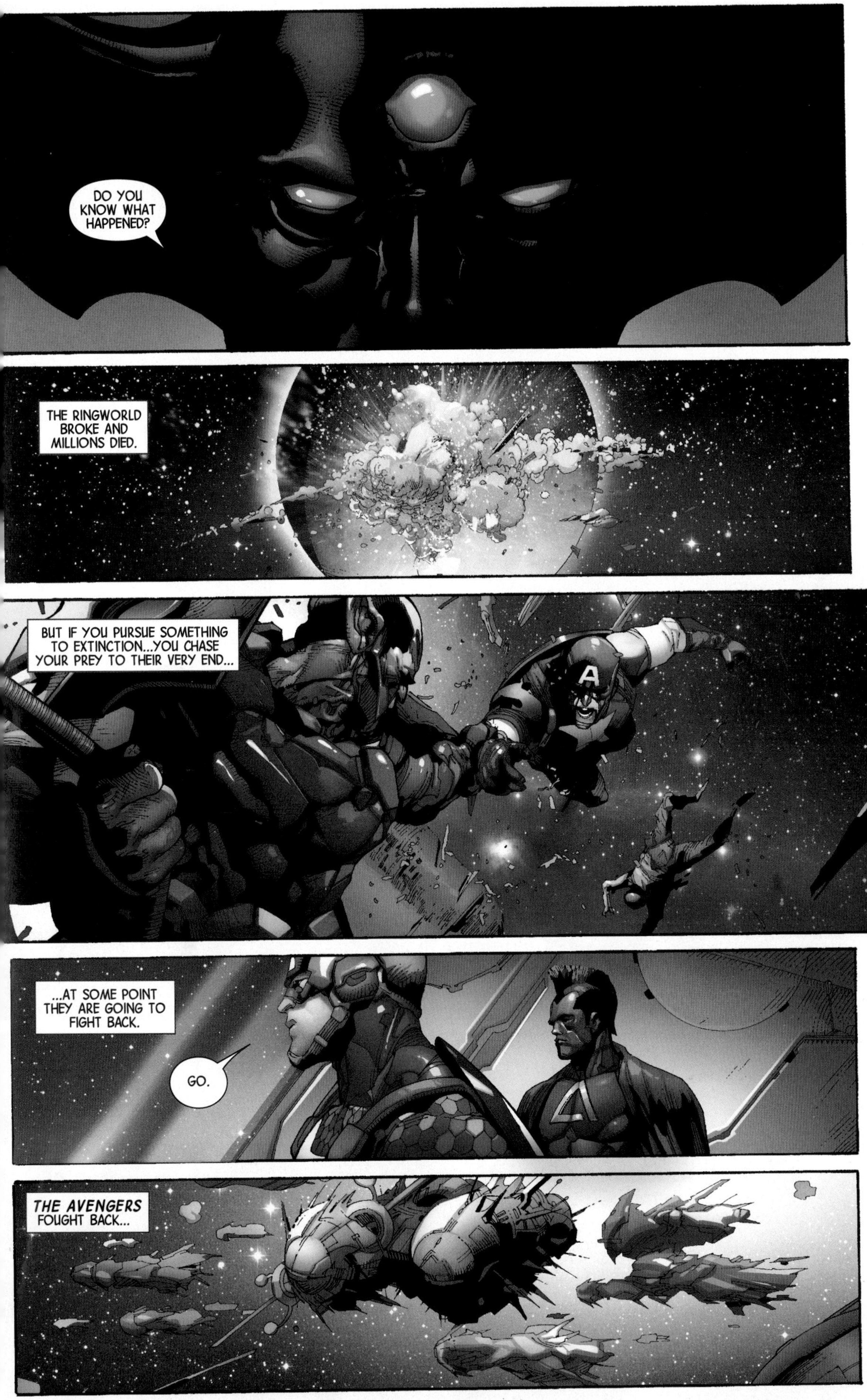
DO YOU KNOW WHAT HAPPENED?
THE RINGWORLD BROKE AND MILLIONS DIED.
BUT IF YOU PURSUE SOMETHING TO EXTINCTION...YOU CHASE YOUR PREY TO THEIR VERY END...
...AT SOME POINT THEY ARE GOING TO FIGHT BACK.
GO.
THE AVENGERS FOUGHT BACK...

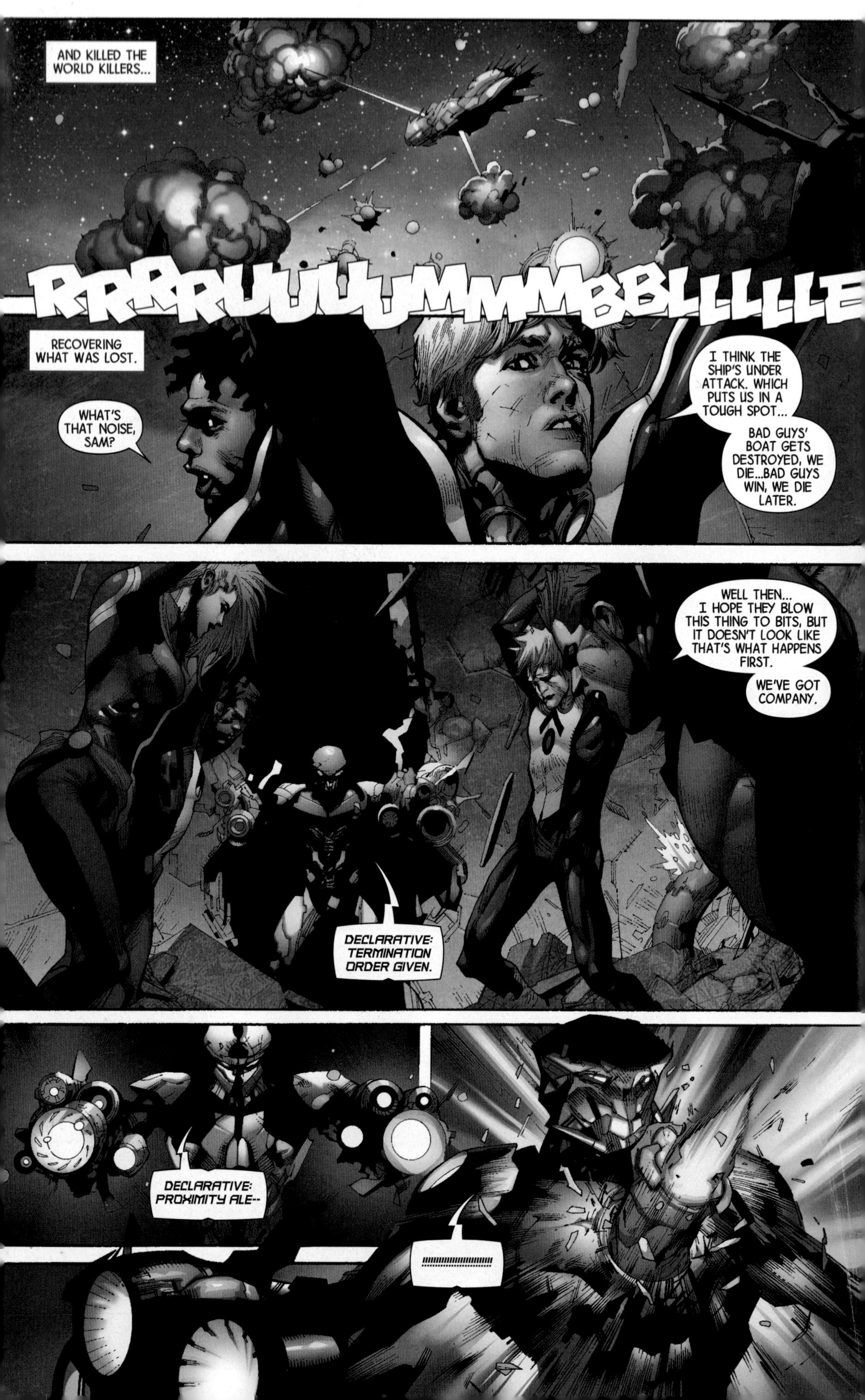
AND KILLED THE WORLD KILLERS...
RRRRUUUUMMMMBBLLLLLE
RECOVERING WHAT WAS LOST.
WHAT'S THAT NOISE, SAM?
I THINK THE SHIP'S UNDER ATTACK. WHICH PUTS US IN A TOUGH SPOT...
BAD GUYS' BOAT GETS DESTROYED, WE DIE...BAD GUYS WIN, WE DIE LATER.
WELL THEN... I HOPE THEY BLOW THIS THING TO BITS, BUT IT DOESN'T LOOK LIKE THAT'S WHAT HAPPENS FIRST.
WE'VE GOT COMPANY.
DECLARATIVE: TERMINATION ORDER GIVEN.
DECLARATIVE: PROXIMITY ALE--

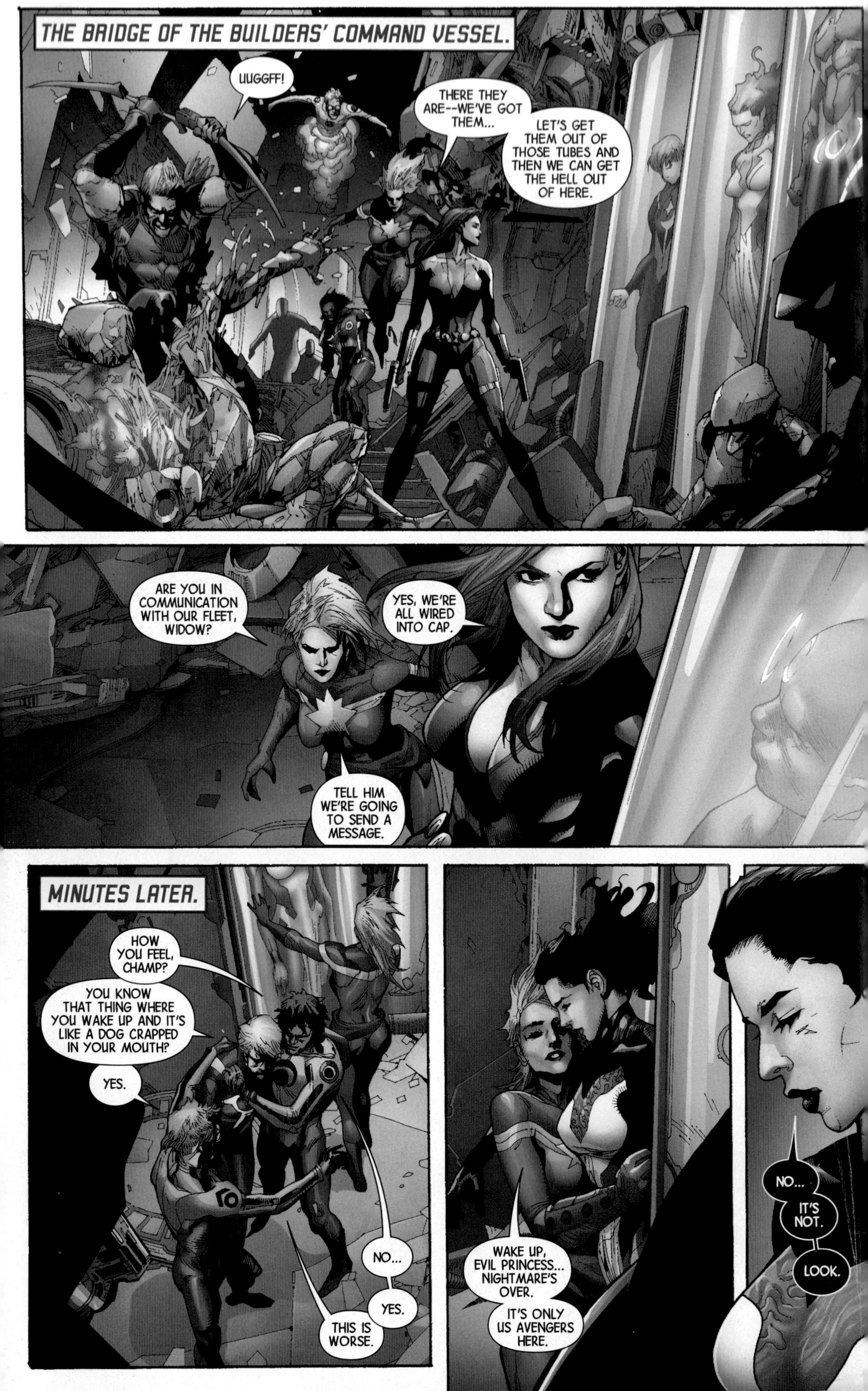
THE BRIDGE OF THE BUILDERS' COMMAND VESSEL.
UUGGFF!
THERE THEY ARE--WE'VE GOT THEM...
LET'S GET THEM OUT OF THOSE TUBES AND THEN WE CAN GET THE HELL OUT OF HERE.
ARE YOU IN COMMUNICATION WITH OUR FLEET, WIDOW?
YES, WE'RE ALL WIRED INTO CAP.
TELL HIM WE'RE GOING TO SEND A MESSAGE.
MINUTES LATER.
HOW YOU FEEL, CHAMP?
YOU KNOW THAT THING WHERE YOU WAKE UP AND IT'S LIKE A DOG CRAPPED IN YOUR MOUTH?
YES.
NO...
YES.
THIS IS WORSE.
WAKE UP, EVIL PRINCESS... NIGHTMARE'S OVER.
IT'S ONLY US AVENGERS HERE.
NO...
IT'S NOT.
LOOK.

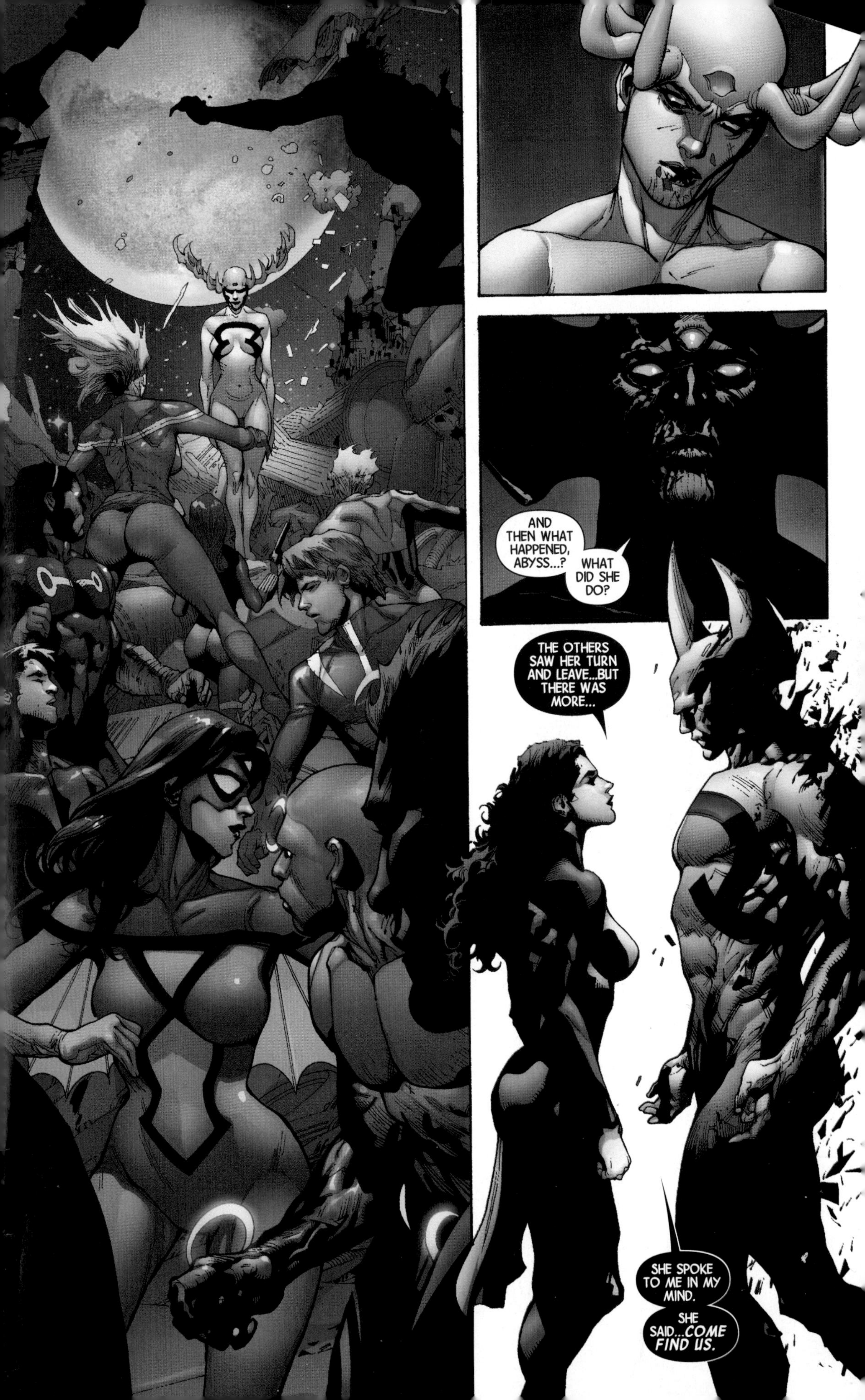
AND THEN WHAT HAPPENED, ABYSS...?
WHAT DID SHE DO?
THE OTHERS SAW HER TURN AND LEAVE...BUT THERE WAS MORE...
SHE SPOKE TO ME IN MY MIND.
SHE SAID...COME FIND US.

THE EDGE OF
ANNIHILATION

◆

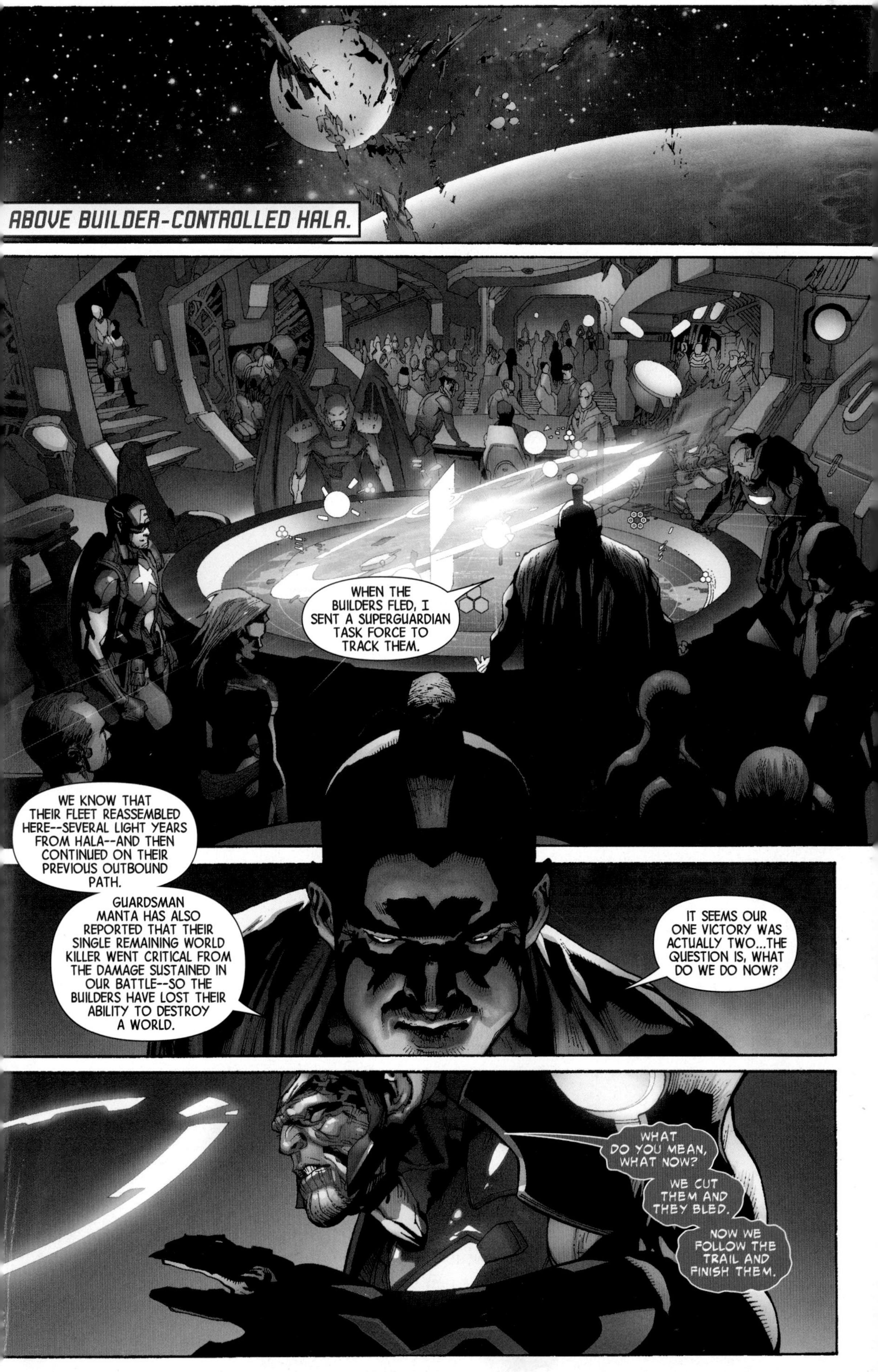
ABOVE BUILDER-CONTROLLED HALA.
WHEN THE BUILDERS FLED, I SENT A SUPERGUARDIAN TASK FORCE TO TRACK THEM.
WE KNOW THAT THEIR FLEET REASSEMBLED HERE--SEVERAL LIGHT YEARS FROM HALA--AND THEN CONTINUED ON THEIR PREVIOUS OUTBOUND PATH.
GUARDSMAN MANTA HAS ALSO REPORTED THAT THEIR SINGLE REMAINING WORLD KILLER WENT CRITICAL FROM THE DAMAGE SUSTAINED IN OUR BATTLE--SO THE BUILDERS HAVE LOST THEIR ABILITY TO DESTROY A WORLD.
IT SEEMS OUR ONE VICTORY WAS ACTUALLY TWO...THE QUESTION IS, WHAT DO WE DO NOW?
WHAT DO YOU MEAN, WHAT NOW?
WE CUT THEM AND THEY BLED.
NOW WE FOLLOW THE TRAIL AND FINISH THEM.

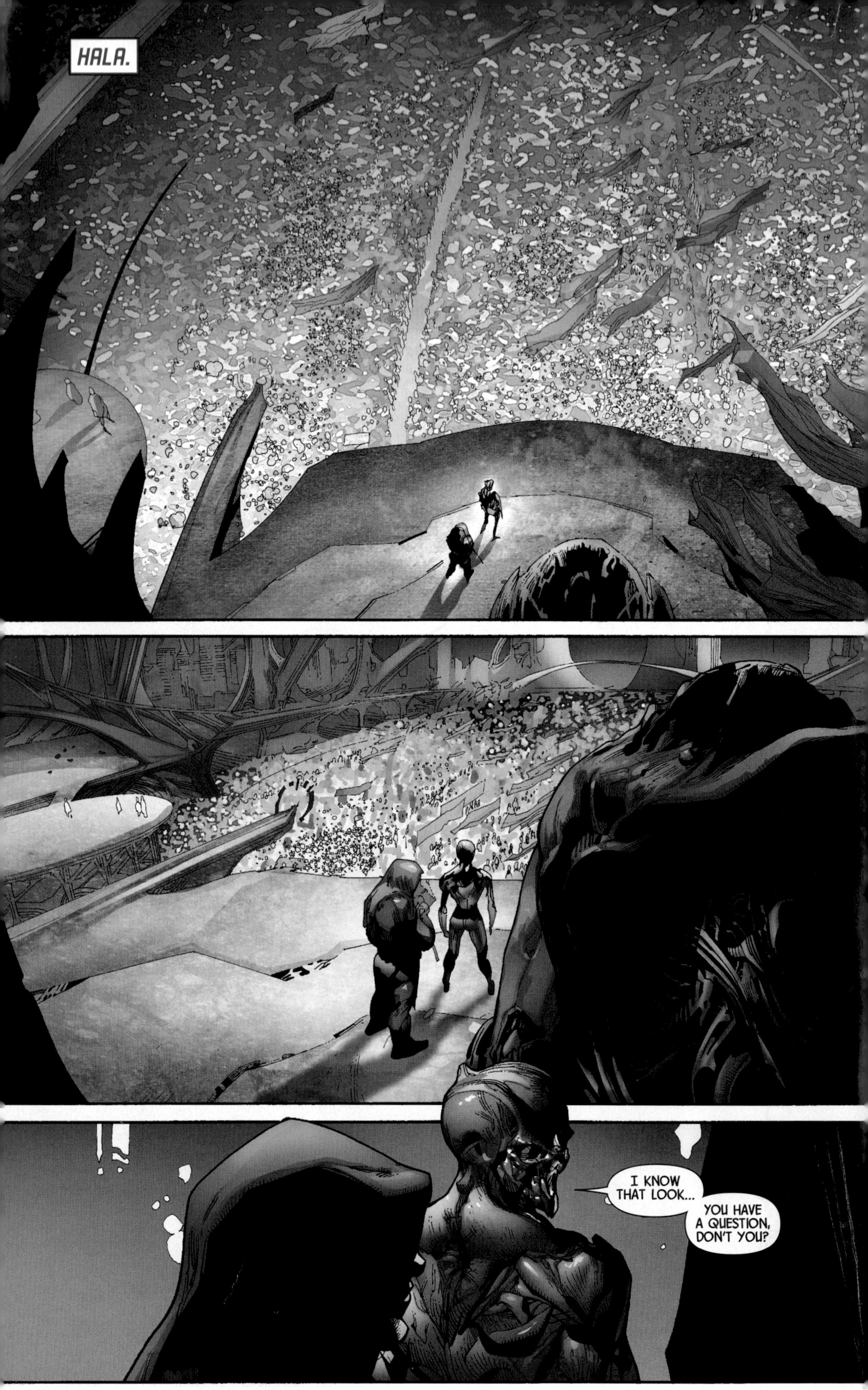
HALA.
I KNOW THAT LOOK...
YOU HAVE A QUESTION, DON'T YOU?

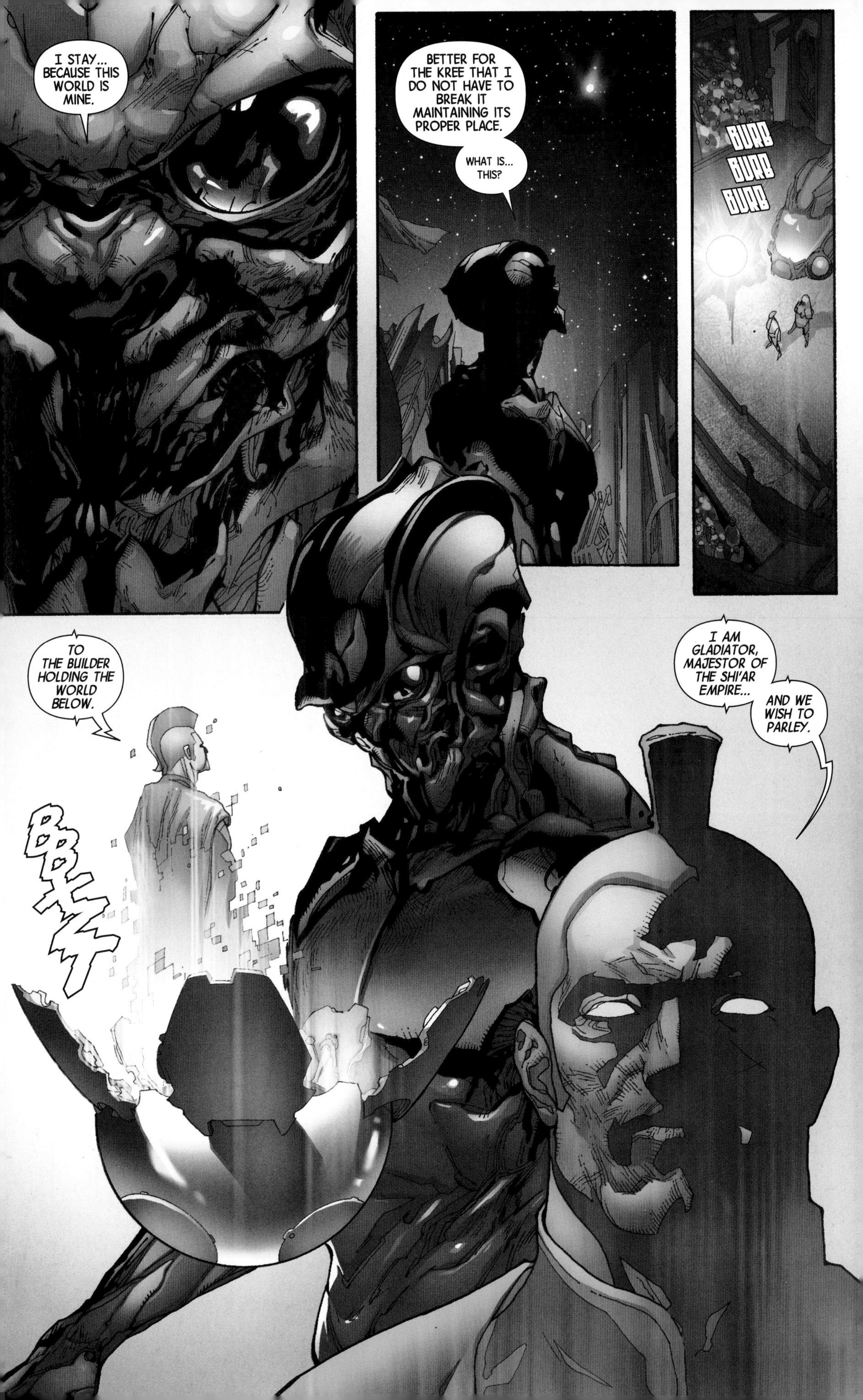
I STAY... BECAUSE THIS WORLD IS MINE.
BETTER FOR THE KREE THAT I DO NOT HAVE TO BREAK IT MAINTAINING ITS PROPER PLACE.
WHAT IS... THIS?
BURB BURB BURB
TO THE BUILDER HOLDING THE WORLD BELOW.
BBZZZT
I AM GLADIATOR, MAJESTOR OF THE SHI'AR EMPIRE...
AND WE WISH TO PARLEY.

WITHOUT JUDGES WE ARE LOST

◆

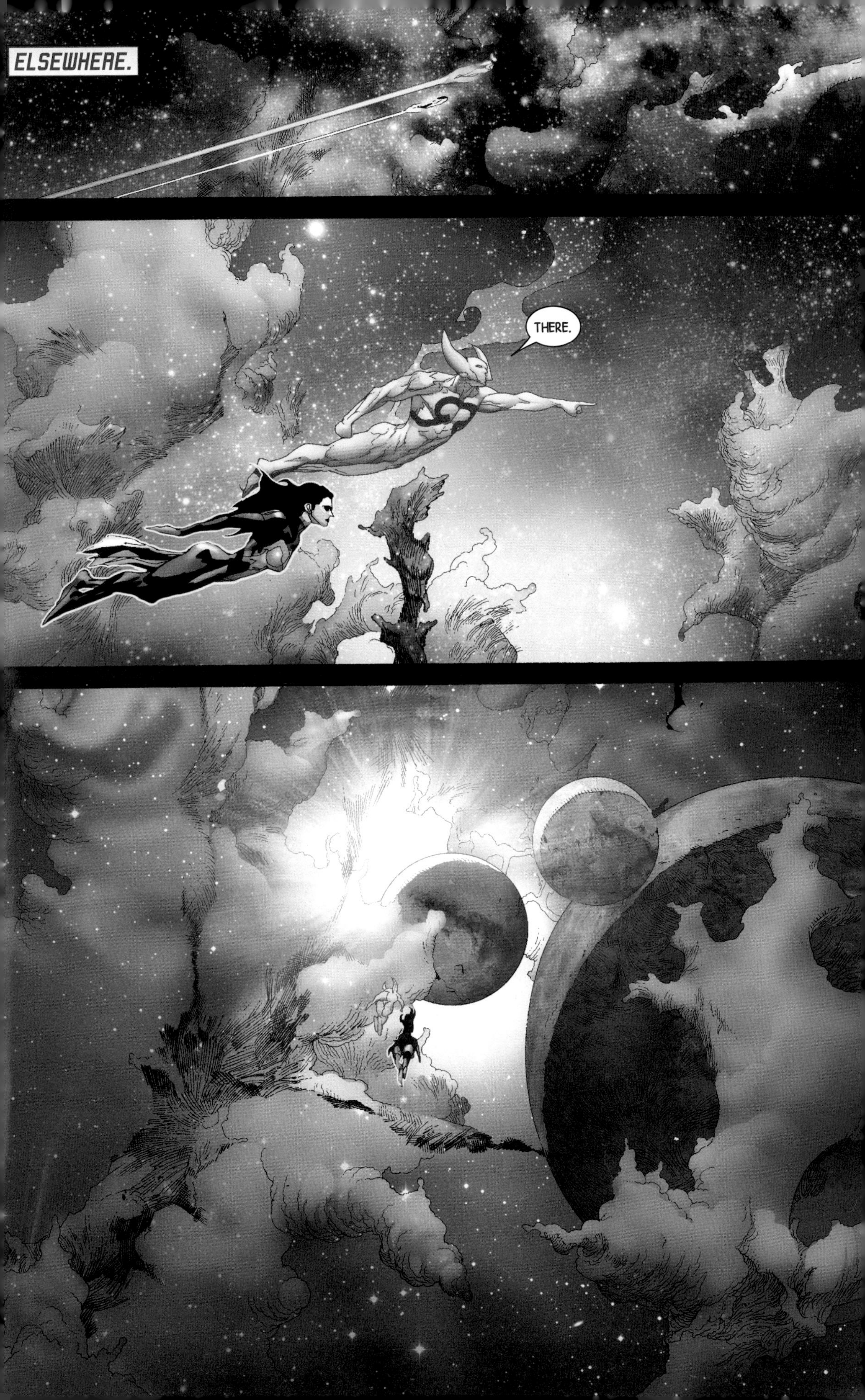
ELSEWHERE.
THERE.

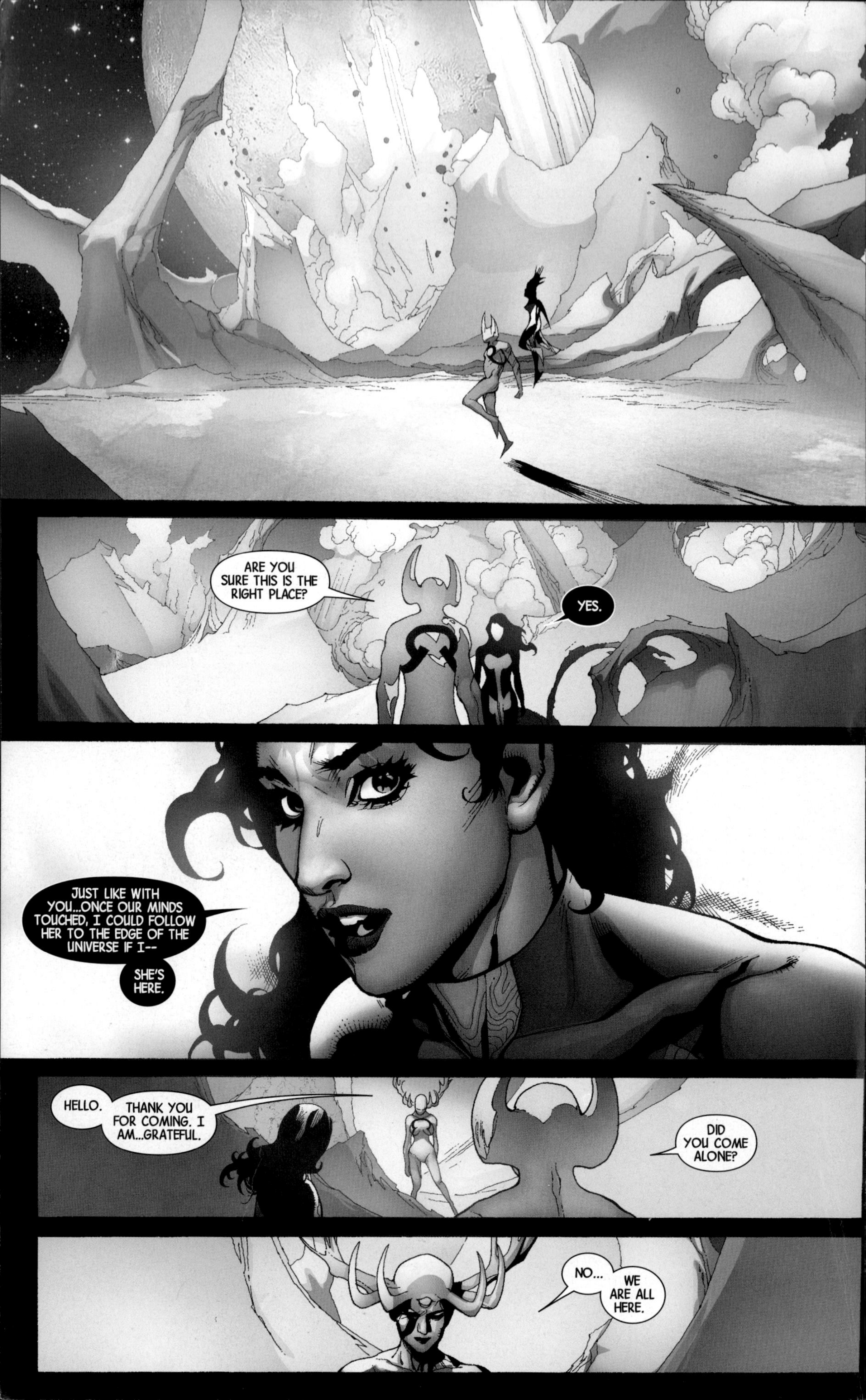
ARE YOU SURE THIS IS THE RIGHT PLACE?
YES.
JUST LIKE WITH YOU...ONCE OUR MINDS TOUCHED, I COULD FOLLOW HER TO THE EDGE OF THE UNIVERSE IF I--
SHE'S HERE.
HELLO.
THANK YOU FOR COMING. I AM...GRATEFUL.
DID YOU COME ALONE?
NO...
WE ARE ALL HERE.

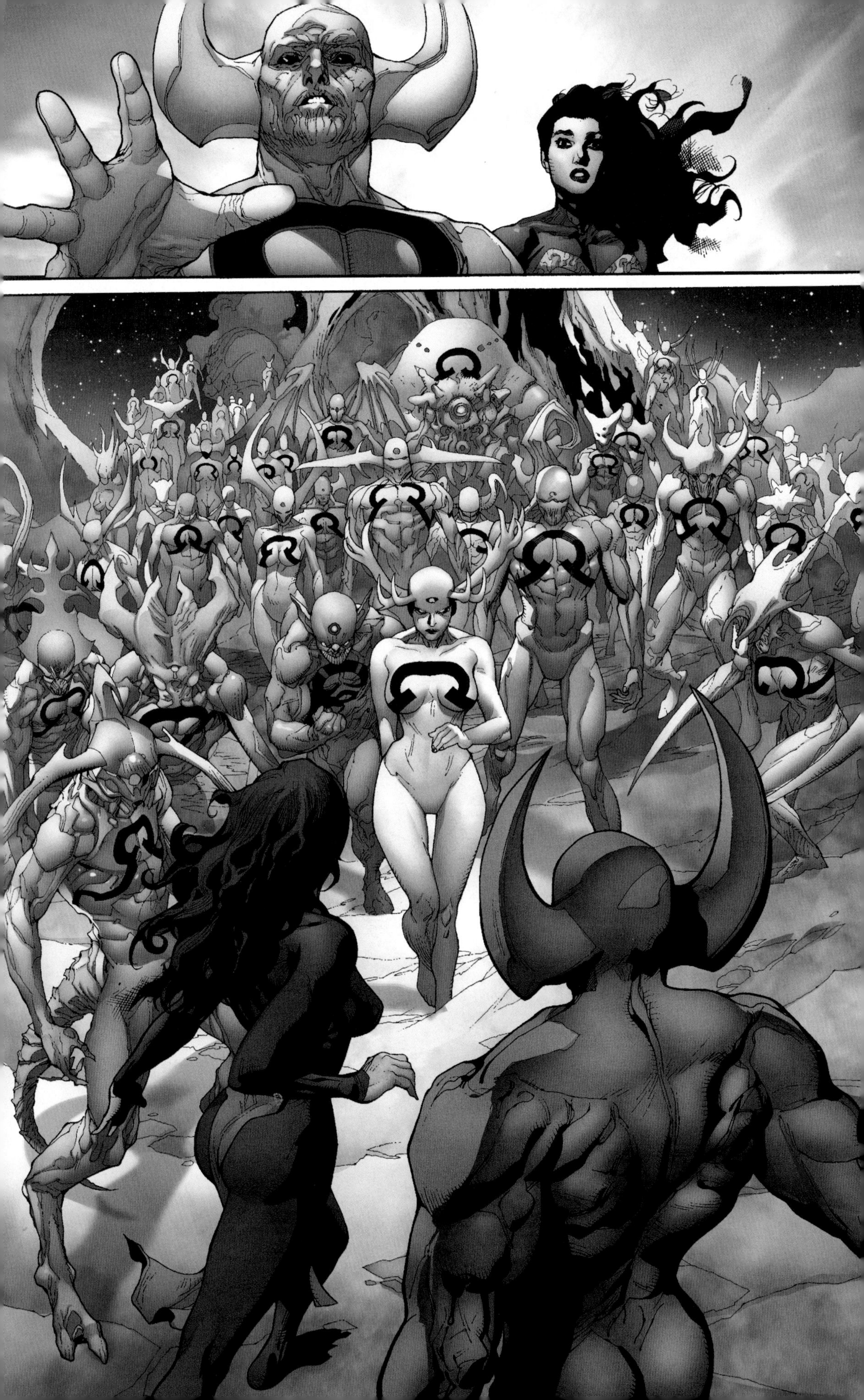

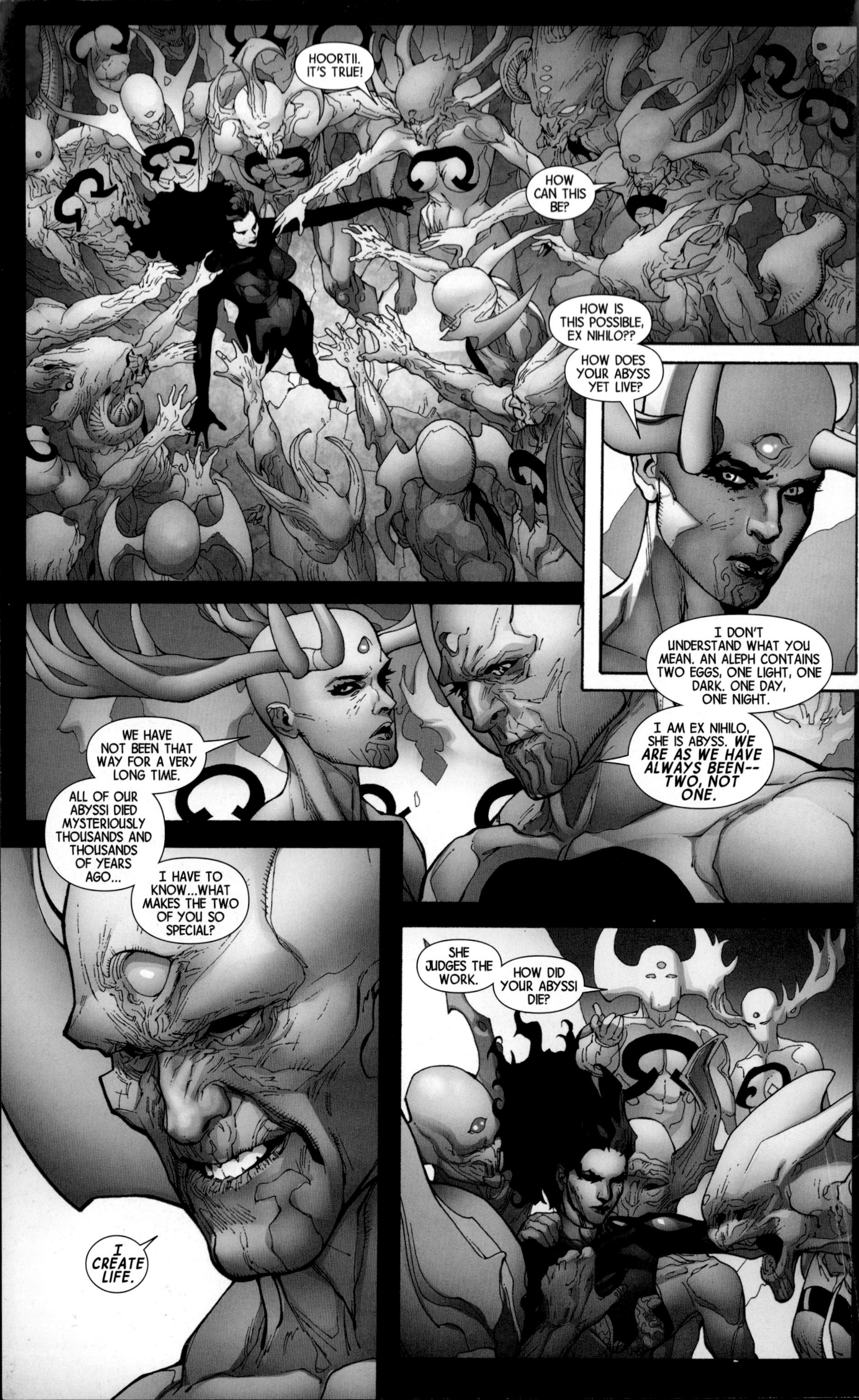
HOORTII. IT'S TRUE!
HOW CAN THIS BE?
HOW IS THIS POSSIBLE, EX NIHILO??
HOW DOES YOUR ABYSS YET LIVE?
I DON'T UNDERSTAND WHAT YOU MEAN. AN ALEPH CONTAINS TWO EGGS, ONE LIGHT, ONE DARK. ONE DAY, ONE NIGHT.
I AM EX NIHILO, SHE IS ABYSS. WE ARE AS WE HAVE ALWAYS BEEN-- TWO, NOT ONE.
WE HAVE NOT BEEN THAT WAY FOR A VERY LONG TIME.
ALL OF OUR ABYSSI DIED MYSTERIOUSLY THOUSANDS AND THOUSANDS OF YEARS AGO...
I HAVE TO KNOW...WHAT MAKES THE TWO OF YOU SO SPECIAL?
I CREATE LIFE.
SHE JUDGES THE WORK.
HOW DID YOUR ABYSSI DIE?

ONE MAN KNEELS

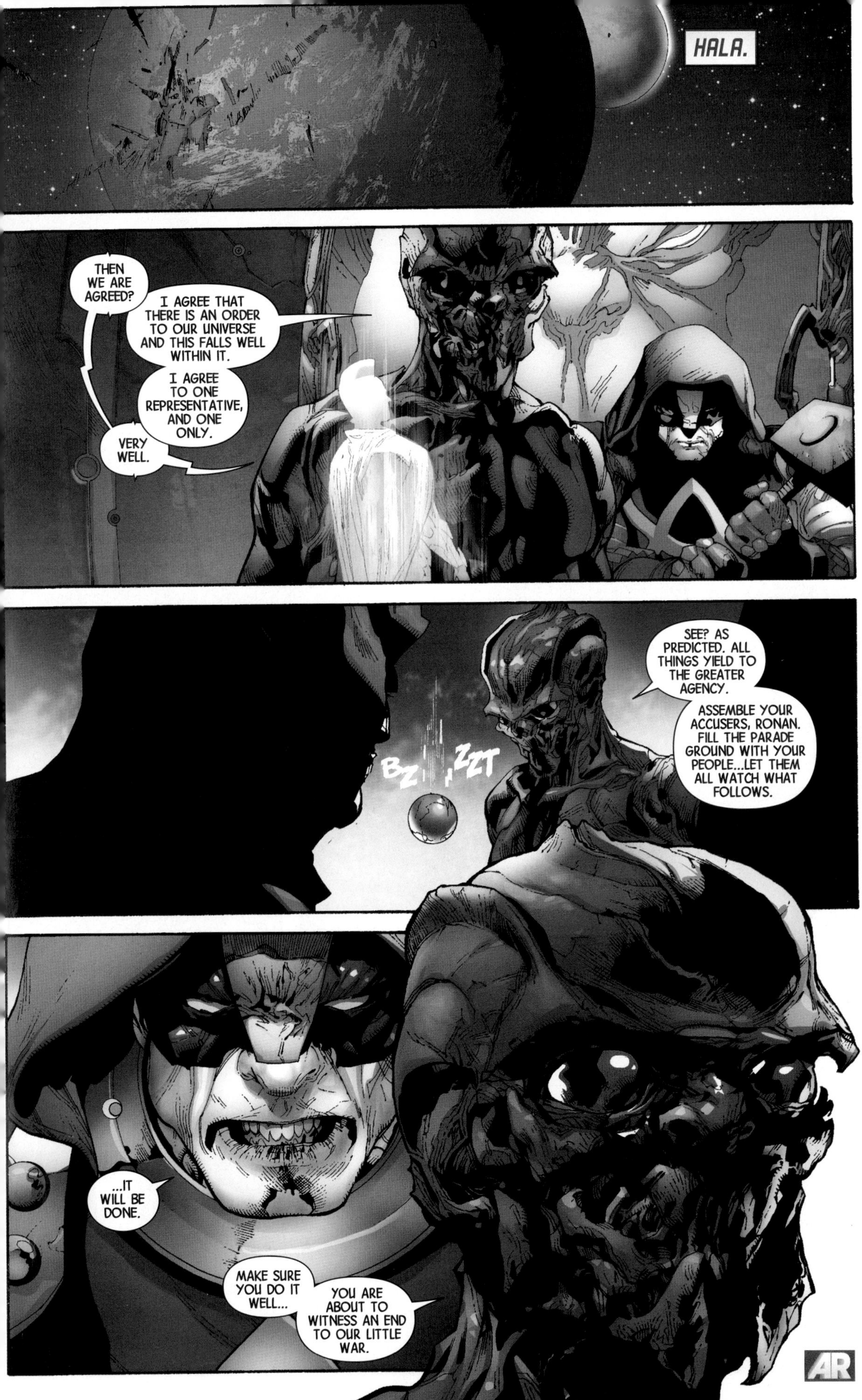
HALA.
THEN WE ARE AGREED?
I AGREE THAT THERE IS AN ORDER TO OUR UNIVERSE AND THIS FALLS WELL WITHIN IT.
I AGREE TO ONE REPRESENTATIVE, AND ONE ONLY.
VERY WELL.
BZZZT
SEE? AS PREDICTED. ALL THINGS YIELD TO THE GREATER AGENCY.
ASSEMBLE YOUR ACCUSERS, RONAN. FILL THE PARADE GROUND WITH YOUR PEOPLE...LET THEM ALL WATCH WHAT FOLLOWS.
...IT WILL BE DONE.
MAKE SURE YOU DO IT WELL...
YOU ARE ABOUT TO WITNESS AN END TO OUR LITTLE WAR.

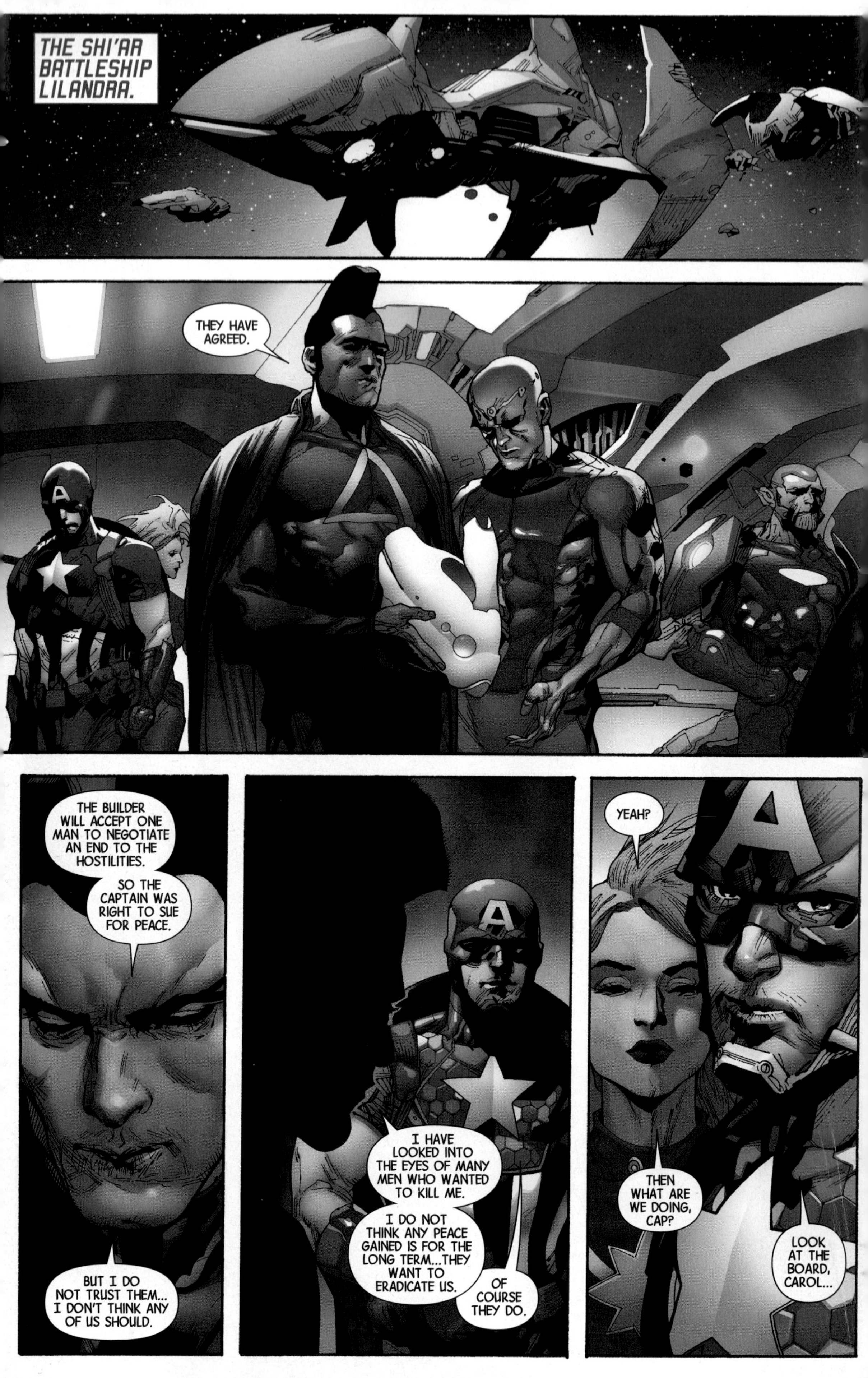

THE SHI'AR BATTLESHIP LILANDRA.
THEY HAVE AGREED.
THE BUILDER WILL ACCEPT ONE MAN TO NEGOTIATE AN END TO THE HOSTILITIES.
SO THE CAPTAIN WAS RIGHT TO SUE FOR PEACE.
BUT I DO NOT TRUST THEM... I DON'T THINK ANY OF US SHOULD.
I HAVE LOOKED INTO THE EYES OF MANY MEN WHO WANTED TO KILL ME.
I DO NOT THINK ANY PEACE GAINED IS FOR THE LONG TERM...THEY WANT TO ERADICATE US.
OF COURSE THEY DO.
YEAH?
THEN WHAT ARE WE DOING, CAP?
LOOK AT THE BOARD, CAROL...

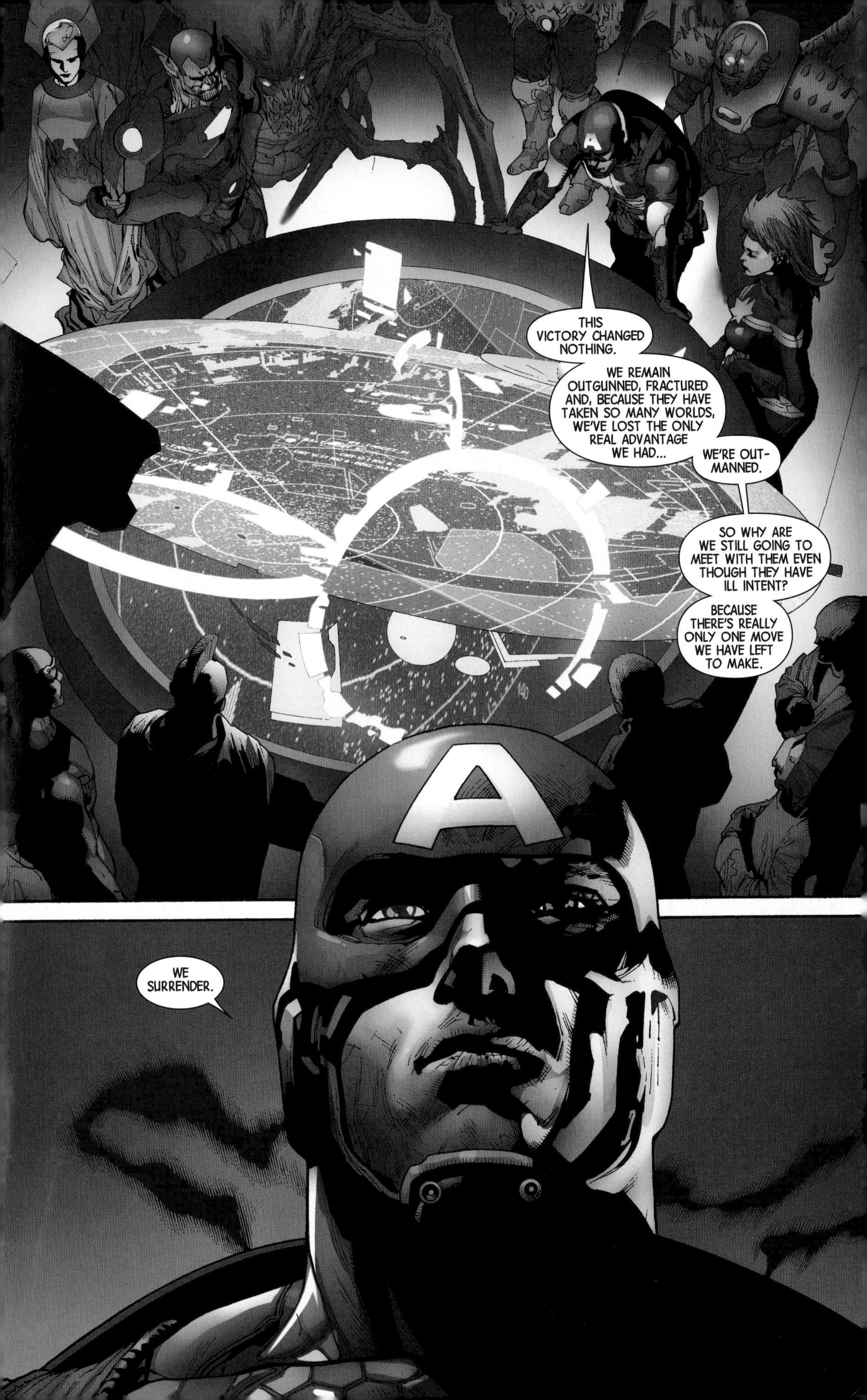
THIS VICTORY CHANGED NOTHING.
WE REMAIN OUTGUNNED, FRACTURED AND, BECAUSE THEY HAVE TAKEN SO MANY WORLDS, WE'VE LOST THE ONLY REAL ADVANTAGE WE HAD...
WE'RE OUT-MANNED.
SO WHY ARE WE STILL GOING TO MEET WITH THEM EVEN THOUGH THEY HAVE ILL INTENT?
BECAUSE THERE'S REALLY ONLY ONE MOVE WE HAVE LEFT TO MAKE.
WE SURRENDER.

"EMANCIPATION"

PREVIOUSLY IN INFINITY

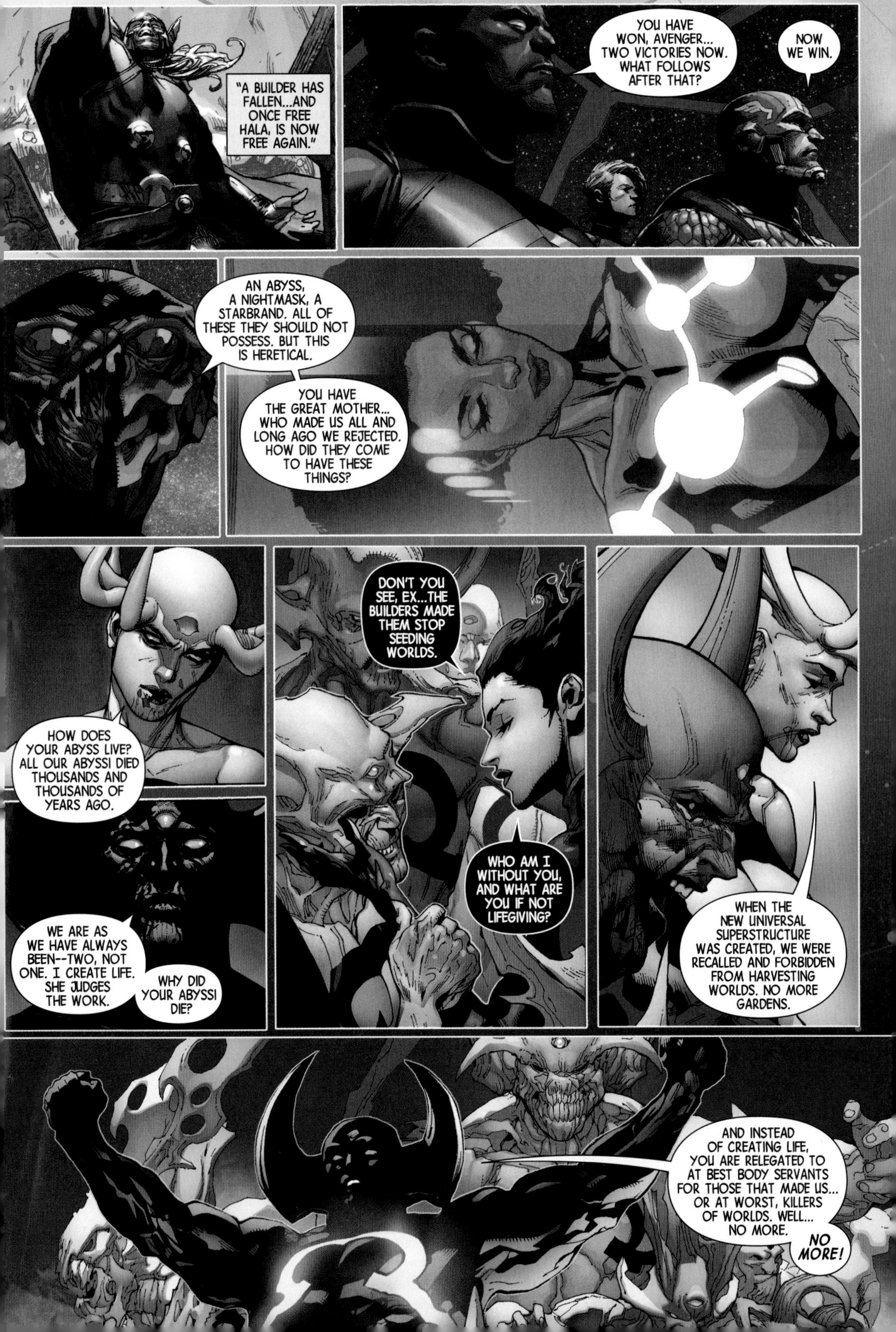
"A BUILDER HAS FALLEN...AND ONCE FREE HALA, IS NOW FREE AGAIN."
YOU HAVE WON, AVENGER... TWO VICTORIES NOW. WHAT FOLLOWS AFTER THAT?
NOW WE WIN.
AN ABYSS, A NIGHTMASK, A STARBRAND. ALL OF THESE THEY SHOULD NOT POSSESS. BUT THIS IS HERETICAL.
YOU HAVE THE GREAT MOTHER... WHO MADE US ALL AND LONG AGO WE REJECTED. HOW DID THEY COME TO HAVE THESE THINGS?
HOW DOES YOUR ABYSS LIVE? ALL OUR ABYSSI DIED THOUSANDS AND THOUSANDS OF YEARS AGO.
WE ARE AS WE HAVE ALWAYS BEEN--TWO, NOT ONE. I CREATE LIFE. SHE JUDGES THE WORK.
WHY DID YOUR ABYSSI DIE?
DON'T YOU SEE, EX...THE BUILDERS MADE THEM STOP SEEDING WORLDS.
WHO AM I WITHOUT YOU, AND WHAT ARE YOU IF NOT LIFEGIVING?
WHEN THE NEW UNIVERSAL SUPERSTRUCTURE WAS CREATED, WE WERE RECALLED AND FORBIDDEN FROM HARVESTING WORLDS. NO MORE GARDENS.
AND INSTEAD OF CREATING LIFE, YOU ARE RELEGATED TO AT BEST BODY SERVANTS FOR THOSE THAT MADE US... OR AT WORST, KILLERS OF WORLDS. WELL... NO MORE.
NO MORE!

CAST

THE AVENGERS

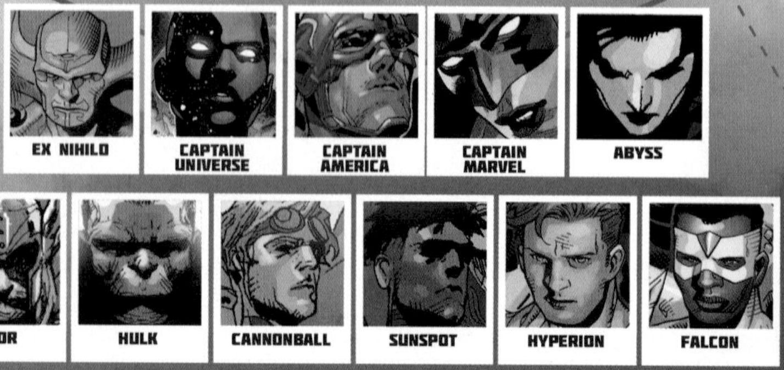

EX NIHILO · CAPTAIN UNIVERSE · CAPTAIN AMERICA · CAPTAIN MARVEL · ABYSS

THOR · HULK · CANNONBALL · SUNSPOT · HYPERION · FALCON

THE BUILDERS

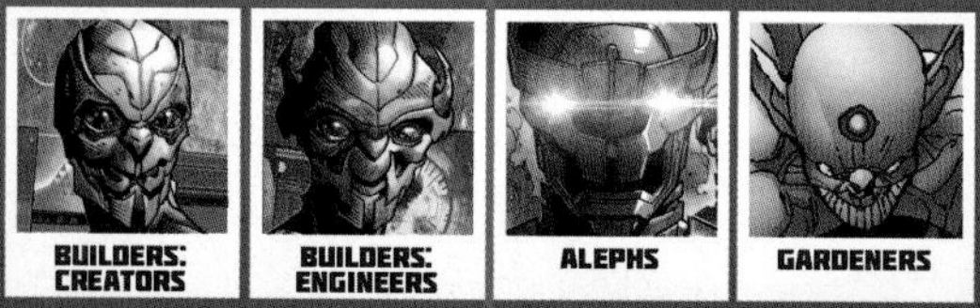

BUILDERS: CREATORS · BUILDERS: ENGINEERS · ALEPHS · GARDENERS

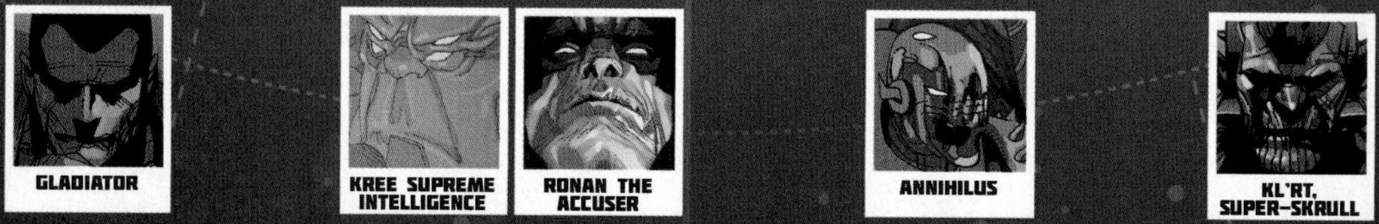

GLADIATOR · KREE SUPREME INTELLIGENCE · RONAN THE ACCUSER · ANNIHILUS · KL'RT, SUPER-SKRULL

SHI'AR IMPERIAL GUARD

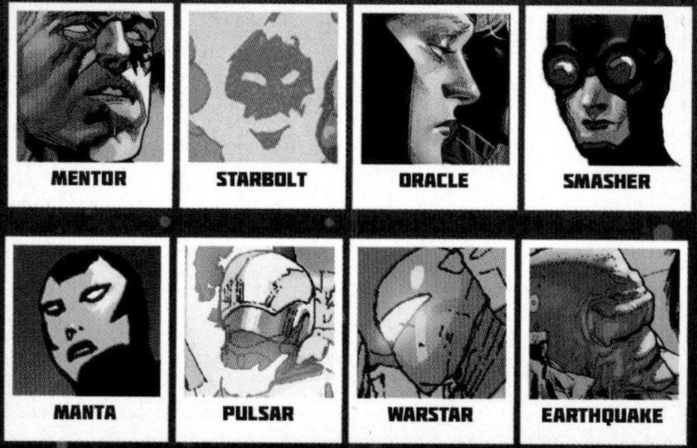

MENTOR · STARBOLT · ORACLE · SMASHER

MANTA · PULSAR · WARSTAR · EARTHQUAKE

SPACEKNIGHTS

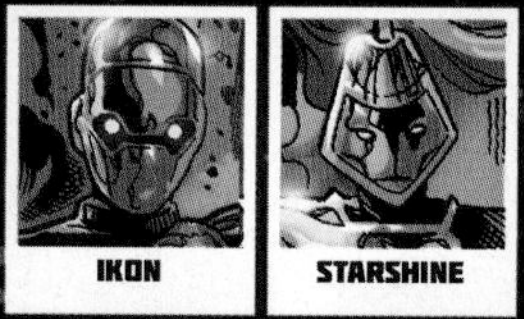

IKON · STARSHINE

THE PROMISE OF THE UNIVERSE

◆

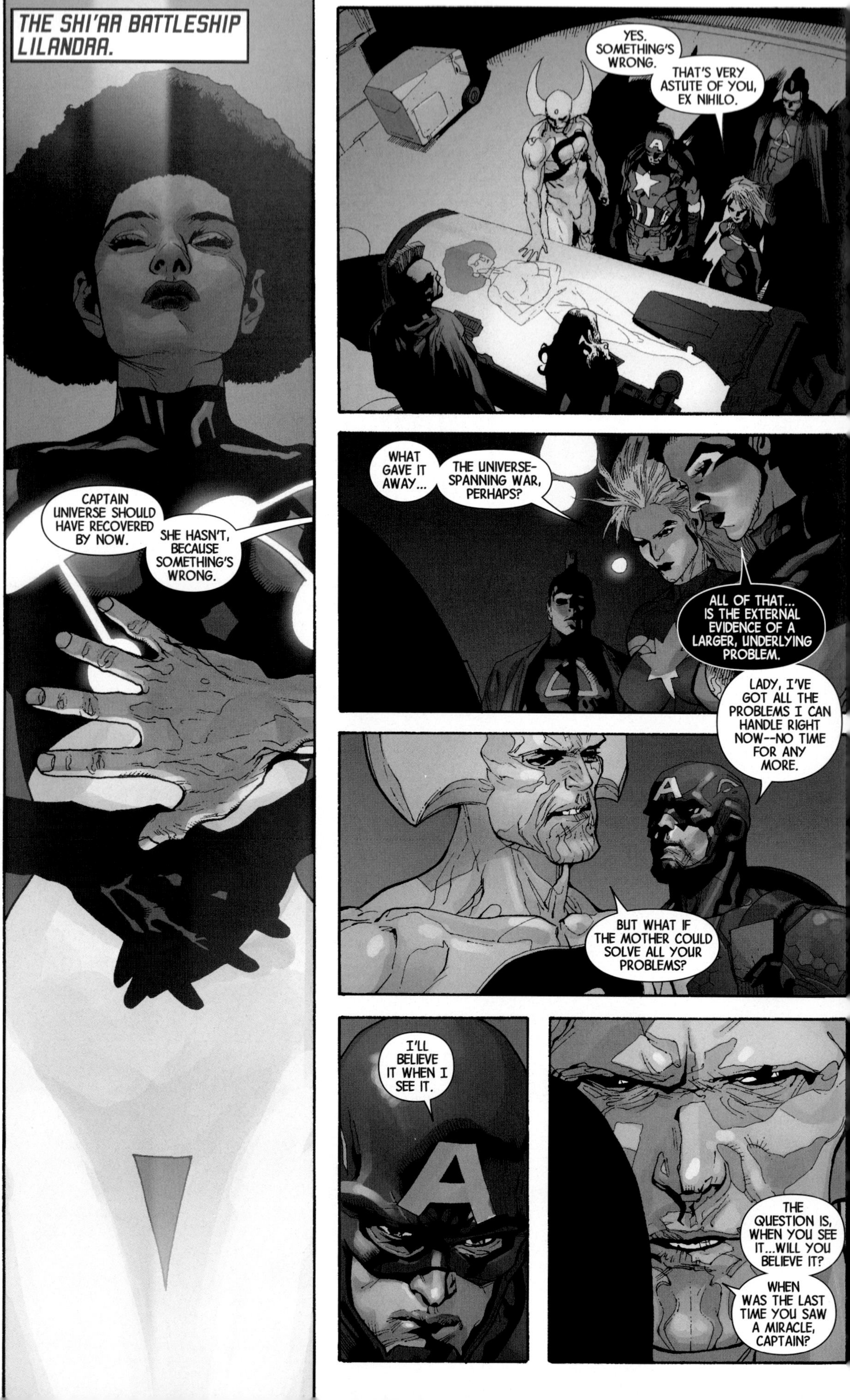

THE SHI'AR BATTLESHIP LILANDRA.
CAPTAIN UNIVERSE SHOULD HAVE RECOVERED BY NOW.
SHE HASN'T, BECAUSE SOMETHING'S WRONG.
YES. SOMETHING'S WRONG.
THAT'S VERY ASTUTE OF YOU, EX NIHILO.
WHAT GAVE IT AWAY...
THE UNIVERSE-SPANNING WAR, PERHAPS?
ALL OF THAT... IS THE EXTERNAL EVIDENCE OF A LARGER, UNDERLYING PROBLEM.
LADY, I'VE GOT ALL THE PROBLEMS I CAN HANDLE RIGHT NOW--NO TIME FOR ANY MORE.
BUT WHAT IF THE MOTHER COULD SOLVE ALL YOUR PROBLEMS?
I'LL BELIEVE IT WHEN I SEE IT.
THE QUESTION IS, WHEN YOU SEE IT...WILL YOU BELIEVE IT?
WHEN WAS THE LAST TIME YOU SAW A MIRACLE, CAPTAIN?

THE SECOND WAVE

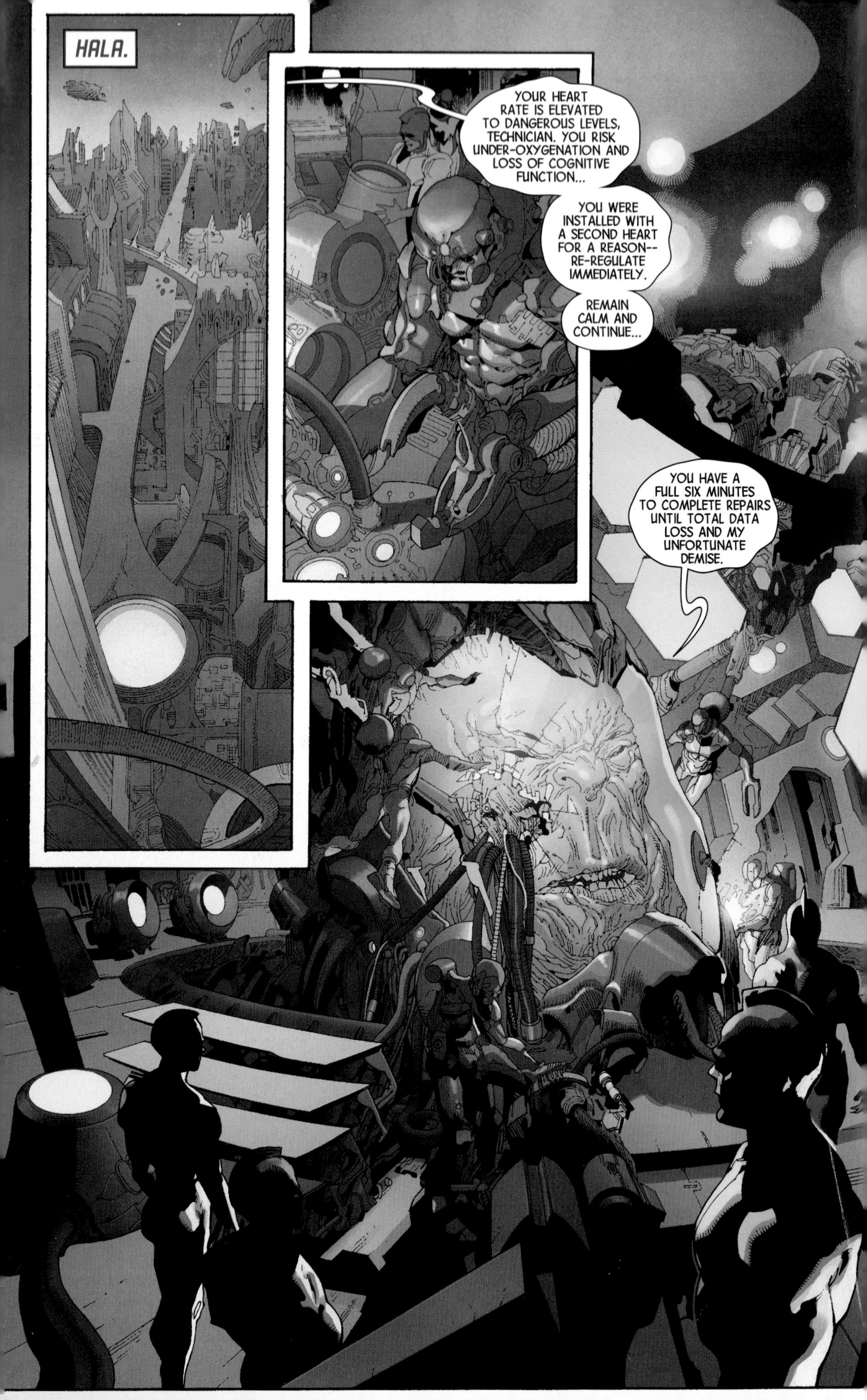
HALA.
YOUR HEART RATE IS ELEVATED TO DANGEROUS LEVELS, TECHNICIAN. YOU RISK UNDER-OXYGENATION AND LOSS OF COGNITIVE FUNCTION...
YOU WERE INSTALLED WITH A SECOND HEART FOR A REASON-- RE-REGULATE IMMEDIATELY.
REMAIN CALM AND CONTINUE...
YOU HAVE A FULL SIX MINUTES TO COMPLETE REPAIRS UNTIL TOTAL DATA LOSS AND MY UNFORTUNATE DEMISE.

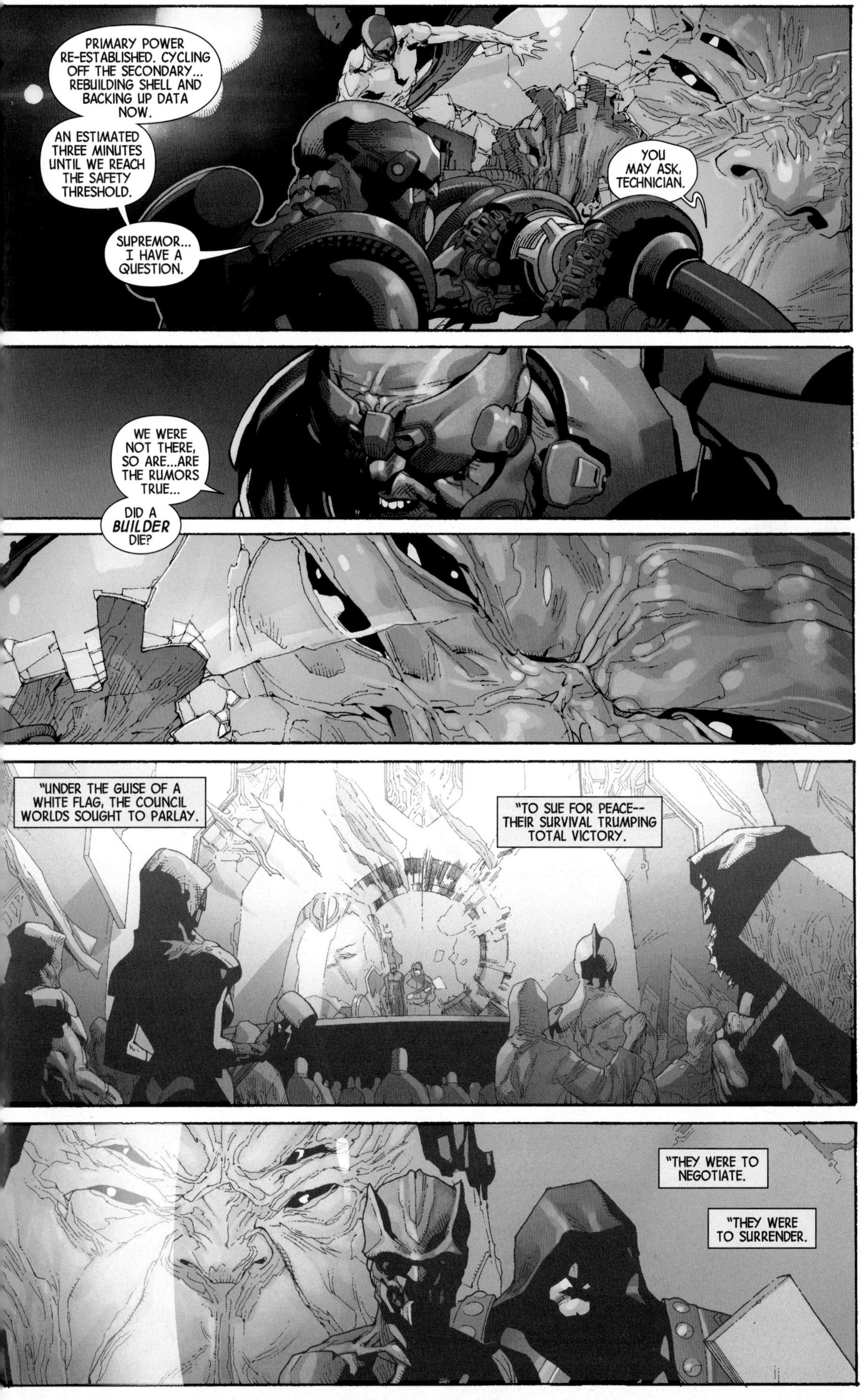
PRIMARY POWER RE-ESTABLISHED. CYCLING OFF THE SECONDARY... REBUILDING SHELL AND BACKING UP DATA NOW.
AN ESTIMATED THREE MINUTES UNTIL WE REACH THE SAFETY THRESHOLD.
SUPREMOR... I HAVE A QUESTION.
YOU MAY ASK, TECHNICIAN.
WE WERE NOT THERE, SO ARE...ARE THE RUMORS TRUE...
DID A *BUILDER* DIE?
"UNDER THE GUISE OF A WHITE FLAG, THE COUNCIL WORLDS SOUGHT TO PARLAY.
"TO SUE FOR PEACE-- THEIR SURVIVAL TRUMPING TOTAL VICTORY.
"THEY WERE TO NEGOTIATE.
"THEY WERE TO SURRENDER.

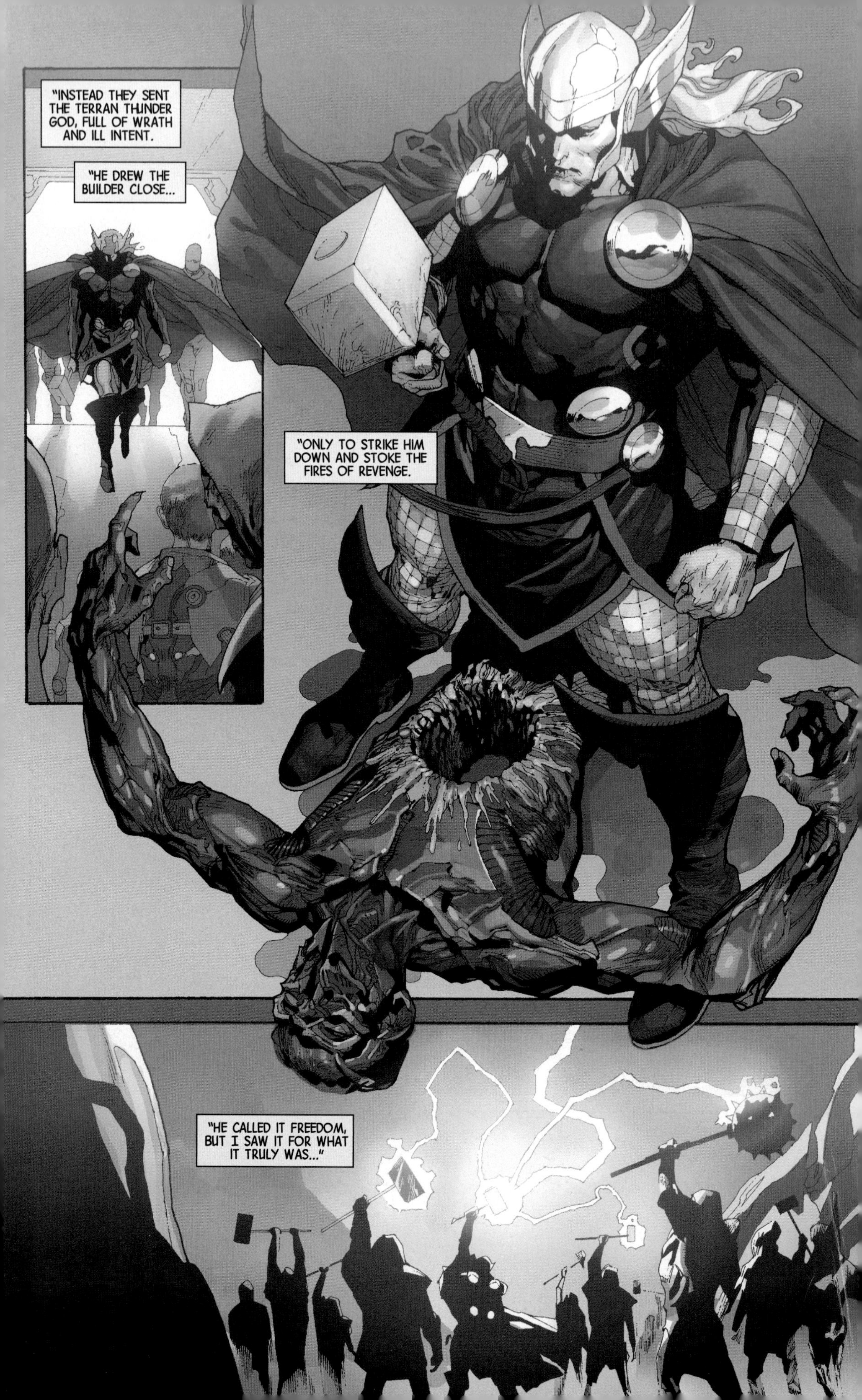
"INSTEAD THEY SENT THE TERRAN THUNDER GOD, FULL OF WRATH AND ILL INTENT.
"HE DREW THE BUILDER CLOSE...
"ONLY TO STRIKE HIM DOWN AND STOKE THE FIRES OF REVENGE.
"HE CALLED IT FREEDOM, BUT I SAW IT FOR WHAT IT TRULY WAS..."

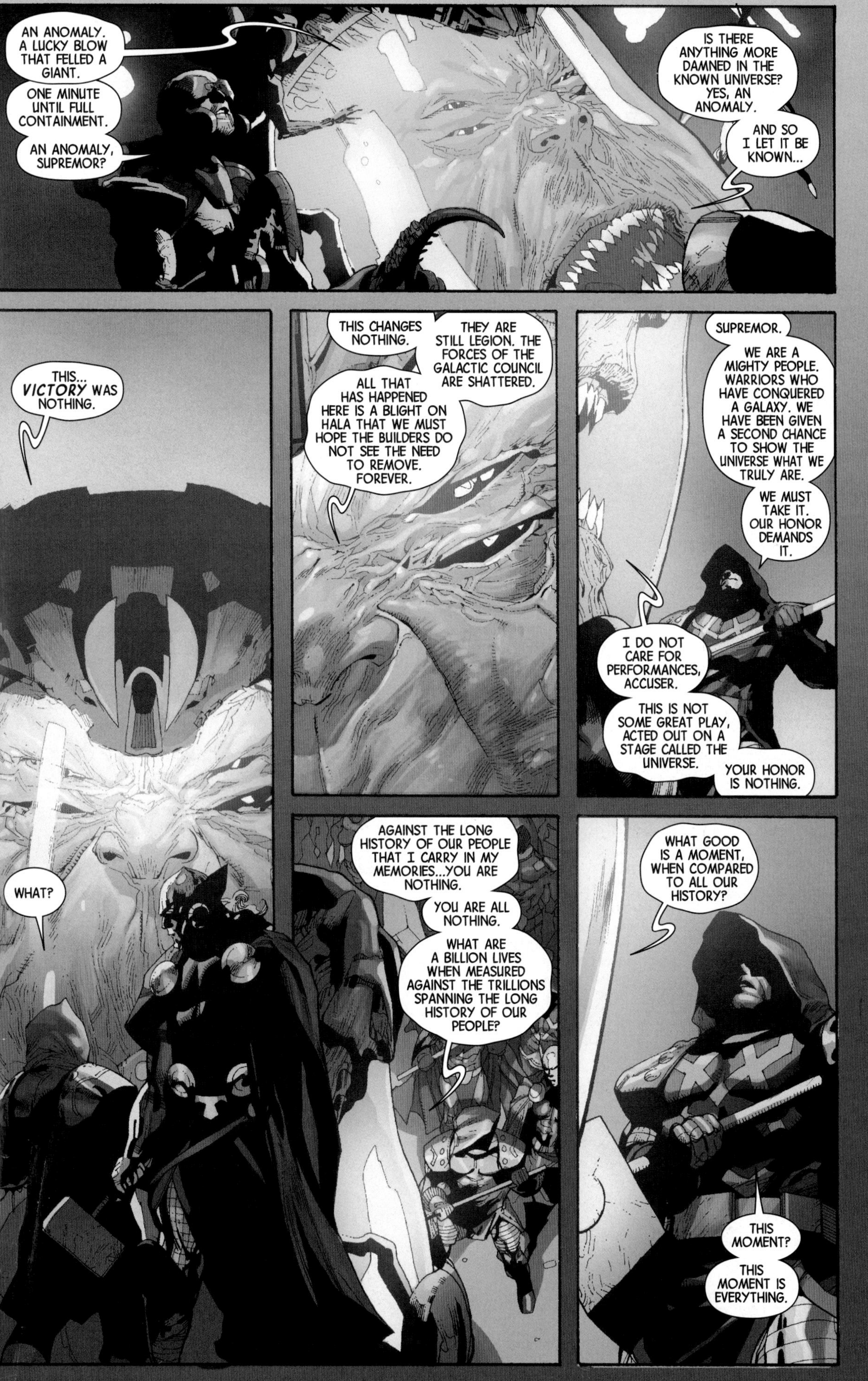
AN ANOMALY. A LUCKY BLOW THAT FELLED A GIANT.
ONE MINUTE UNTIL FULL CONTAINMENT.
AN ANOMALY, SUPREMOR?
IS THERE ANYTHING MORE DAMNED IN THE KNOWN UNIVERSE? YES, AN ANOMALY.
AND SO I LET IT BE KNOWN...
THIS... VICTORY WAS NOTHING.
WHAT?
THIS CHANGES NOTHING.
THEY ARE STILL LEGION. THE FORCES OF THE GALACTIC COUNCIL ARE SHATTERED.
ALL THAT HAS HAPPENED HERE IS A BLIGHT ON HALA THAT WE MUST HOPE THE BUILDERS DO NOT SEE THE NEED TO REMOVE. FOREVER.
SUPREMOR.
WE ARE A MIGHTY PEOPLE. WARRIORS WHO HAVE CONQUERED A GALAXY. WE HAVE BEEN GIVEN A SECOND CHANCE TO SHOW THE UNIVERSE WHAT WE TRULY ARE.
WE MUST TAKE IT. OUR HONOR DEMANDS IT.
I DO NOT CARE FOR PERFORMANCES, ACCUSER.
THIS IS NOT SOME GREAT PLAY, ACTED OUT ON A STAGE CALLED THE UNIVERSE.
YOUR HONOR IS NOTHING.
AGAINST THE LONG HISTORY OF OUR PEOPLE THAT I CARRY IN MY MEMORIES...YOU ARE NOTHING.
YOU ARE ALL NOTHING.
WHAT ARE A BILLION LIVES WHEN MEASURED AGAINST THE TRILLIONS SPANNING THE LONG HISTORY OF OUR PEOPLE?
WHAT GOOD IS A MOMENT, WHEN COMPARED TO ALL OUR HISTORY?
THIS MOMENT?
THIS MOMENT IS EVERYTHING.

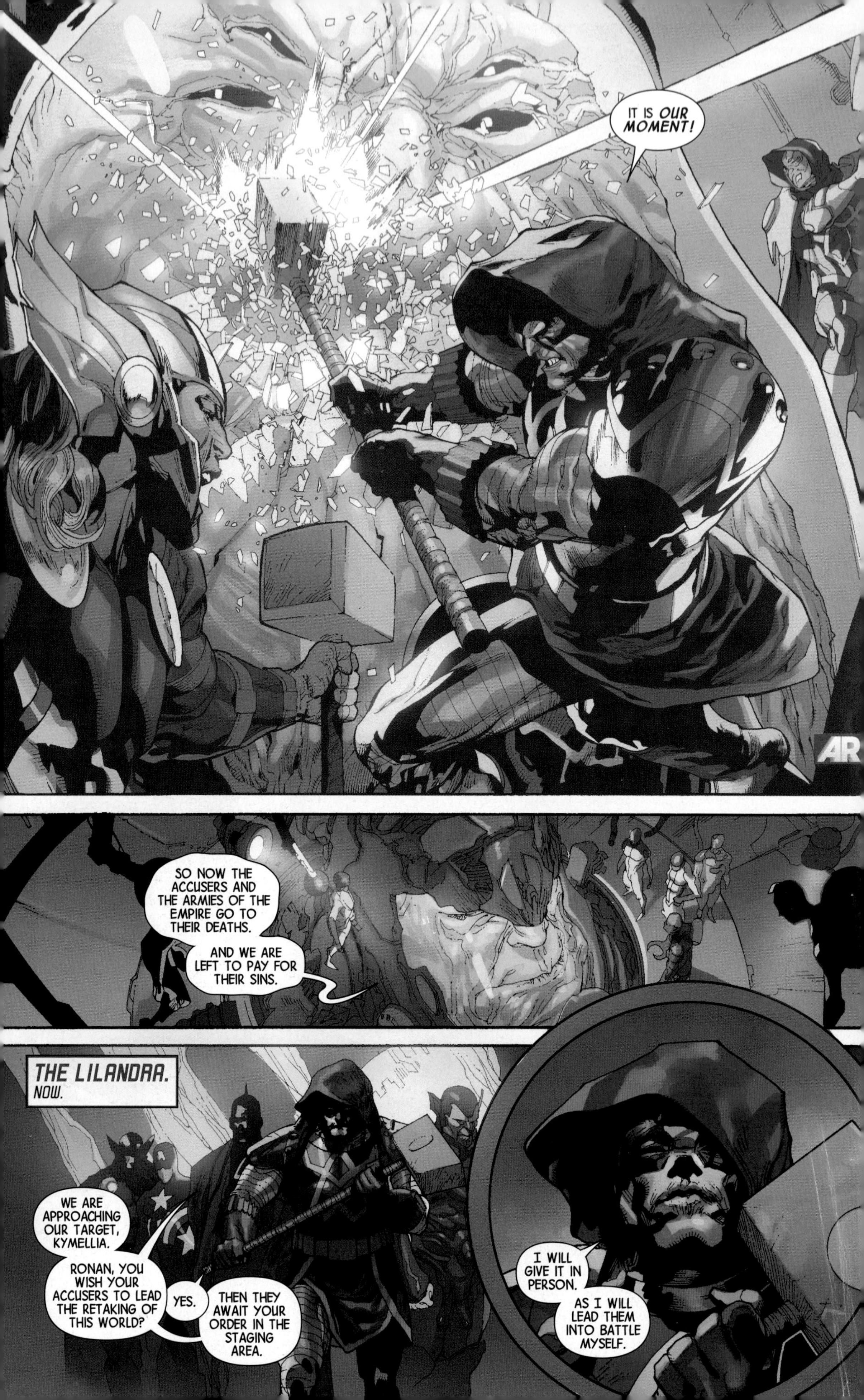
IT IS OUR MOMENT!
SO NOW THE ACCUSERS AND THE ARMIES OF THE EMPIRE GO TO THEIR DEATHS.
AND WE ARE LEFT TO PAY FOR THEIR SINS.
THE LILANDRA. NOW.
WE ARE APPROACHING OUR TARGET, KYMELLIA.
RONAN, YOU WISH YOUR ACCUSERS TO LEAD THE RETAKING OF THIS WORLD?
YES.
THEN THEY AWAIT YOUR ORDER IN THE STAGING AREA.
I WILL GIVE IT IN PERSON.
AS I WILL LEAD THEM INTO BATTLE MYSELF.

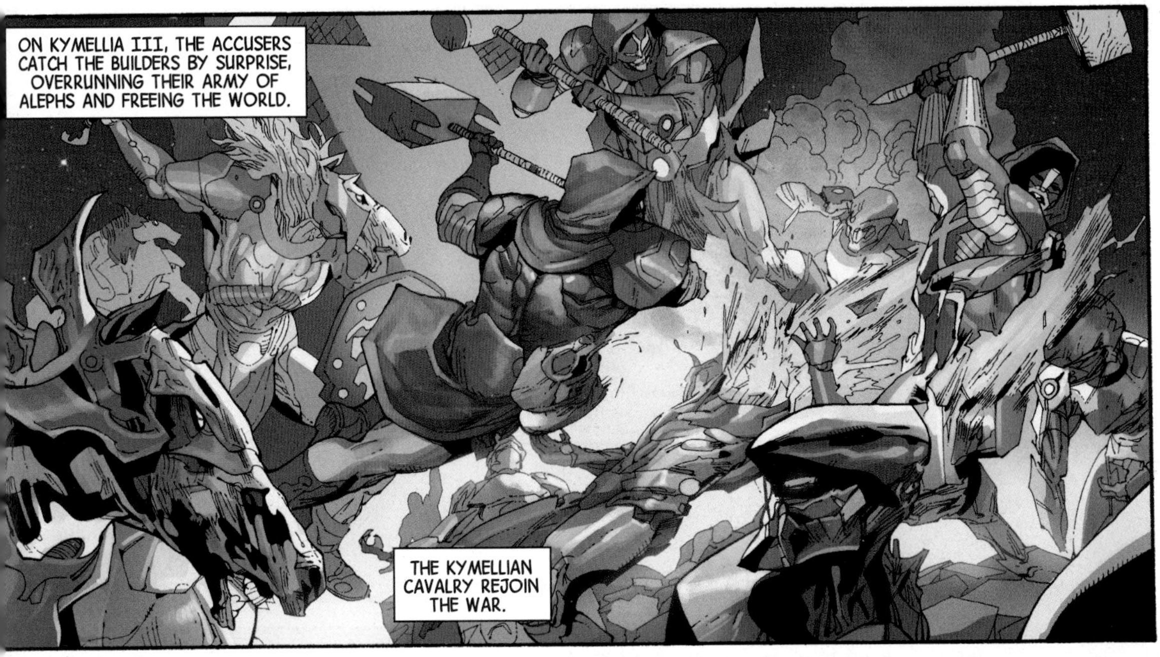
ON KYMELLIA III, THE ACCUSERS CATCH THE BUILDERS BY SURPRISE, OVERRUNNING THEIR ARMY OF ALEPHS AND FREEING THE WORLD.
THE KYMELLIAN CAVALRY REJOIN THE WAR.

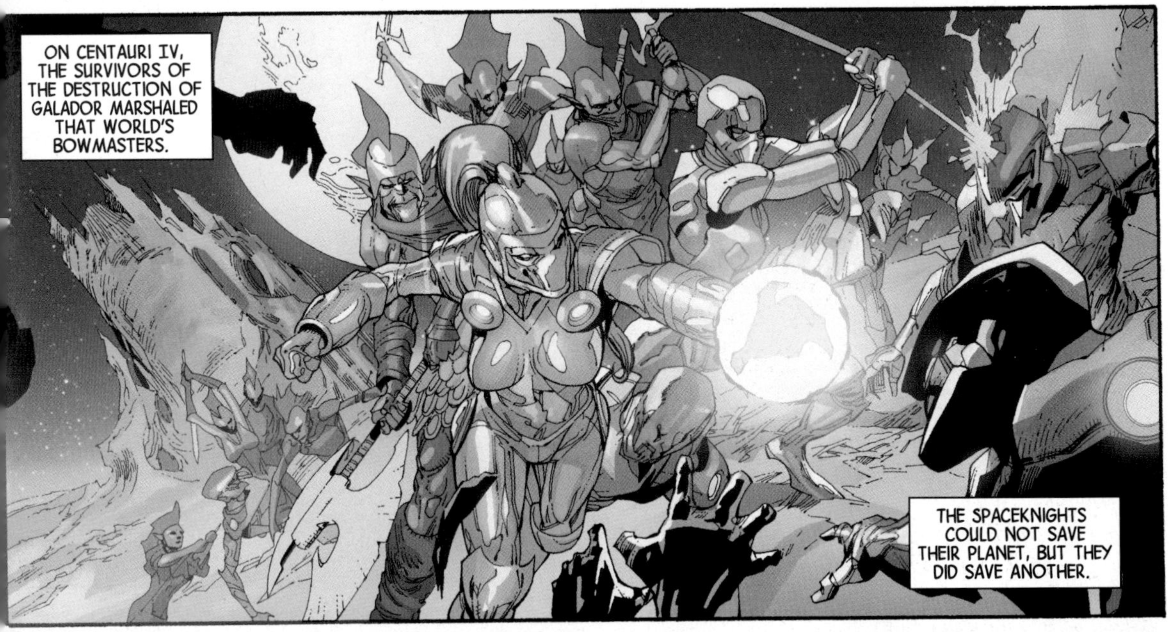
ON CENTAURI IV, THE SURVIVORS OF THE DESTRUCTION OF GALADOR MARSHALED THAT WORLD'S BOWMASTERS.
THE SPACEKNIGHTS COULD NOT SAVE THEIR PLANET, BUT THEY DID SAVE ANOTHER.

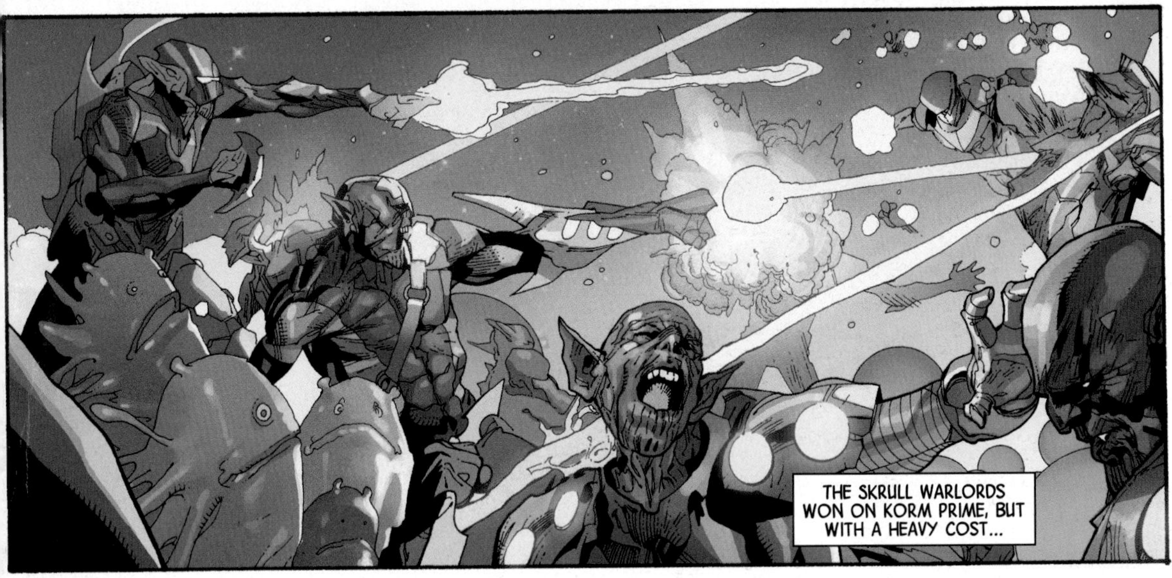
THE SKRULL WARLORDS WON ON KORM PRIME, BUT WITH A HEAVY COST...

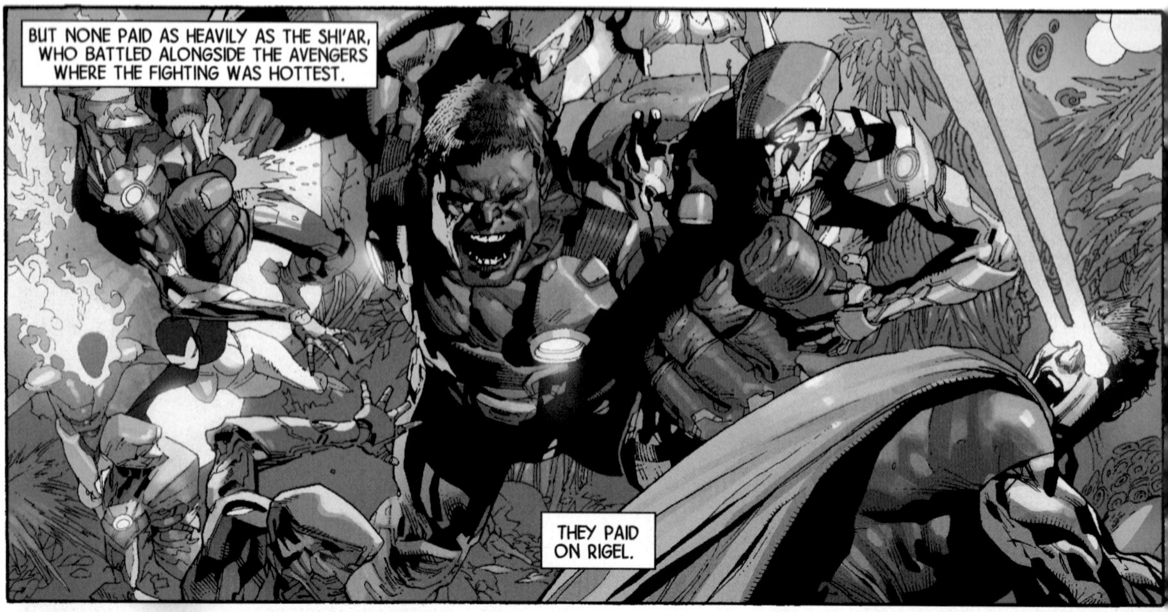
BUT NONE PAID AS HEAVILY AS THE SHI'AR, WHO BATTLED ALONGSIDE THE AVENGERS WHERE THE FIGHTING WAS HOTTEST.
THEY PAID ON RIGEL.

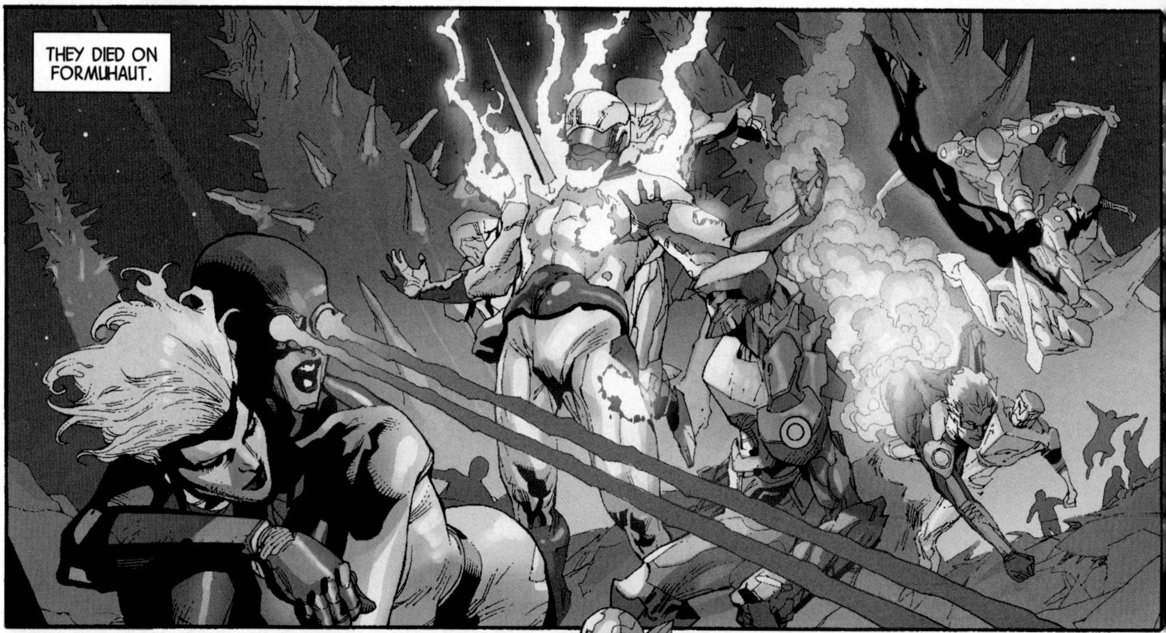
THEY DIED ON FORMUHAUT.

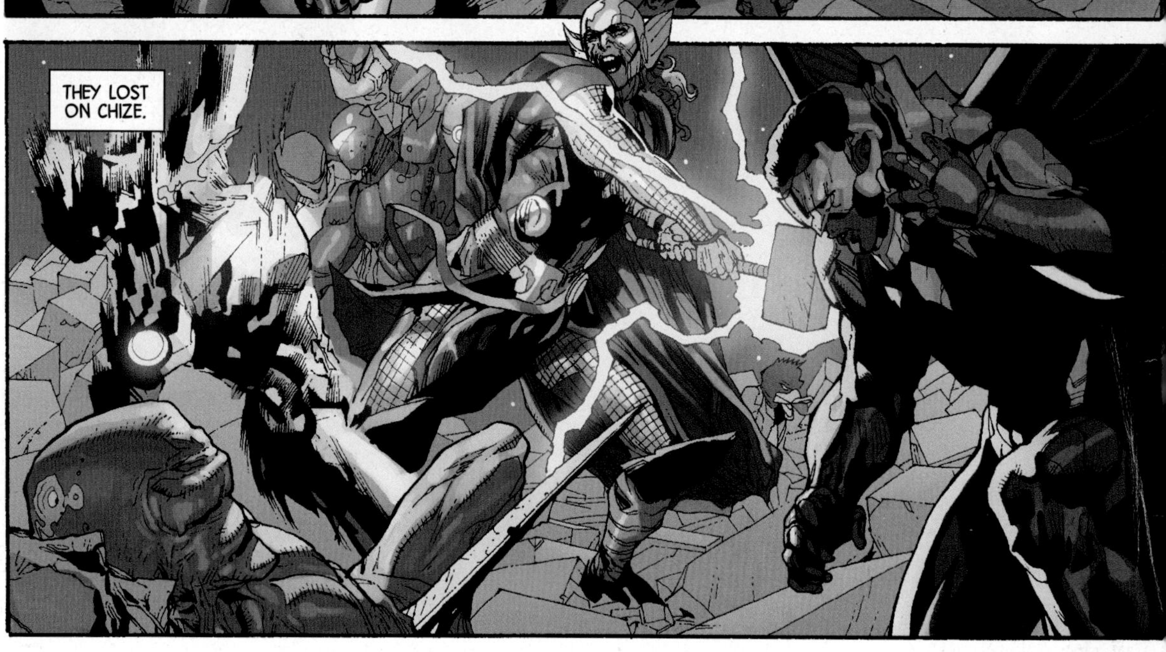
THEY LOST ON CHIZE.

THE LILANDRA.

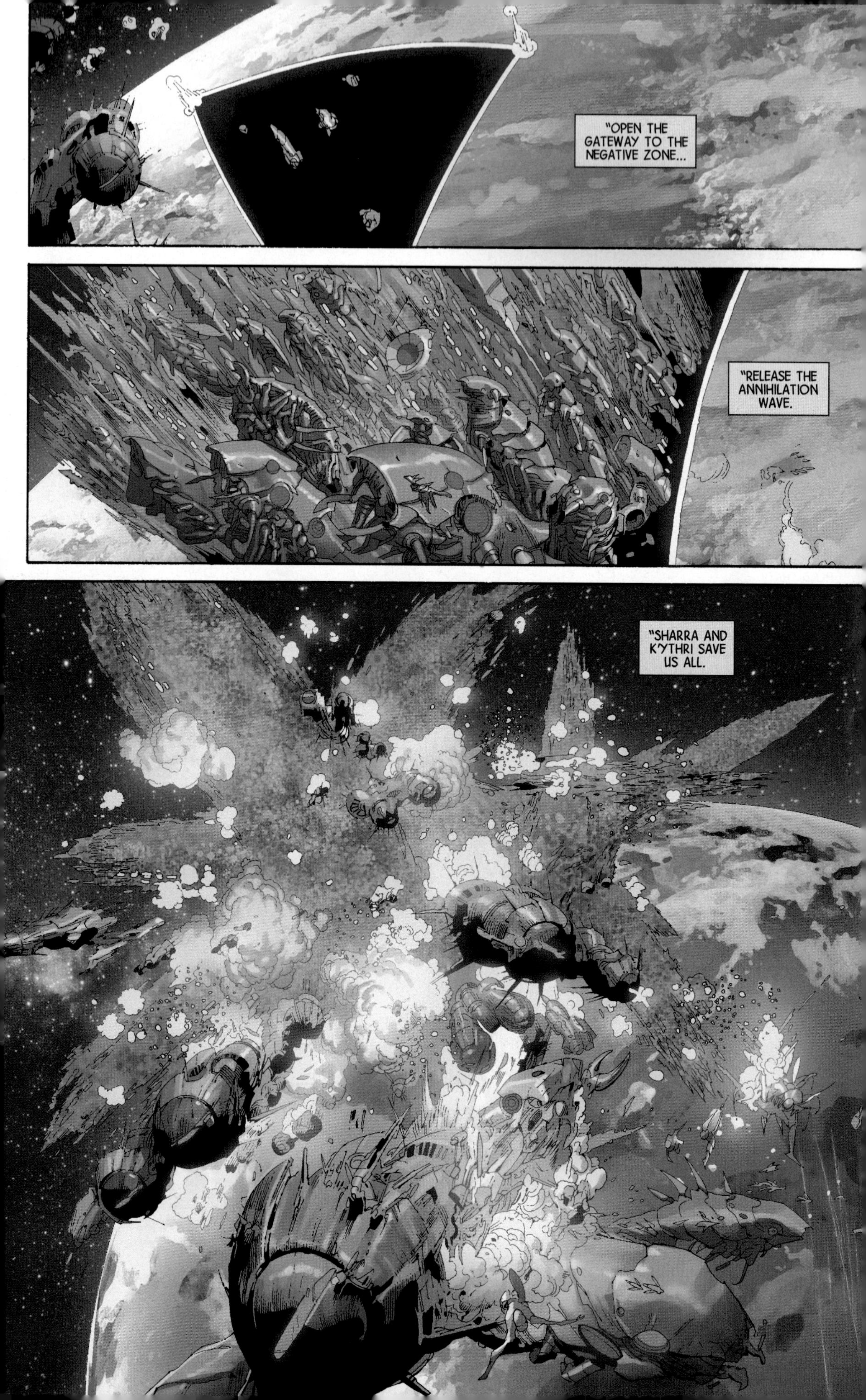
"OPEN THE GATEWAY TO THE NEGATIVE ZONE...
"RELEASE THE ANNIHILATION WAVE.
"SHARRA AND K'YTHRI SAVE US ALL.

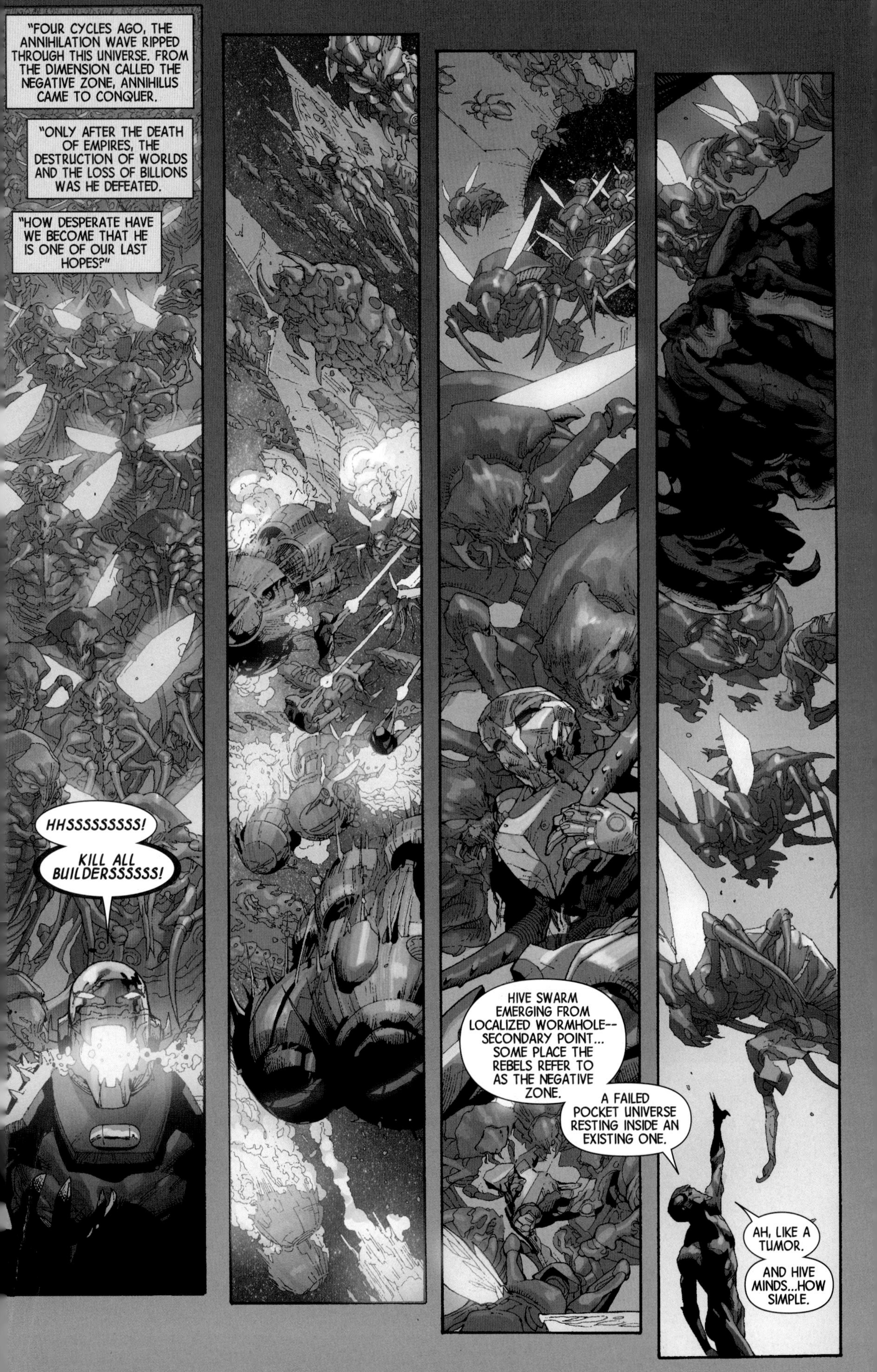
"FOUR CYCLES AGO, THE ANNIHILATION WAVE RIPPED THROUGH THIS UNIVERSE. FROM THE DIMENSION CALLED THE NEGATIVE ZONE, ANNIHILUS CAME TO CONQUER.
"ONLY AFTER THE DEATH OF EMPIRES, THE DESTRUCTION OF WORLDS AND THE LOSS OF BILLIONS WAS HE DEFEATED.
"HOW DESPERATE HAVE WE BECOME THAT HE IS ONE OF OUR LAST HOPES?"
HHSSSSSSSSSS!
KILL ALL BUILDERSSSSSS!
HIVE SWARM EMERGING FROM LOCALIZED WORMHOLE--SECONDARY POINT... SOME PLACE THE REBELS REFER TO AS THE NEGATIVE ZONE.
A FAILED POCKET UNIVERSE RESTING INSIDE AN EXISTING ONE.
AH, LIKE A TUMOR.
AND HIVE MINDS...HOW SIMPLE.

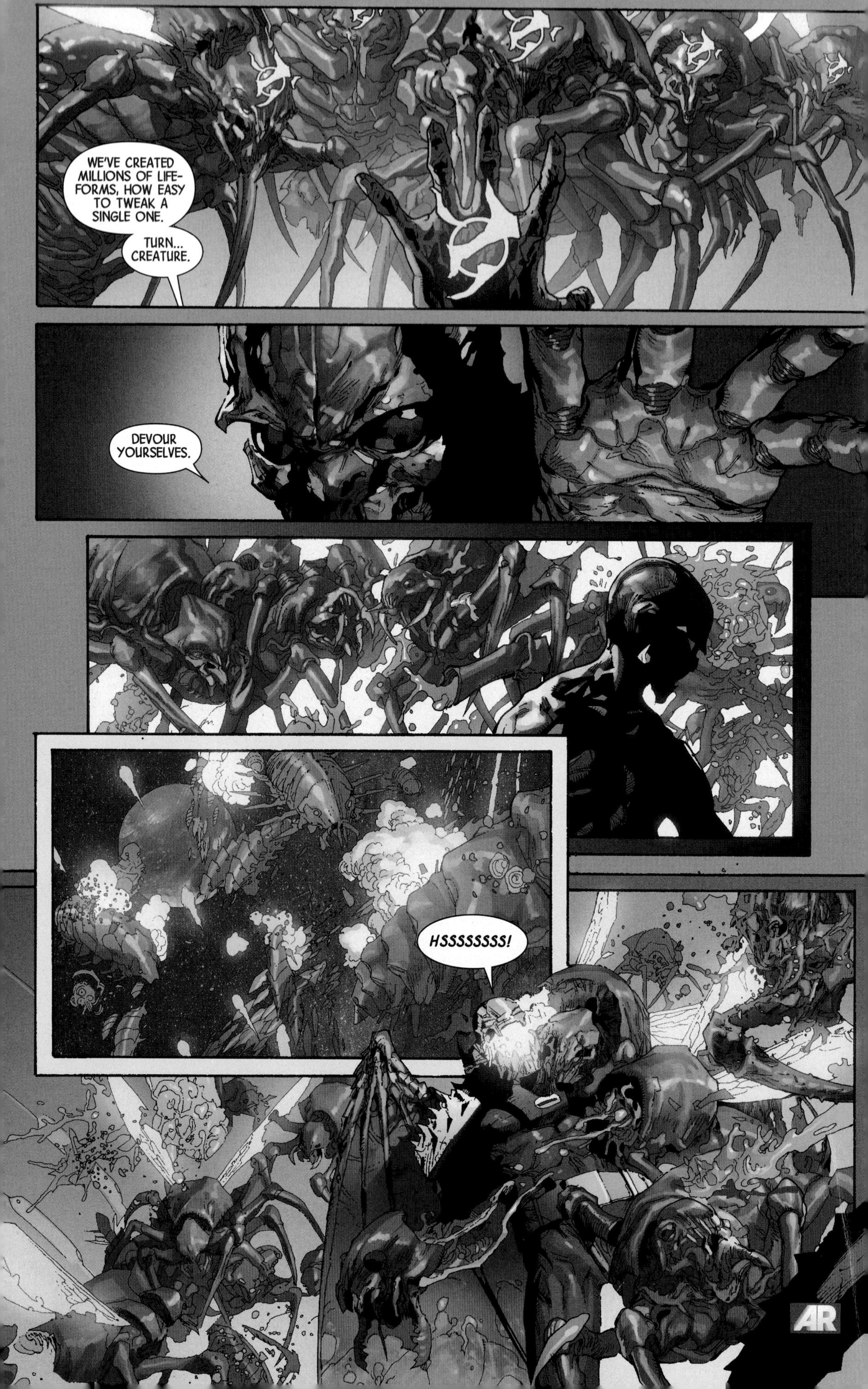
WE'VE CREATED MILLIONS OF LIFE-FORMS, HOW EASY TO TWEAK A SINGLE ONE.
TURN... CREATURE.
DEVOUR YOURSELVES.
HSSSSSSSS!

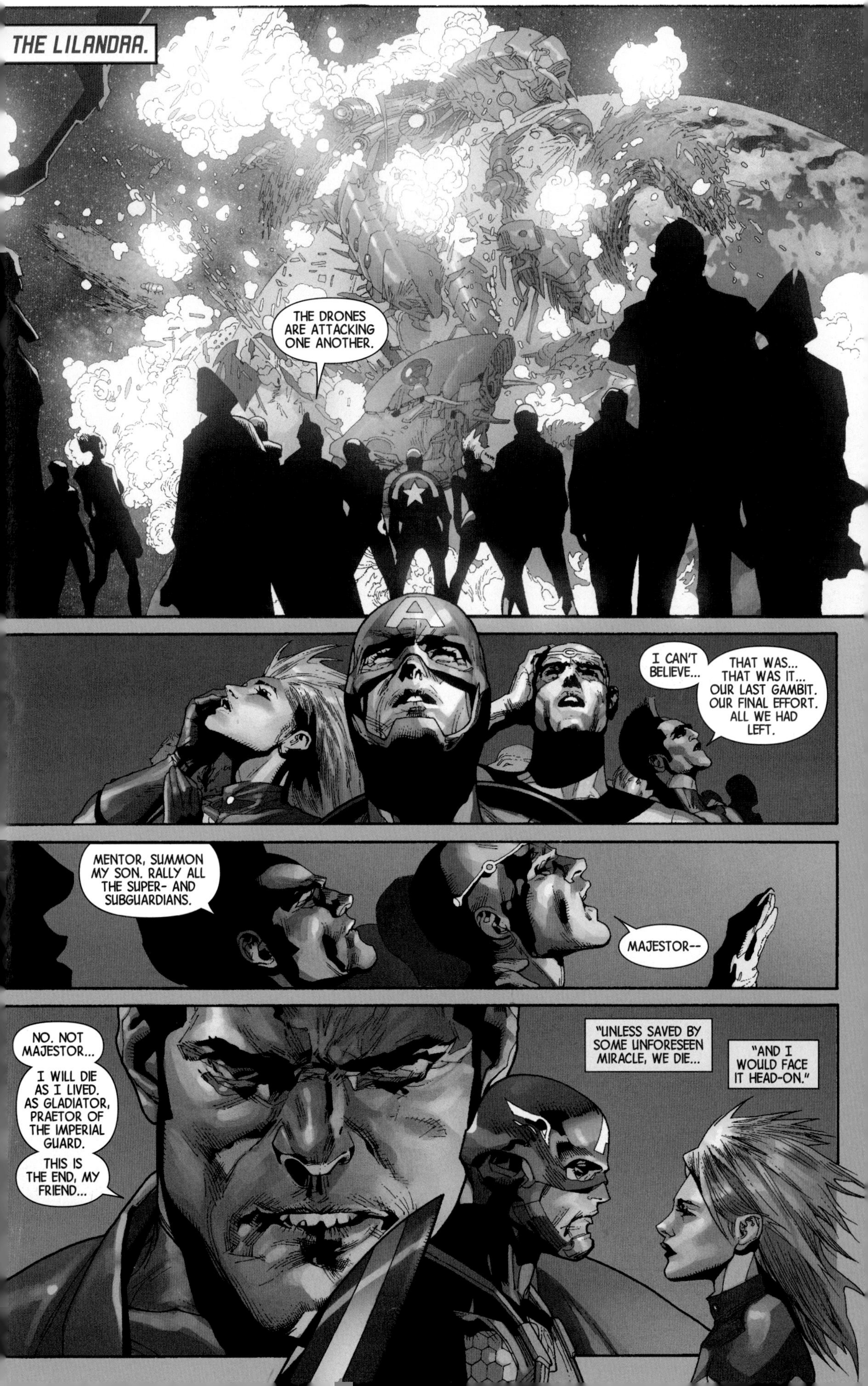
THE LILANDRA.
THE DRONES ARE ATTACKING ONE ANOTHER.
I CAN'T BELIEVE...
THAT WAS... THAT WAS IT... OUR LAST GAMBIT. OUR FINAL EFFORT. ALL WE HAD LEFT.
MENTOR, SUMMON MY SON. RALLY ALL THE SUPER- AND SUBGUARDIANS.
MAJESTOR--
NO. NOT MAJESTOR...
I WILL DIE AS I LIVED. AS GLADIATOR, PRAETOR OF THE IMPERIAL GUARD.
THIS IS THE END, MY FRIEND...
"UNLESS SAVED BY SOME UNFORESEEN MIRACLE, WE DIE...
"AND I WOULD FACE IT HEAD-ON."

THE PROMISE
FULFILLED

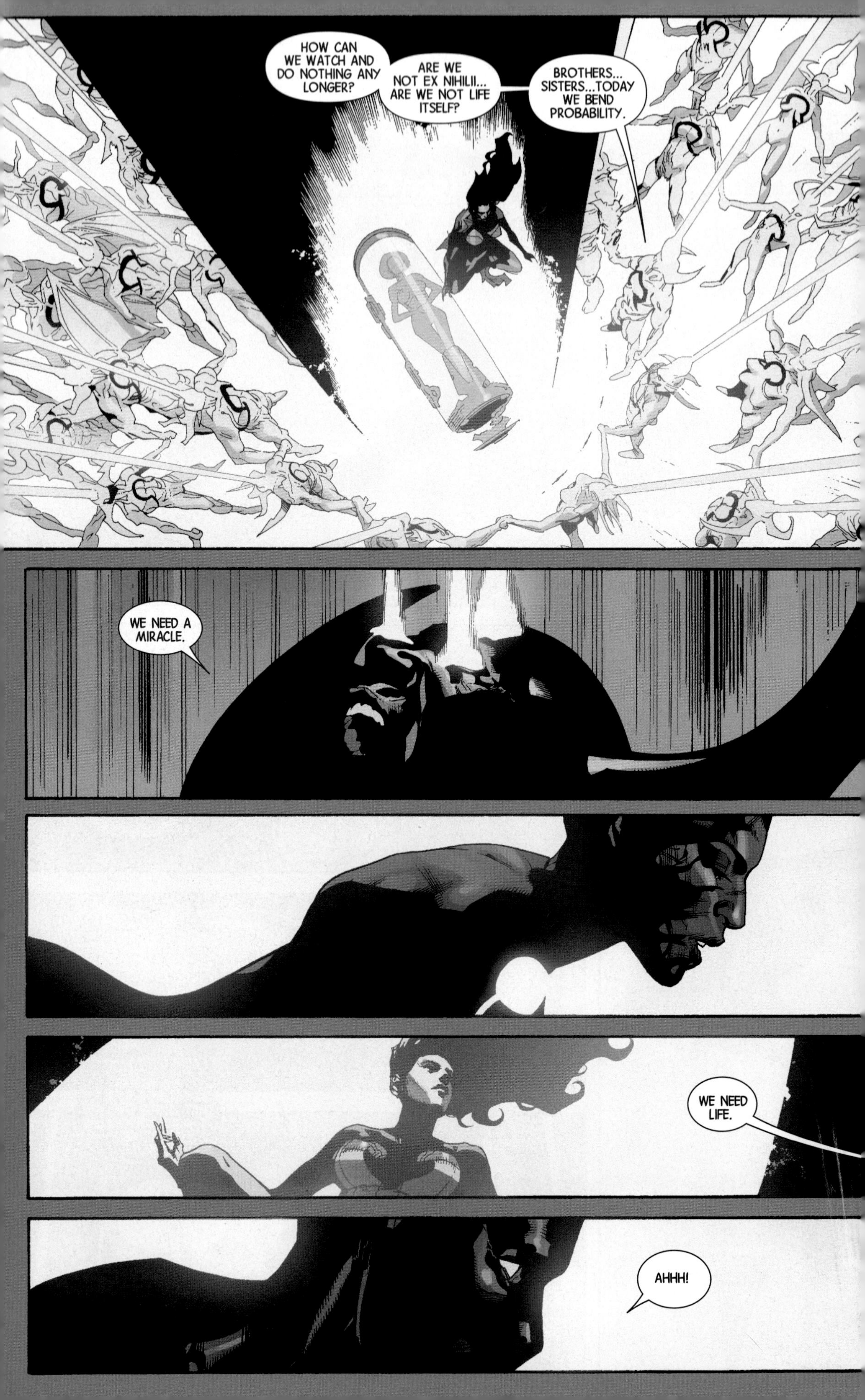
HOW CAN WE WATCH AND DO NOTHING ANY LONGER?
ARE WE NOT EX NIHILII... ARE WE NOT LIFE ITSELF?
BROTHERS... SISTERS...TODAY WE BEND PROBABILITY.
WE NEED A MIRACLE.
WE NEED LIFE.
AHHH!

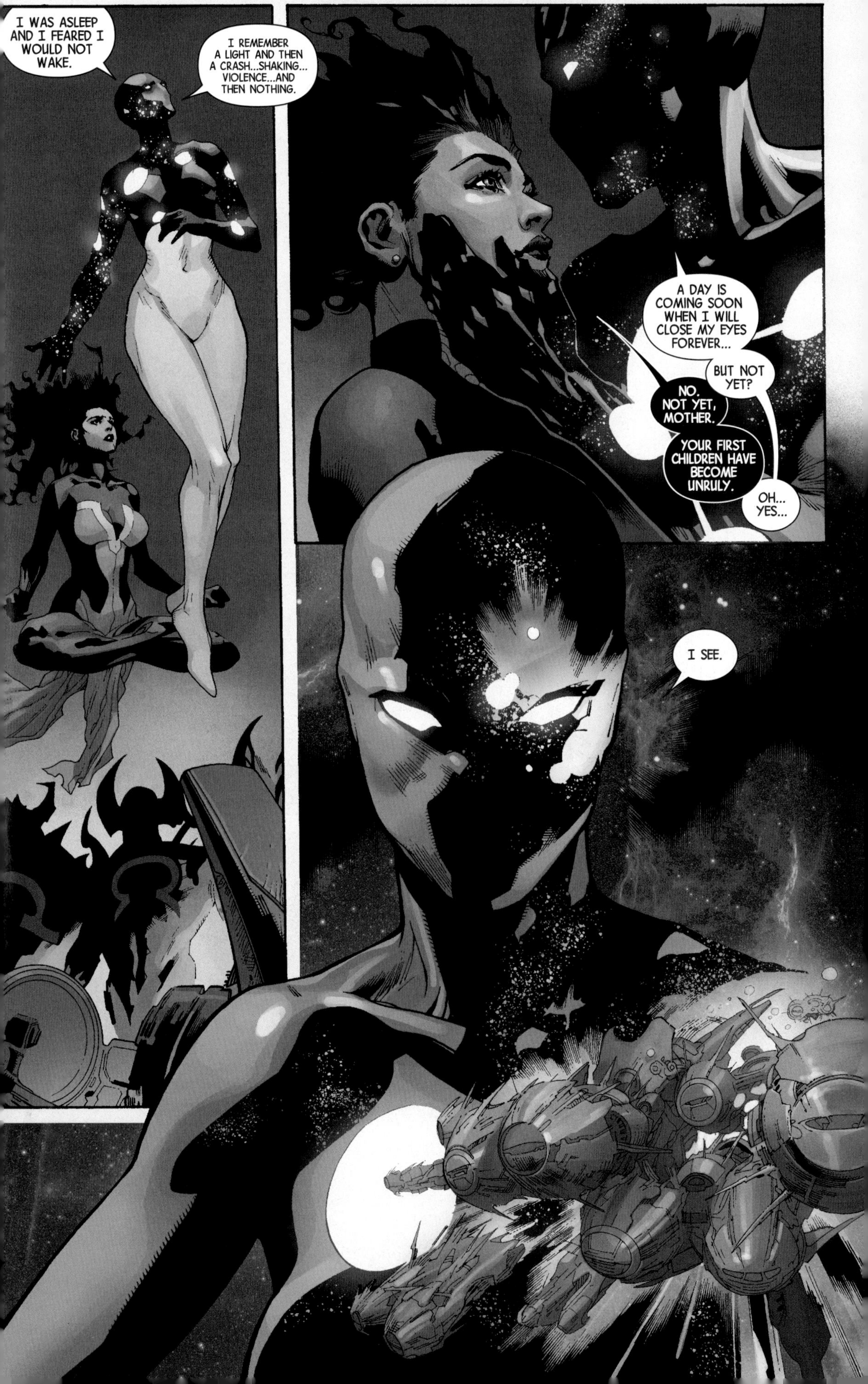
I WAS ASLEEP AND I FEARED I WOULD NOT WAKE.
I REMEMBER A LIGHT AND THEN A CRASH...SHAKING... VIOLENCE...AND THEN NOTHING.
A DAY IS COMING SOON WHEN I WILL CLOSE MY EYES FOREVER...
BUT NOT YET?
NO. NOT YET, MOTHER.
YOUR FIRST CHILDREN HAVE BECOME UNRULY.
OH... YES...
I SEE.

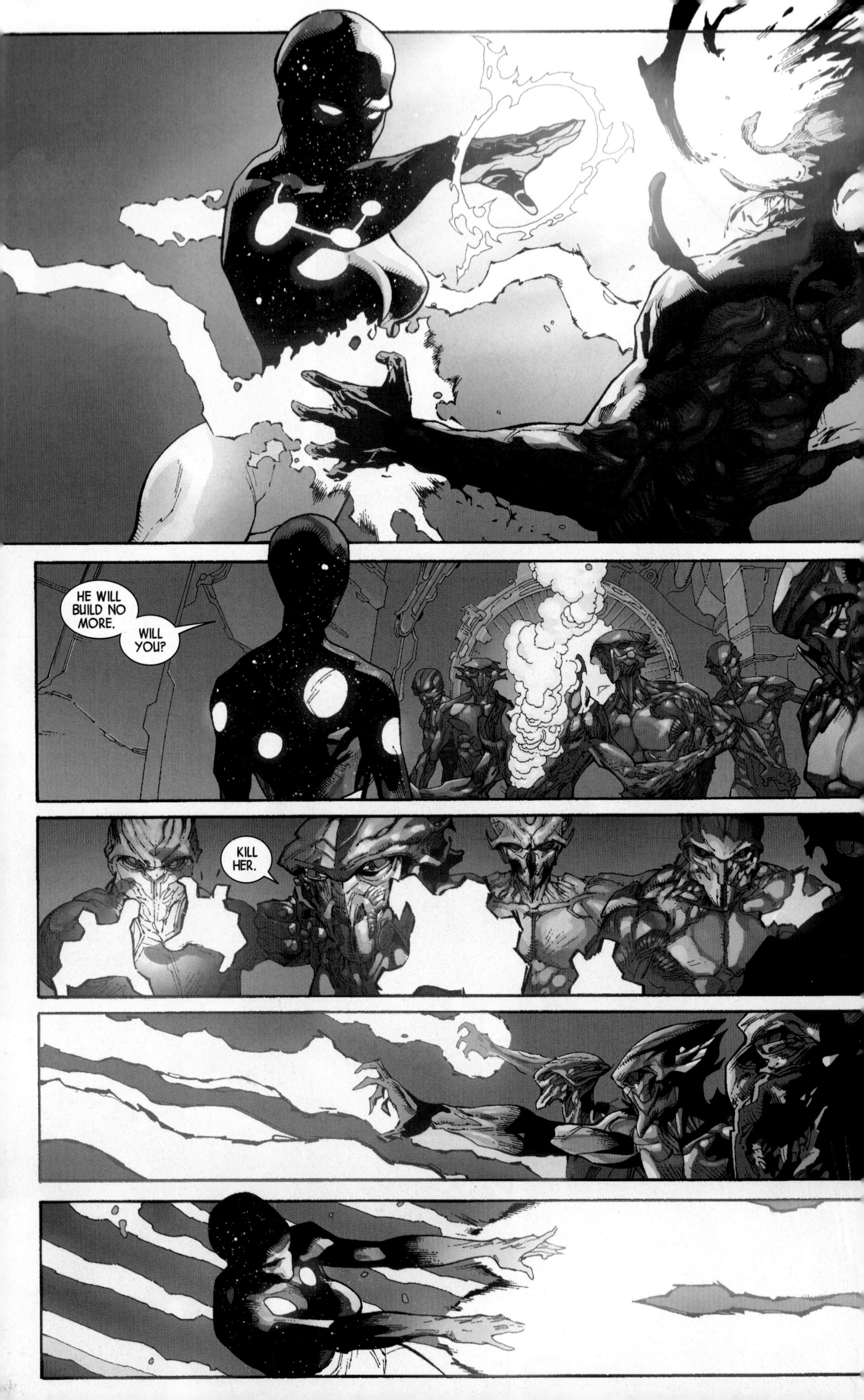
HE WILL BUILD NO MORE.
WILL YOU?
KILL HER.

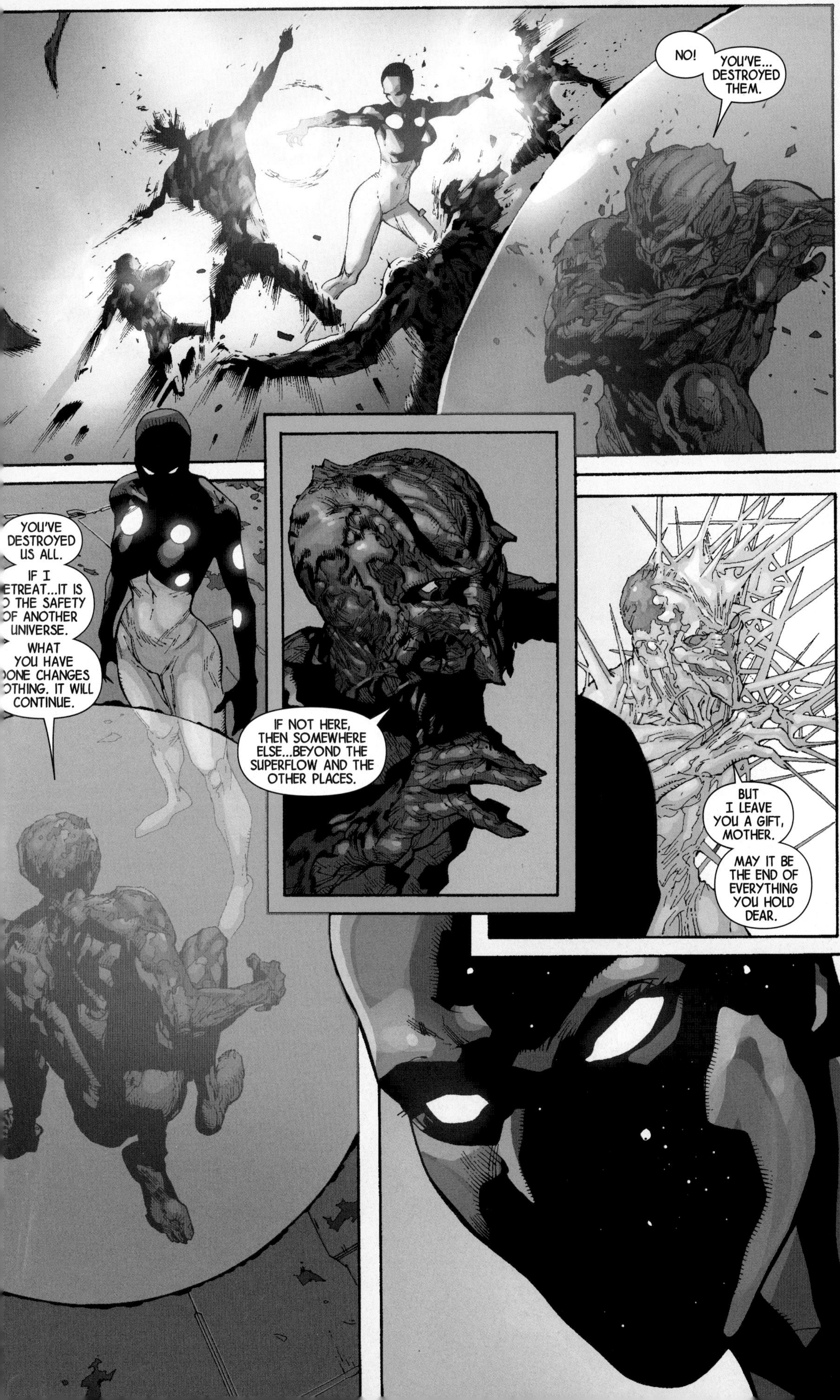
NO!
YOU'VE... DESTROYED THEM.
YOU'VE DESTROYED US ALL.
IF I ETREAT...IT IS O THE SAFETY OF ANOTHER UNIVERSE.
WHAT YOU HAVE ONE CHANGES OTHING. IT WILL CONTINUE.
IF NOT HERE, THEN SOMEWHERE ELSE...BEYOND THE SUPERFLOW AND THE OTHER PLACES.
BUT I LEAVE YOU A GIFT, MOTHER.
MAY IT BE THE END OF EVERYTHING YOU HOLD DEAR.

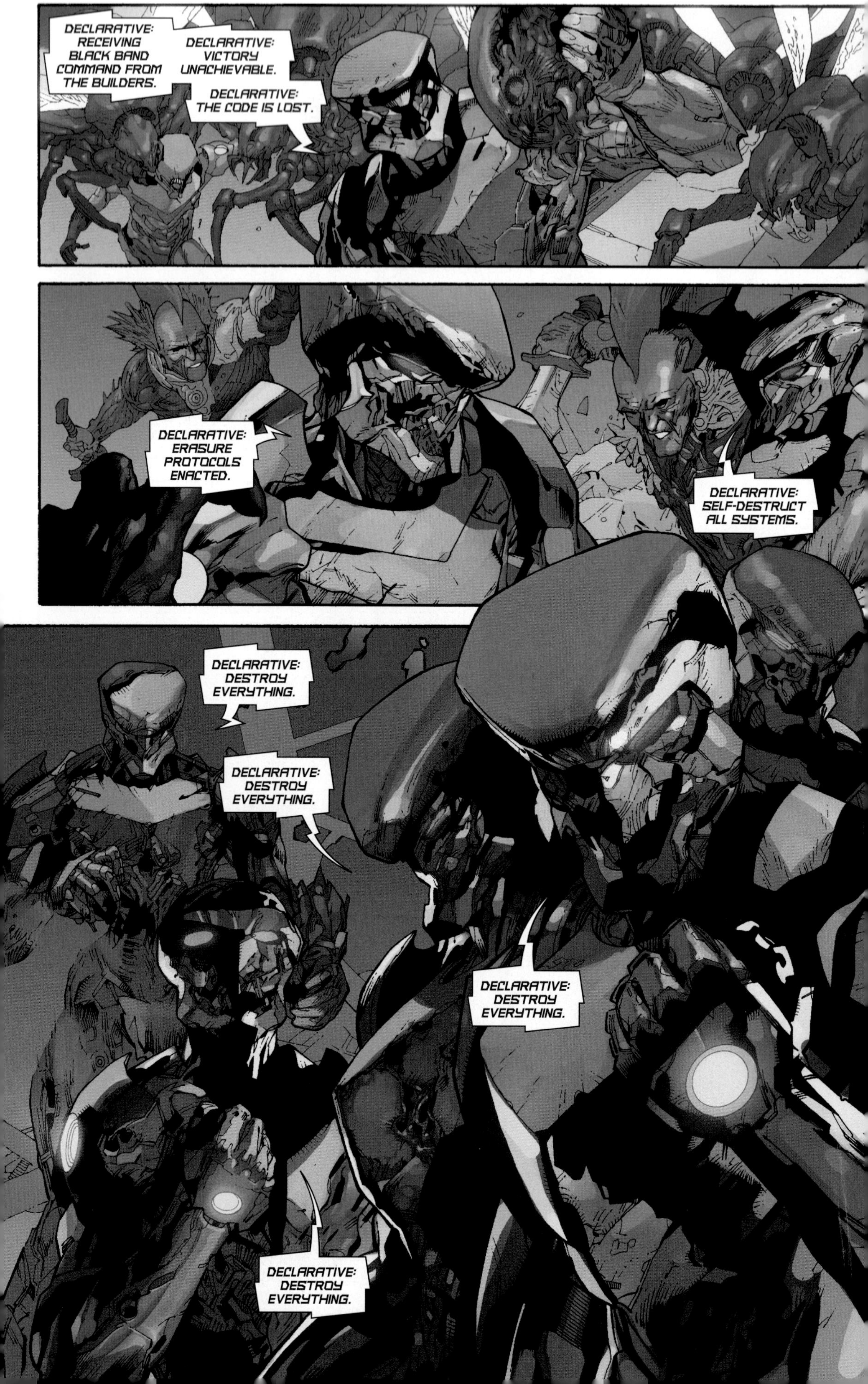
DECLARATIVE: RECEIVING BLACK BAND COMMAND FROM THE BUILDERS.
DECLARATIVE: VICTORY UNACHIEVABLE.
DECLARATIVE: THE CODE IS LOST.
DECLARATIVE: ERASURE PROTOCOLS ENACTED.
DECLARATIVE: SELF-DESTRUCT ALL SYSTEMS.
DECLARATIVE: DESTROY EVERYTHING.
DECLARATIVE: DESTROY EVERYTHING.
DECLARATIVE: DESTROY EVERYTHING.
DECLARATIVE: DESTROY EVERYTHING.

"TO THE EARTH..."

CAST

THE AVENGERS

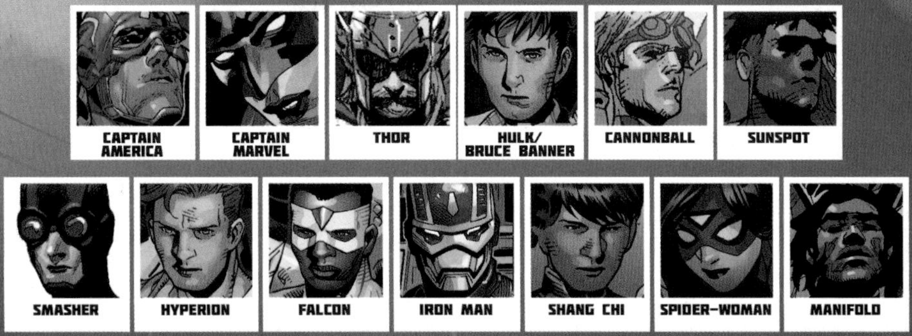
CAPTAIN AMERICA
CAPTAIN MARVEL
THOR
HULK/ BRUCE BANNER
CANNONBALL
SUNSPOT
SMASHER
HYPERION
FALCON
IRON MAN
SHANG CHI
SPIDER-WOMAN
MANIFOLD

THE BLACK ORDER/CULL OBSIDIAN

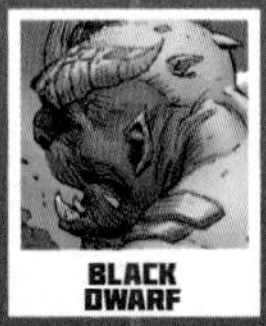
BLACK DWARF

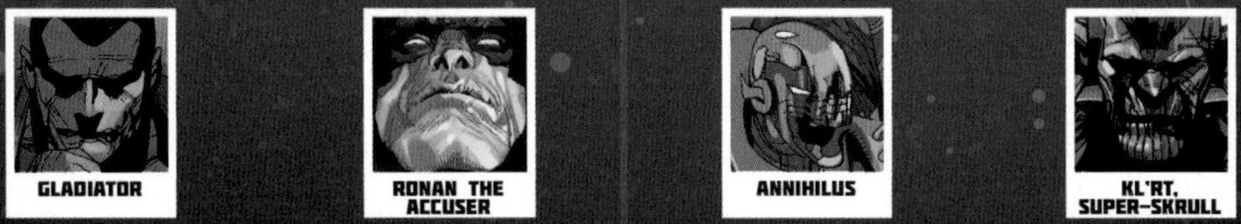
GLADIATOR
RONAN THE ACCUSER
ANNIHILUS
KL'RT, SUPER-SKRULL

SHI'AR IMPERIAL GUARD

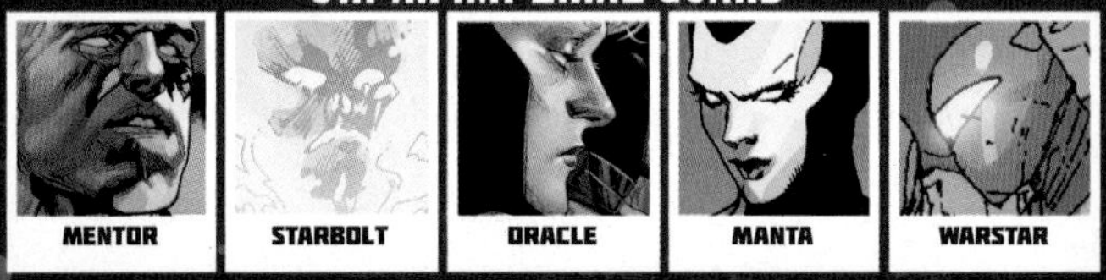
MENTOR
STARBOLT
ORACLE
MANTA
WARSTAR

HOMECOMING

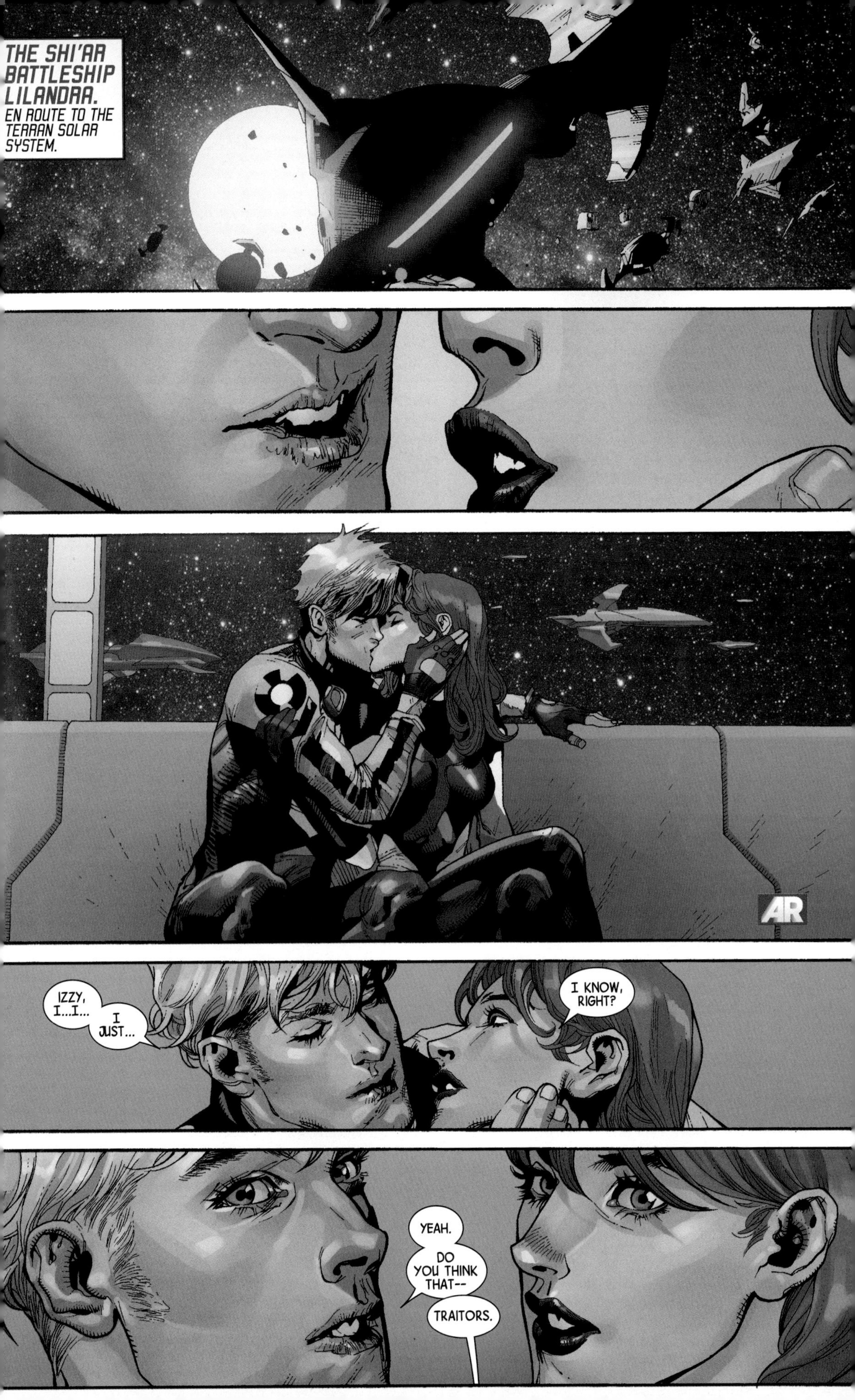
THE SHI'AR BATTLESHIP LILANDRA.
EN ROUTE TO THE TERRAN SOLAR SYSTEM.
IZZY, I...I...
I JUST...
I KNOW, RIGHT?
YEAH.
DO YOU THINK THAT--
TRAITORS.

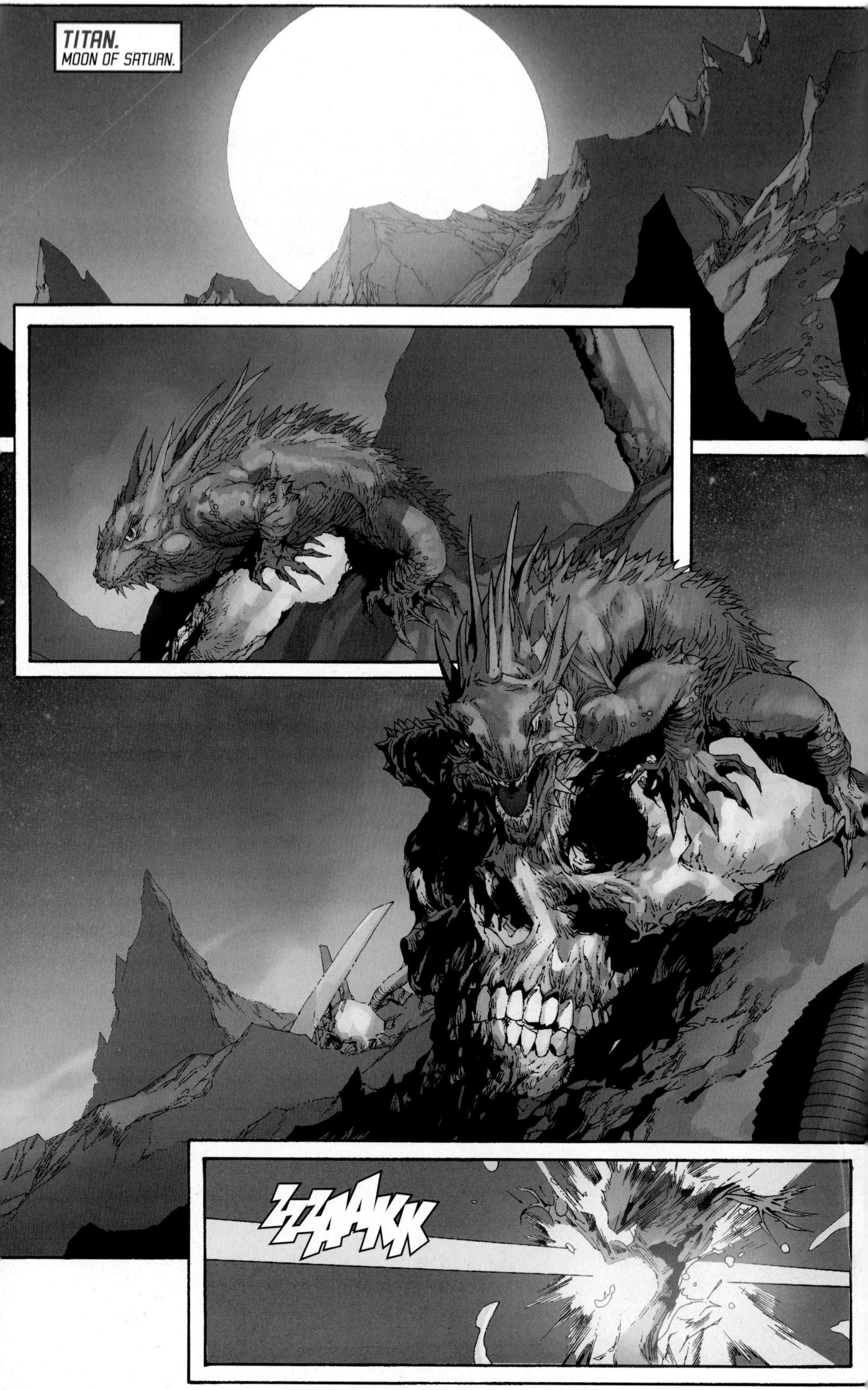
TITAN.
MOON OF SATURN.
ZZZAAKK

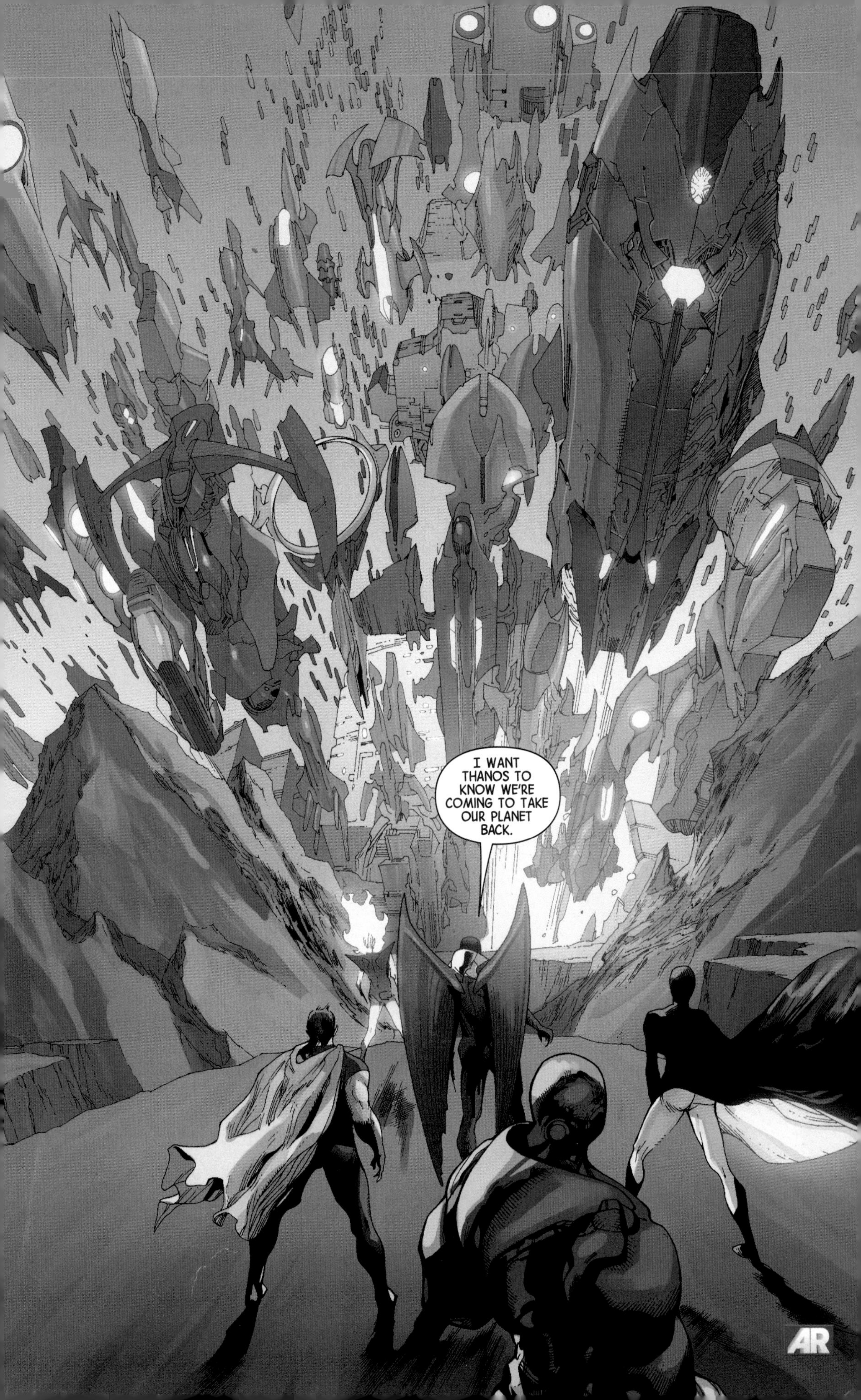
I WANT THANOS TO KNOW WE'RE COMING TO TAKE OUR PLANET BACK.

PLANS AND INTENTIONS

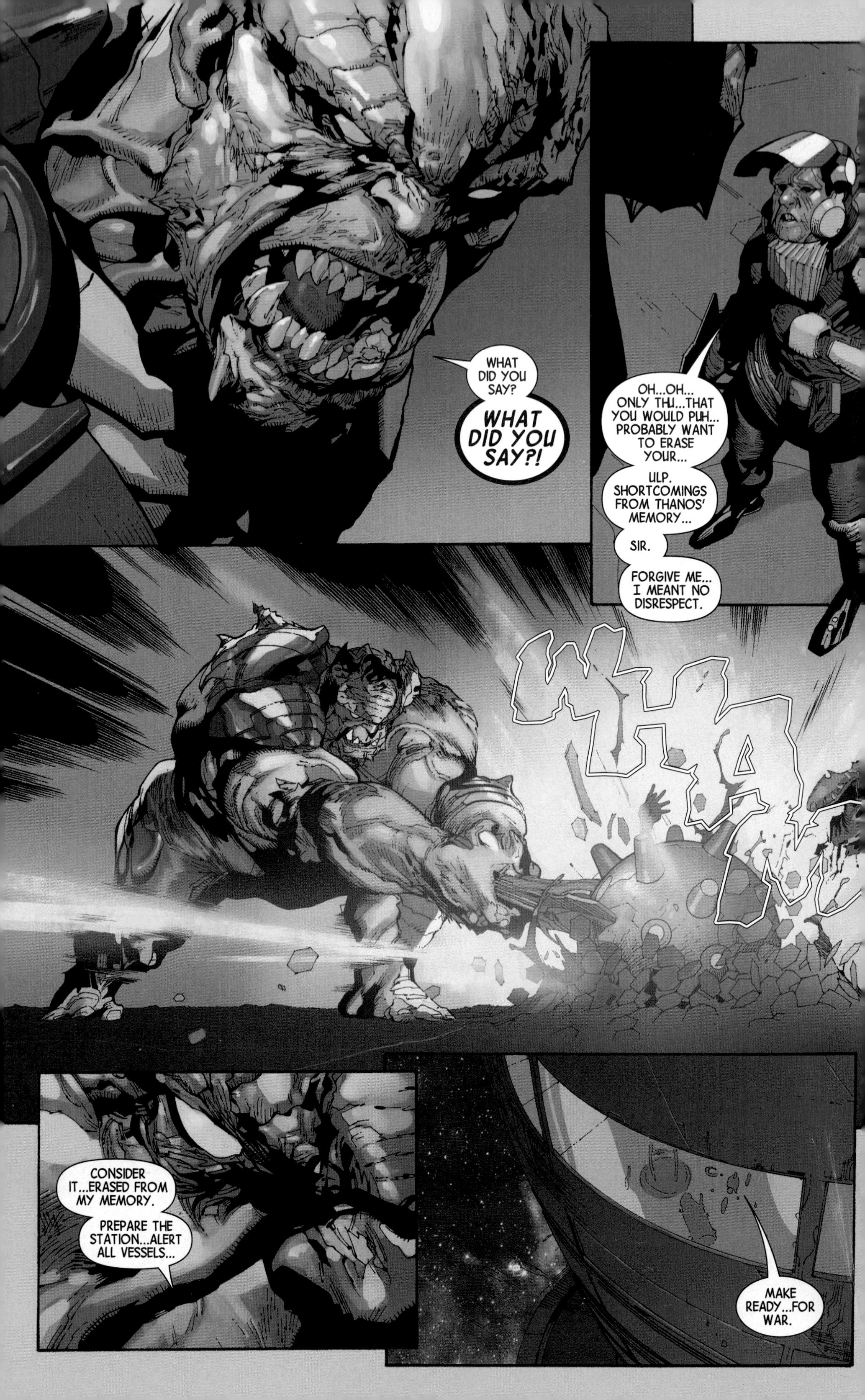
WHAT DID YOU SAY?
WHAT DID YOU SAY?!
OH...OH... ONLY THU...THAT YOU WOULD PUH... PROBABLY WANT TO ERASE YOUR...
ULP. SHORTCOMINGS FROM THANOS' MEMORY...
SIR.
FORGIVE ME... I MEANT NO DISRESPECT.
CONSIDER IT...ERASED FROM MY MEMORY.
PREPARE THE STATION...ALERT ALL VESSELS...
MAKE READY...FOR WAR.

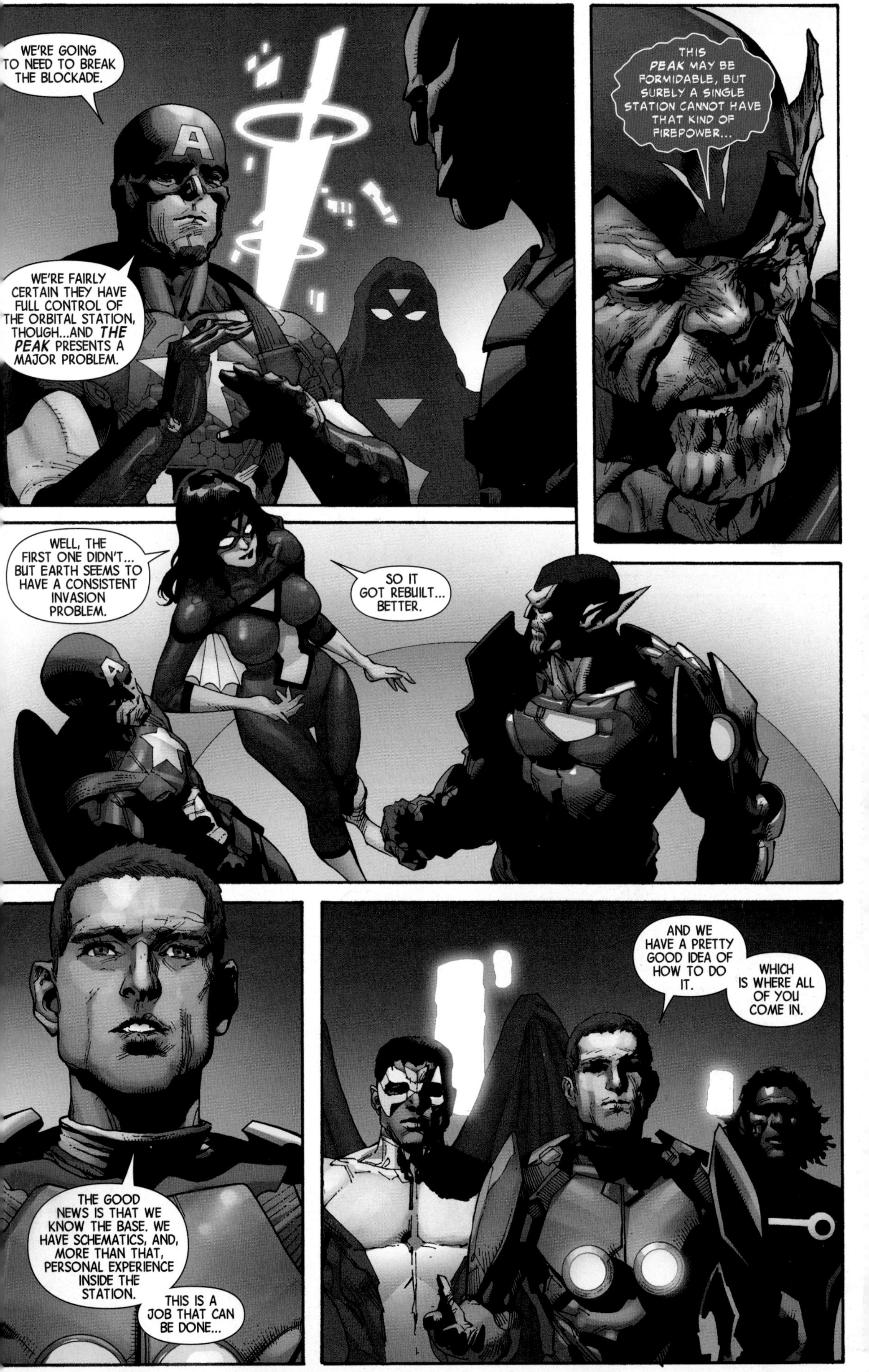
WE'RE GOING TO NEED TO BREAK THE BLOCKADE.
WE'RE FAIRLY CERTAIN THEY HAVE FULL CONTROL OF THE ORBITAL STATION, THOUGH...AND THE PEAK PRESENTS A MAJOR PROBLEM.
THIS PEAK MAY BE FORMIDABLE, BUT SURELY A SINGLE STATION CANNOT HAVE THAT KIND OF FIREPOWER...
WELL, THE FIRST ONE DIDN'T... BUT EARTH SEEMS TO HAVE A CONSISTENT INVASION PROBLEM.
SO IT GOT REBUILT... BETTER.
THE GOOD NEWS IS THAT WE KNOW THE BASE. WE HAVE SCHEMATICS, AND, MORE THAN THAT, PERSONAL EXPERIENCE INSIDE THE STATION.
THIS IS A JOB THAT CAN BE DONE...
AND WE HAVE A PRETTY GOOD IDEA OF HOW TO DO IT.
WHICH IS WHERE ALL OF YOU COME IN.

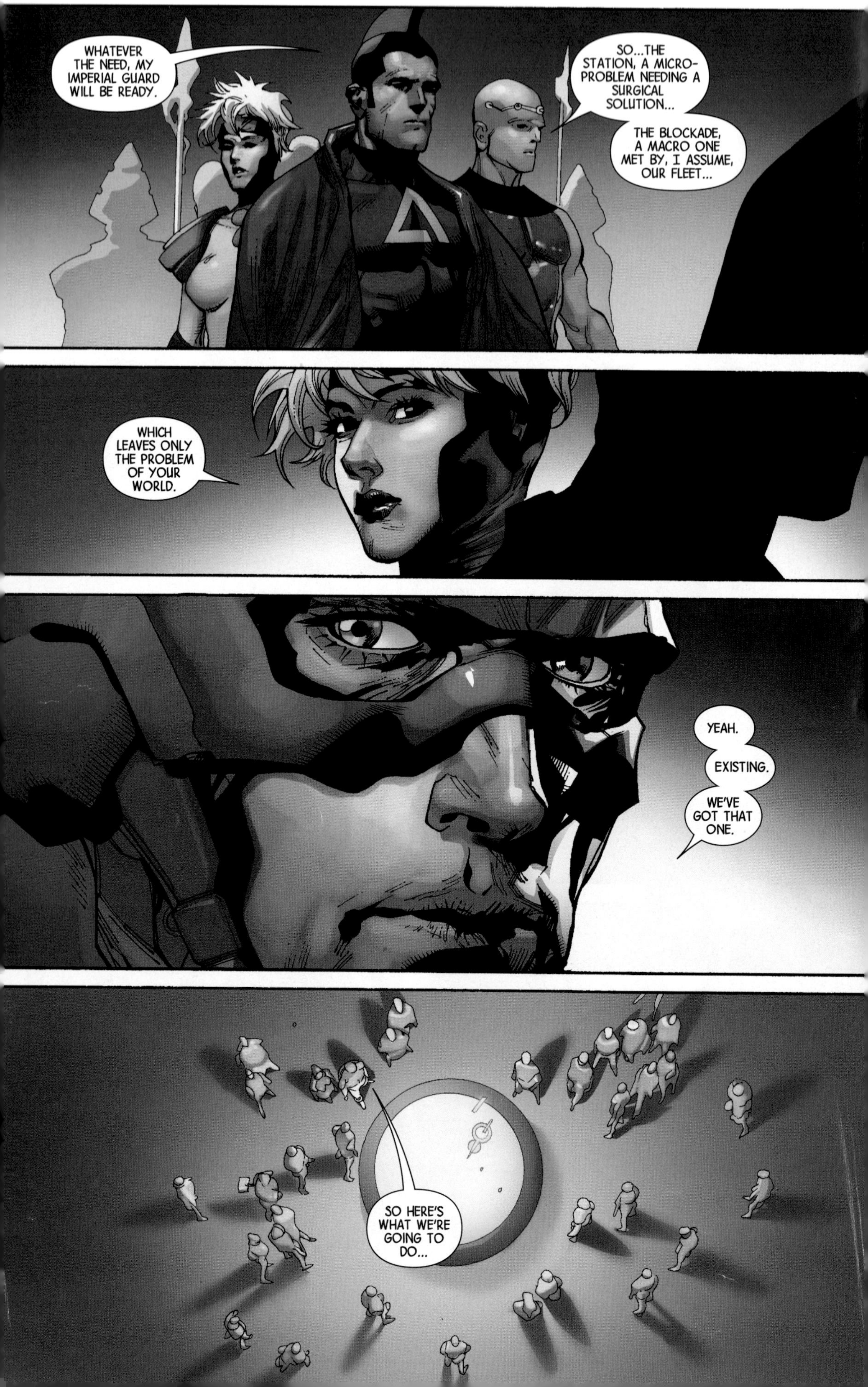
WHATEVER THE NEED, MY IMPERIAL GUARD WILL BE READY.
SO...THE STATION, A MICRO-PROBLEM NEEDING A SURGICAL SOLUTION...
THE BLOCKADE, A MACRO ONE MET BY, I ASSUME, OUR FLEET...
WHICH LEAVES ONLY THE PROBLEM OF YOUR WORLD.
YEAH.
EXISTING.
WE'VE GOT THAT ONE.
SO HERE'S WHAT WE'RE GOING TO DO...

A GREATER PURPOSE

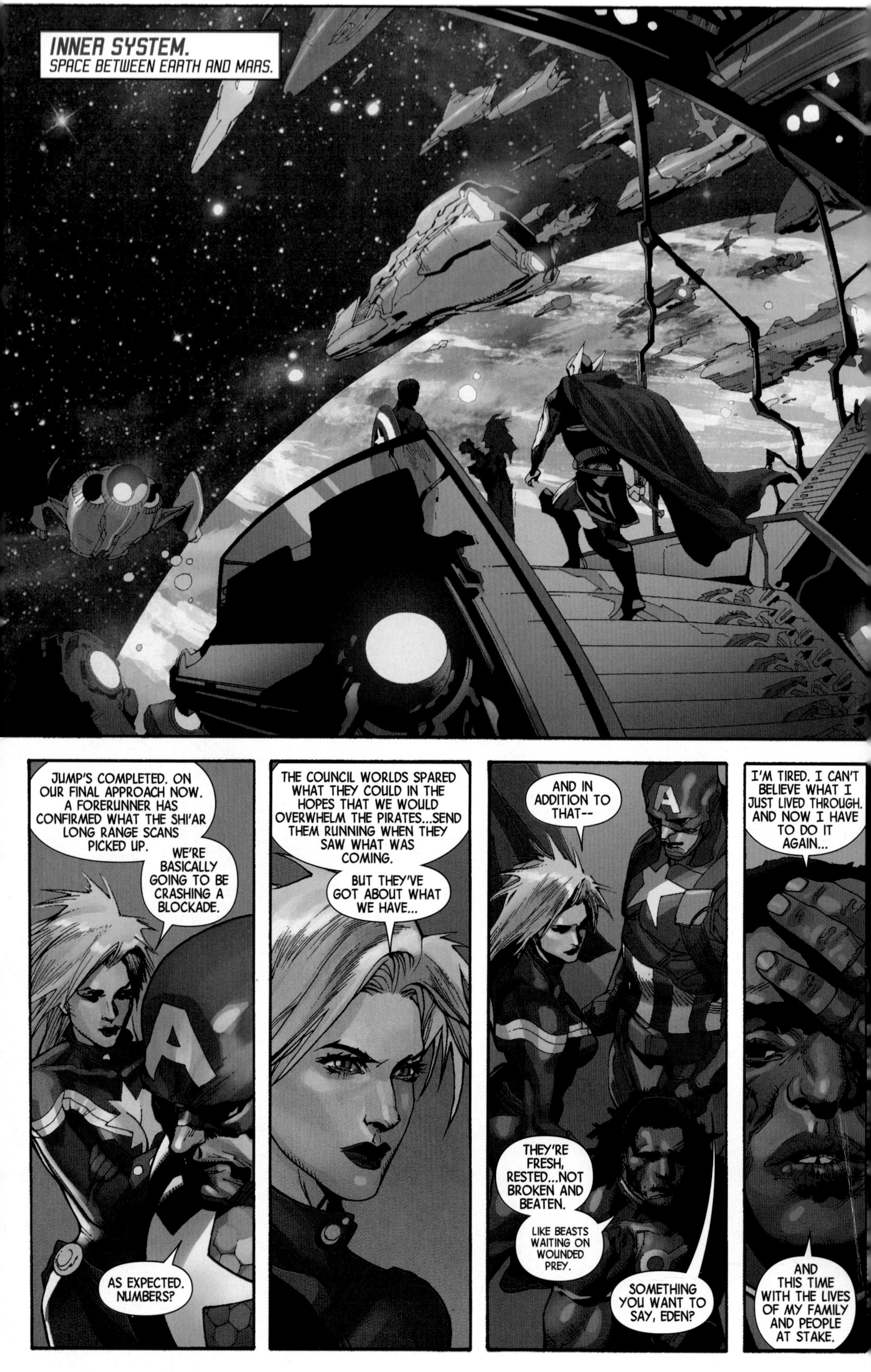
INNER SYSTEM.
SPACE BETWEEN EARTH AND MARS.
JUMP'S COMPLETED. ON OUR FINAL APPROACH NOW. A FORERUNNER HAS CONFIRMED WHAT THE SHI'AR LONG RANGE SCANS PICKED UP.
WE'RE BASICALLY GOING TO BE CRASHING A BLOCKADE.
AS EXPECTED. NUMBERS?
THE COUNCIL WORLDS SPARED WHAT THEY COULD IN THE HOPES THAT WE WOULD OVERWHELM THE PIRATES...SEND THEM RUNNING WHEN THEY SAW WHAT WAS COMING.
BUT THEY'VE GOT ABOUT WHAT WE HAVE...
AND IN ADDITION TO THAT--
THEY'RE FRESH, RESTED...NOT BROKEN AND BEATEN.
LIKE BEASTS WAITING ON WOUNDED PREY.
SOMETHING YOU WANT TO SAY, EDEN?
I'M TIRED. I CAN'T BELIEVE WHAT I JUST LIVED THROUGH. AND NOW I HAVE TO DO IT AGAIN...
AND THIS TIME WITH THE LIVES OF MY FAMILY AND PEOPLE AT STAKE.

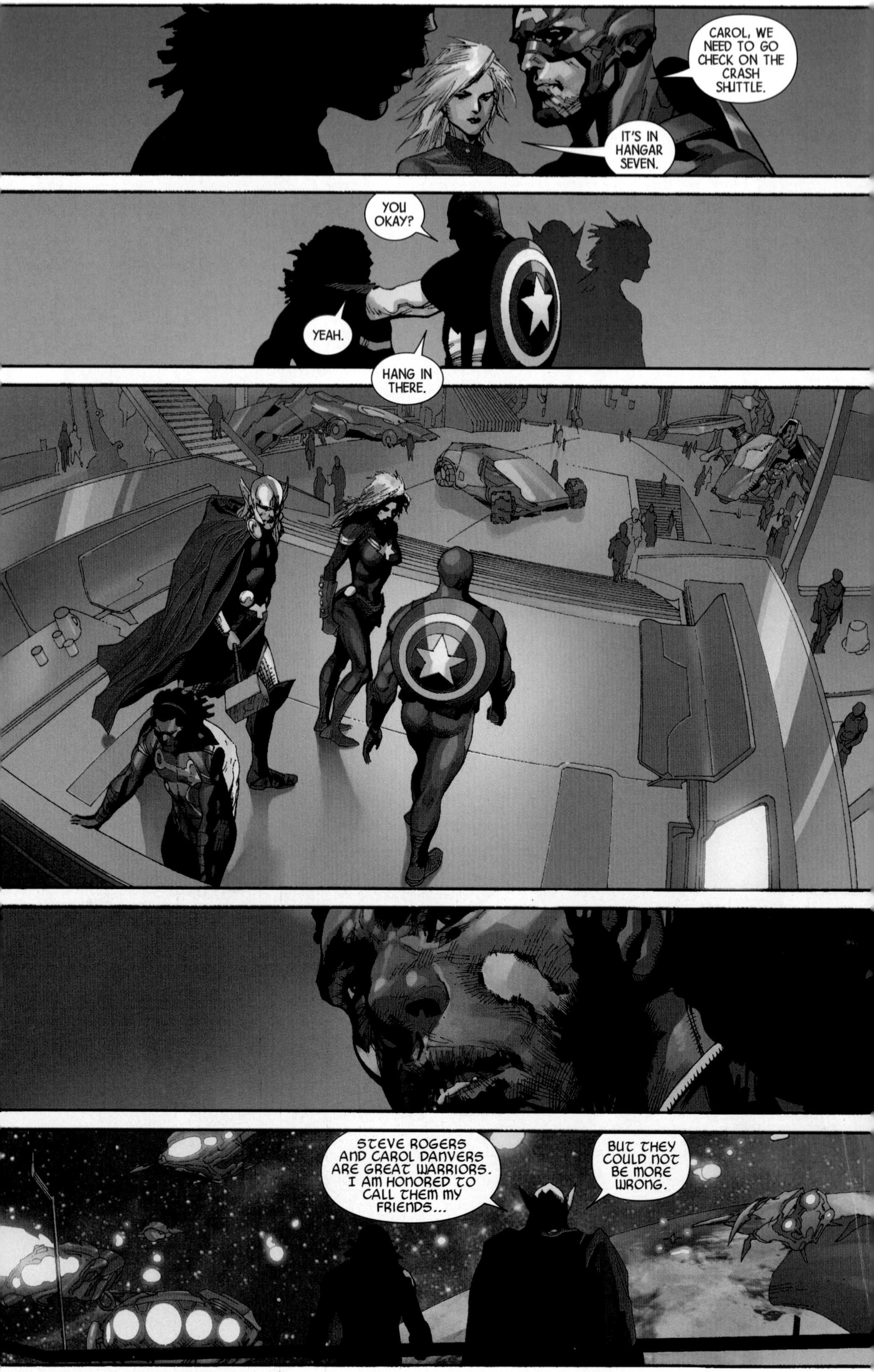
CAROL, WE NEED TO GO CHECK ON THE CRASH SHUTTLE.
IT'S IN HANGAR SEVEN.
YOU OKAY?
YEAH.
HANG IN THERE.
STEVE ROGERS AND CAROL DANVERS ARE GREAT WARRIORS. I AM HONORED TO CALL THEM MY FRIENDS...
BUT THEY COULD NOT BE MORE WRONG.

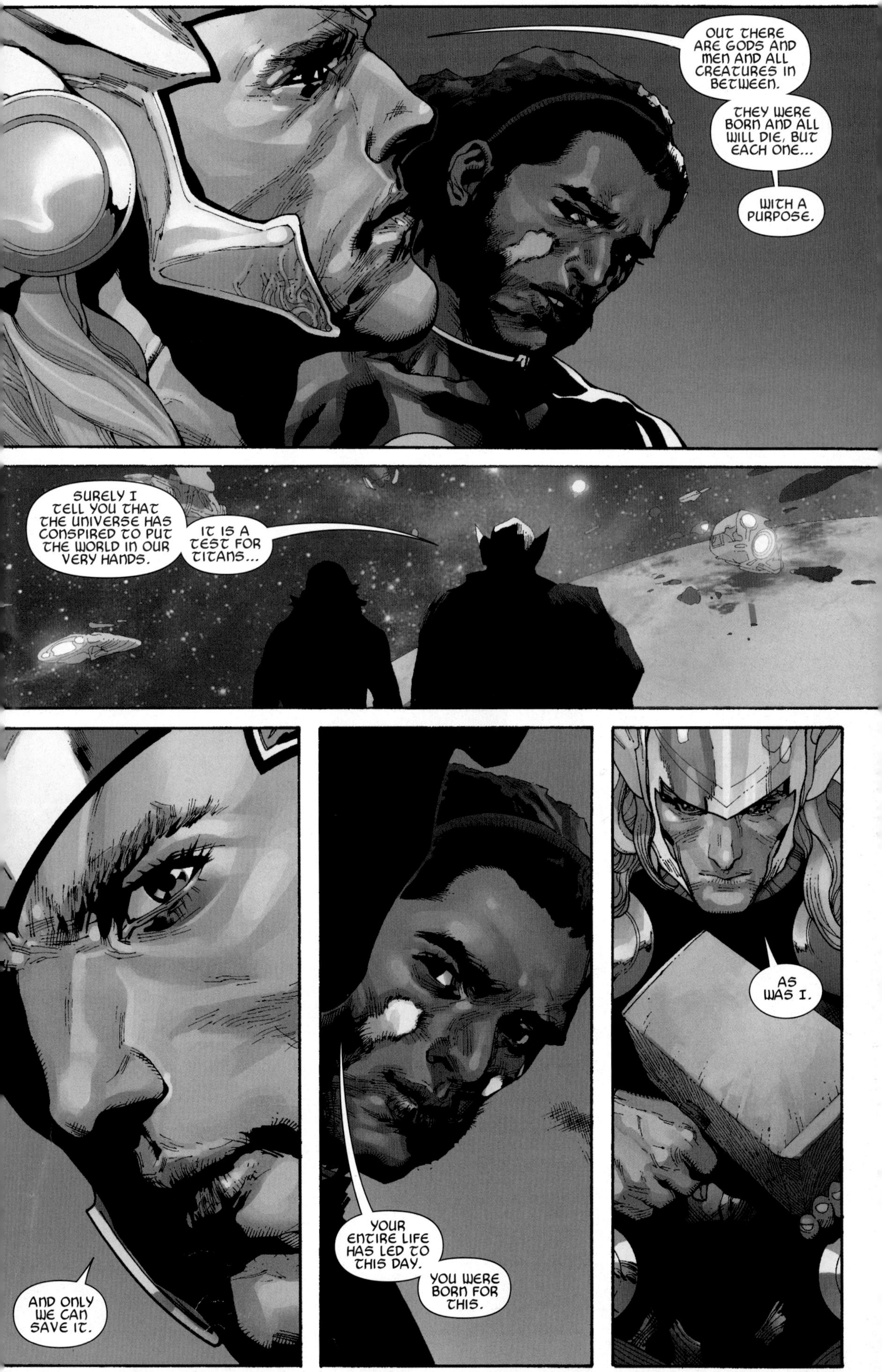
OUT THERE ARE GODS AND MEN AND ALL CREATURES IN BETWEEN.
THEY WERE BORN AND ALL WILL DIE, BUT EACH ONE...
WITH A PURPOSE.
SURELY I TELL YOU THAT THE UNIVERSE HAS CONSPIRED TO PUT THE WORLD IN OUR VERY HANDS.
IT IS A TEST FOR TITANS...
AND ONLY WE CAN SAVE IT.
YOUR ENTIRE LIFE HAS LED TO THIS DAY.
YOU WERE BORN FOR THIS.
AS WAS I.

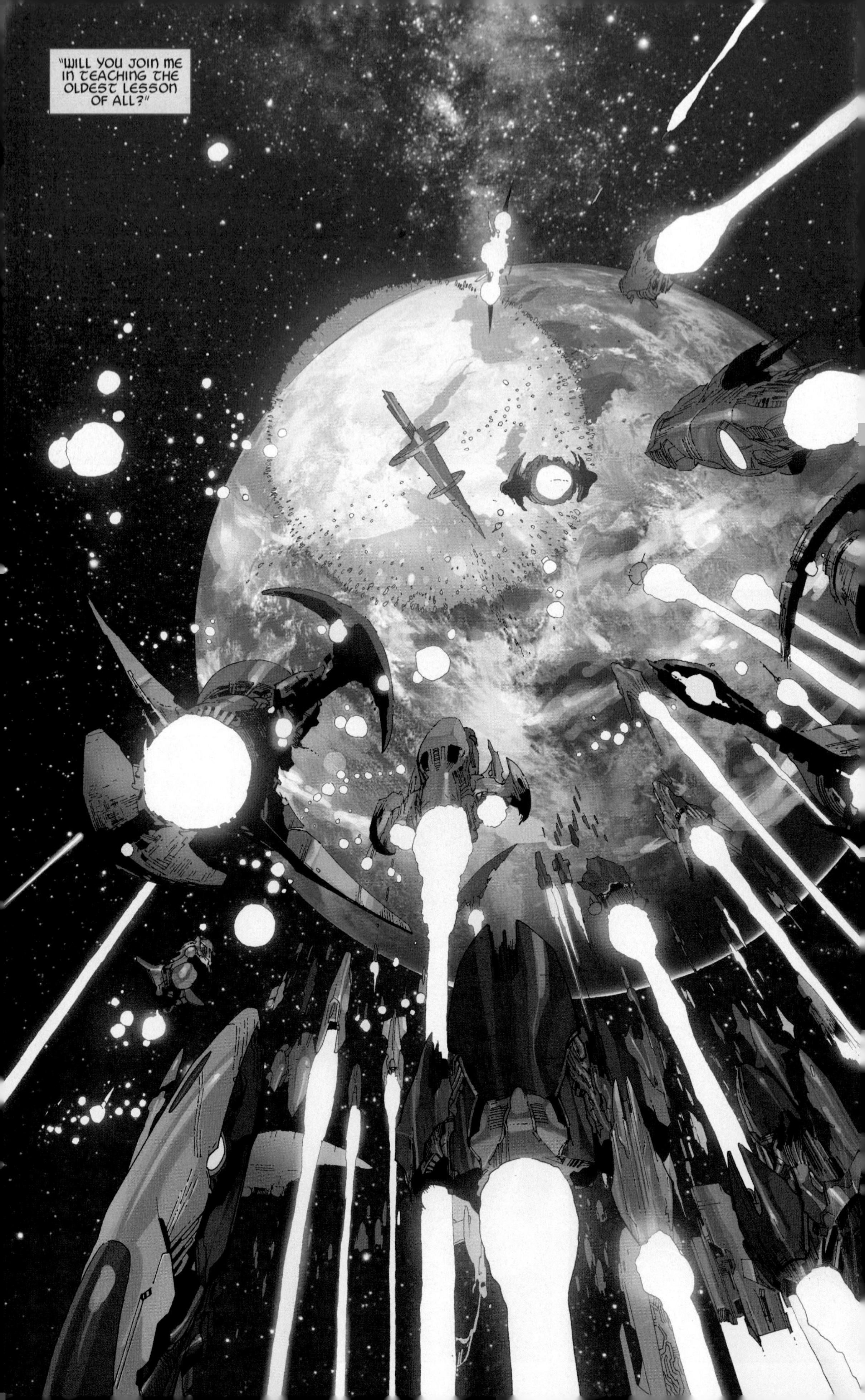
"WILL YOU JOIN ME IN TEACHING THE OLDEST LESSON OF ALL?"

"...TO THE VERY END"

TITAN.

WE SECURED THE MOON, SCUTTLED ANY VESSELS THEY HAD, KNOCKED OUT ALL WEAPONS SYSTEMS. THE PERIMETER WATCH...DO YOU WANT ME TO SEND SOMEONE AFTER HIM?

DON'T BOTHER, MANTA... IF HE CALLS, HE CALLS. HELL, LET 'EM...

I WANT THANOS TO KNOW WE'RE COMING TO TAKE OUR PLANET BACK.

IS IT READY?

IT IS, BLACK DWARF...CREATED EXACTLY AS REQUESTED.

THE PEAK.

GOOD. WE RECEIVED WORD FROM THANOS, WHO HEARD THE SCREAMS FROM TITAN...WE ARE TO EXPECT VISITORS.

LET THEM COME! WE WILL BE READY FOR THEM!

THE MAD TITAN THANOS HAS INVADED EARTH. HIS ARMADA SURROUNDS THE PLANET. WE'RE GOING TO NEED TO BREAK THE BLOCKADE. WE'RE FAIRLY CERTAIN THEY HAVE CONTROL OF THE ORBITAL STATION, AND THE PEAK PRESENTS A MAJOR PROBLEM.

SHALL WE WAGE ONE MORE BATTLE FOR THE AGES?

I DID NOT DRAG A PORTION OF MY REMAINING FLEET ALL THE WAY OUT HERE FOR LEISURE, GLADIATOR. ACCUSER?

I CAME TO JUDGE THE GUILTY.

THEN CONSIDER THE ORDER GIVEN...

"THERE'S ONE LAST WORLD THAT NEEDS SAVING."

CAST

THE AVENGERS

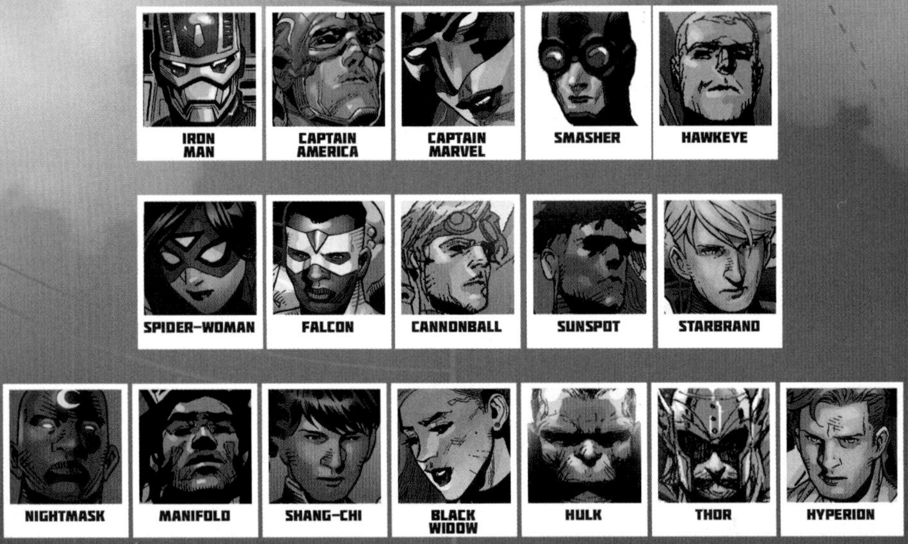
IRON MAN
CAPTAIN AMERICA
CAPTAIN MARVEL
SMASHER
HAWKEYE
SPIDER-WOMAN
FALCON
CANNONBALL
SUNSPOT
STARBRAND
NIGHTMASK
MANIFOLD
SHANG-CHI
BLACK WIDOW
HULK
THOR
HYPERION

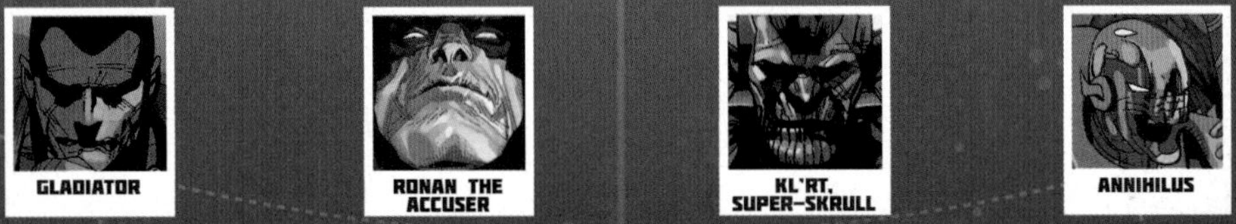
GLADIATOR
RONAN THE ACCUSER
KL'RT, SUPER-SKRULL
ANNIHILUS

SHI'AR IMPERIAL GUARD

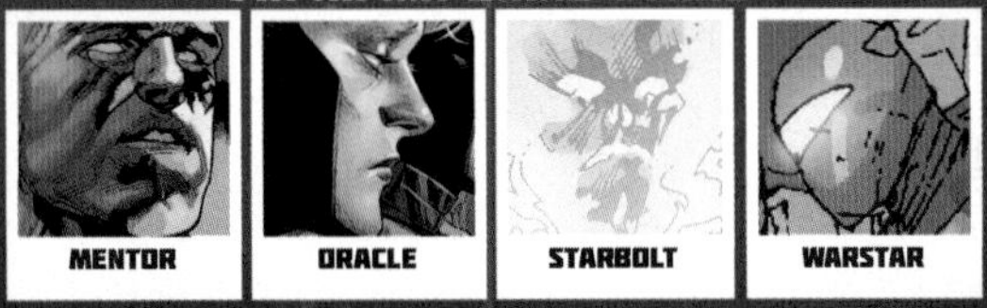
MENTOR
ORACLE
STARBOLT
WARSTAR

GUARDIANS OF THE GALAXY

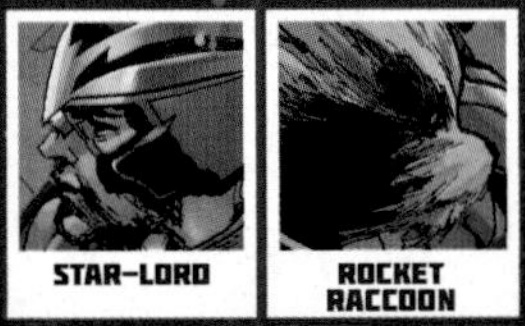
STAR-LORD
ROCKET RACCOON

THE BLACK ORDER/CULL OBSIDIAN

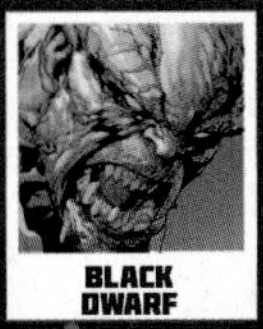
BLACK DWARF

A WORD FROM THE HEAVENS

◆

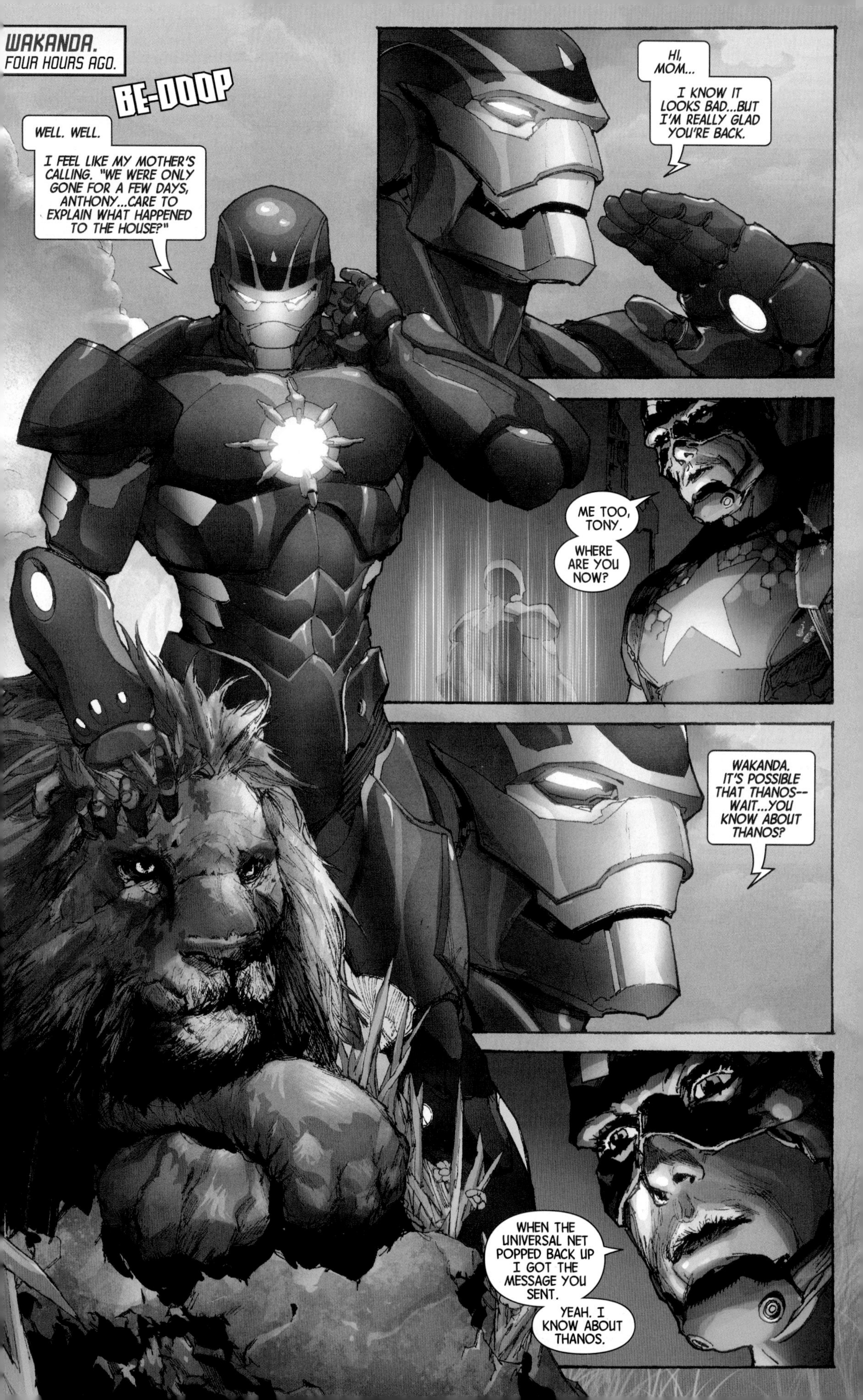
WAKANDA. FOUR HOURS AGO.
BE-DOOP
WELL. WELL.
I FEEL LIKE MY MOTHER'S CALLING. "WE WERE ONLY GONE FOR A FEW DAYS, ANTHONY...CARE TO EXPLAIN WHAT HAPPENED TO THE HOUSE?"
HI, MOM...
I KNOW IT LOOKS BAD...BUT I'M REALLY GLAD YOU'RE BACK.
ME TOO, TONY.
WHERE ARE YOU NOW?
WAKANDA. IT'S POSSIBLE THAT THANOS--WAIT...YOU KNOW ABOUT THANOS?
WHEN THE UNIVERSAL NET POPPED BACK UP I GOT THE MESSAGE YOU SENT.
YEAH. I KNOW ABOUT THANOS.

HOMECOMING

◆

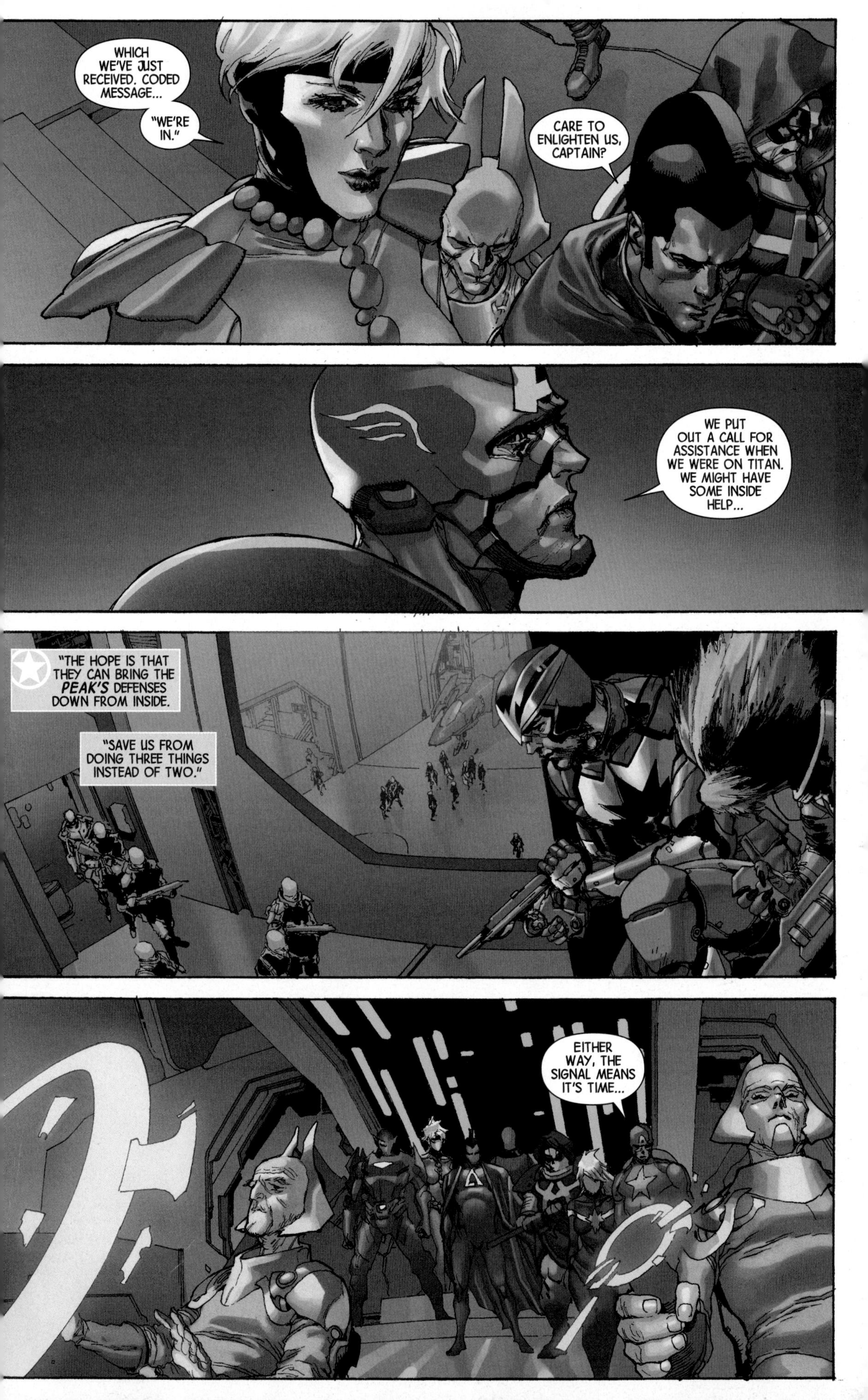
WHICH WE'VE JUST RECEIVED. CODED MESSAGE...
"WE'RE IN."
CARE TO ENLIGHTEN US, CAPTAIN?
WE PUT OUT A CALL FOR ASSISTANCE WHEN WE WERE ON TITAN. WE MIGHT HAVE SOME INSIDE HELP...
"THE HOPE IS THAT THEY CAN BRING THE PEAK'S DEFENSES DOWN FROM INSIDE.
"SAVE US FROM DOING THREE THINGS INSTEAD OF TWO."
EITHER WAY, THE SIGNAL MEANS IT'S TIME...

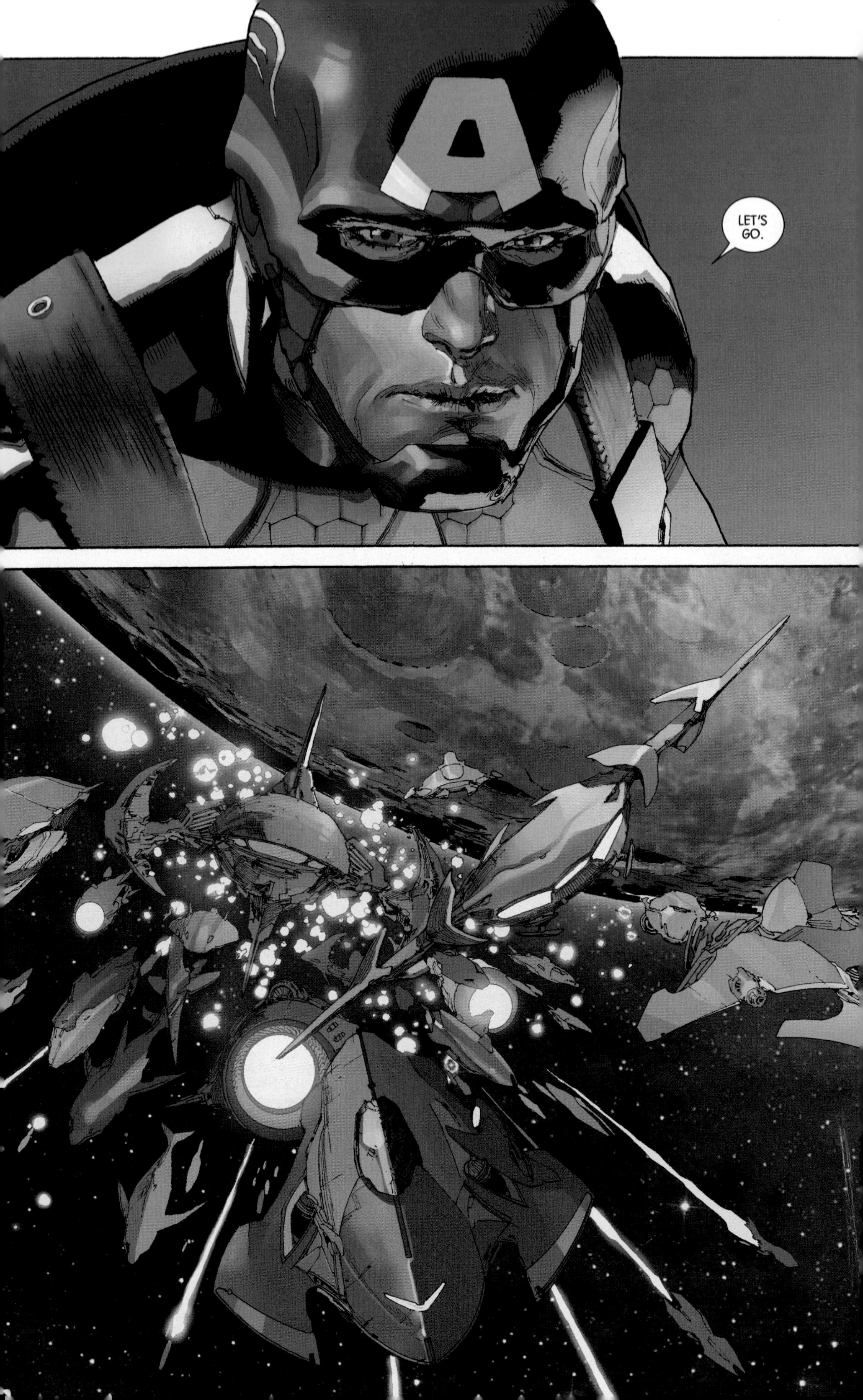
LET'S GO.

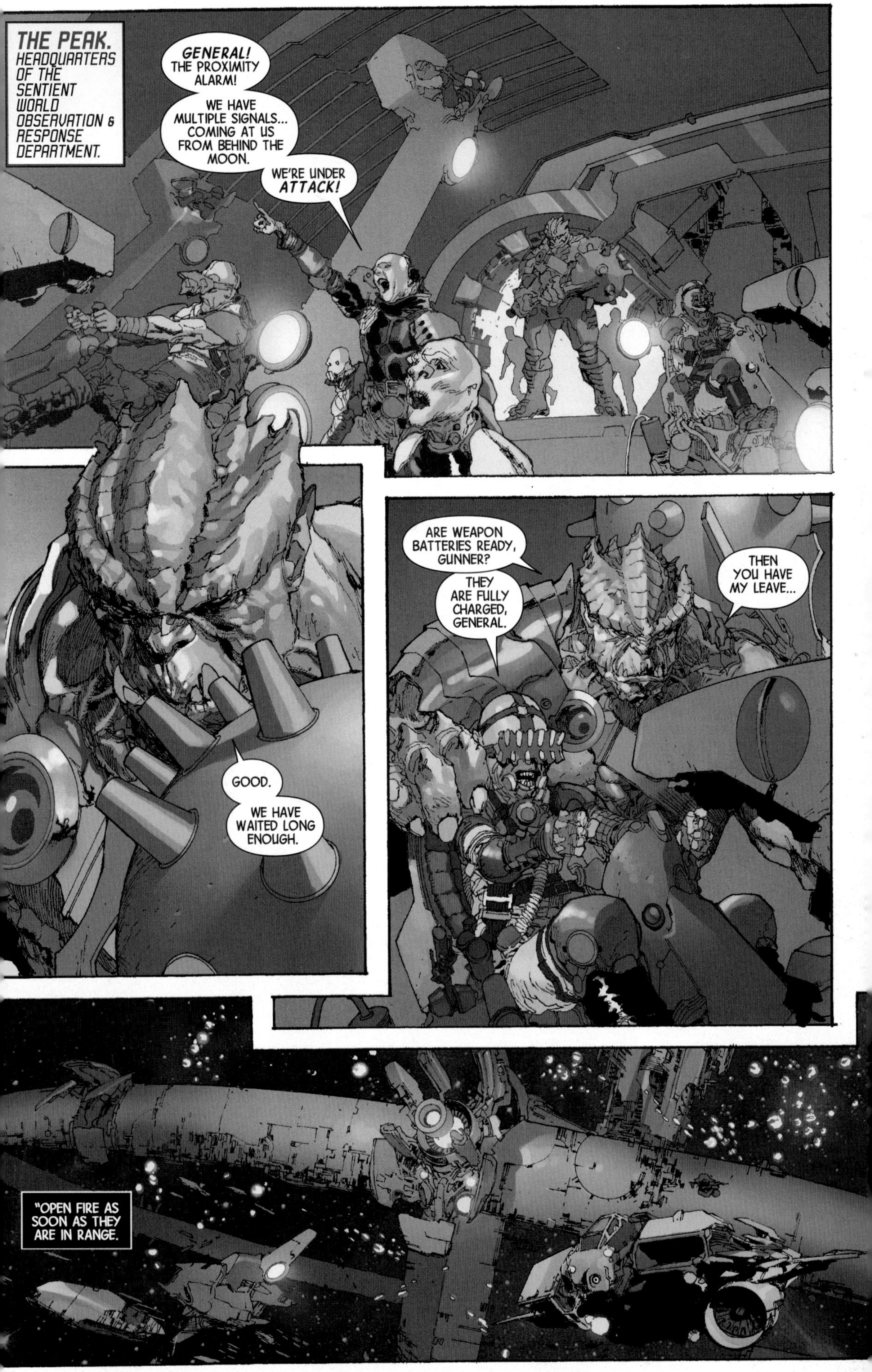
THE PEAK. HEADQUARTERS OF THE SENTIENT WORLD OBSERVATION & RESPONSE DEPARTMENT.
GENERAL! THE PROXIMITY ALARM!
WE HAVE MULTIPLE SIGNALS... COMING AT US FROM BEHIND THE MOON.
WE'RE UNDER ATTACK!
GOOD.
WE HAVE WAITED LONG ENOUGH.
ARE WEAPON BATTERIES READY, GUNNER?
THEY ARE FULLY CHARGED, GENERAL.
THEN YOU HAVE MY LEAVE...
"OPEN FIRE AS SOON AS THEY ARE IN RANGE.

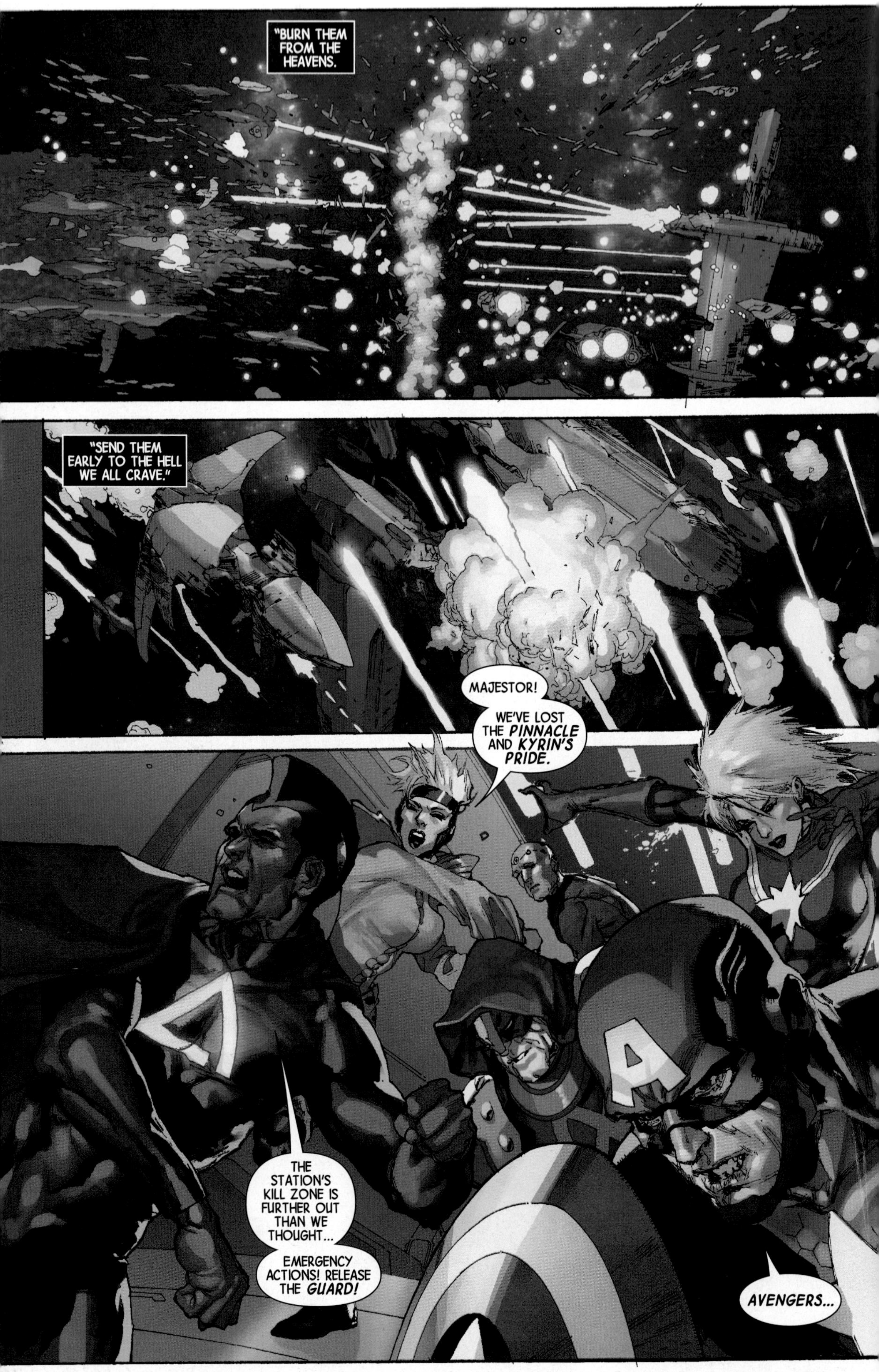
"BURN THEM FROM THE HEAVENS.
"SEND THEM EARLY TO THE HELL WE ALL CRAVE."
MAJESTOR!
WE'VE LOST THE PINNACLE AND KYRIN'S PRIDE.
THE STATION'S KILL ZONE IS FURTHER OUT THAN WE THOUGHT...
EMERGENCY ACTIONS! RELEASE THE GUARD!
AVENGERS...

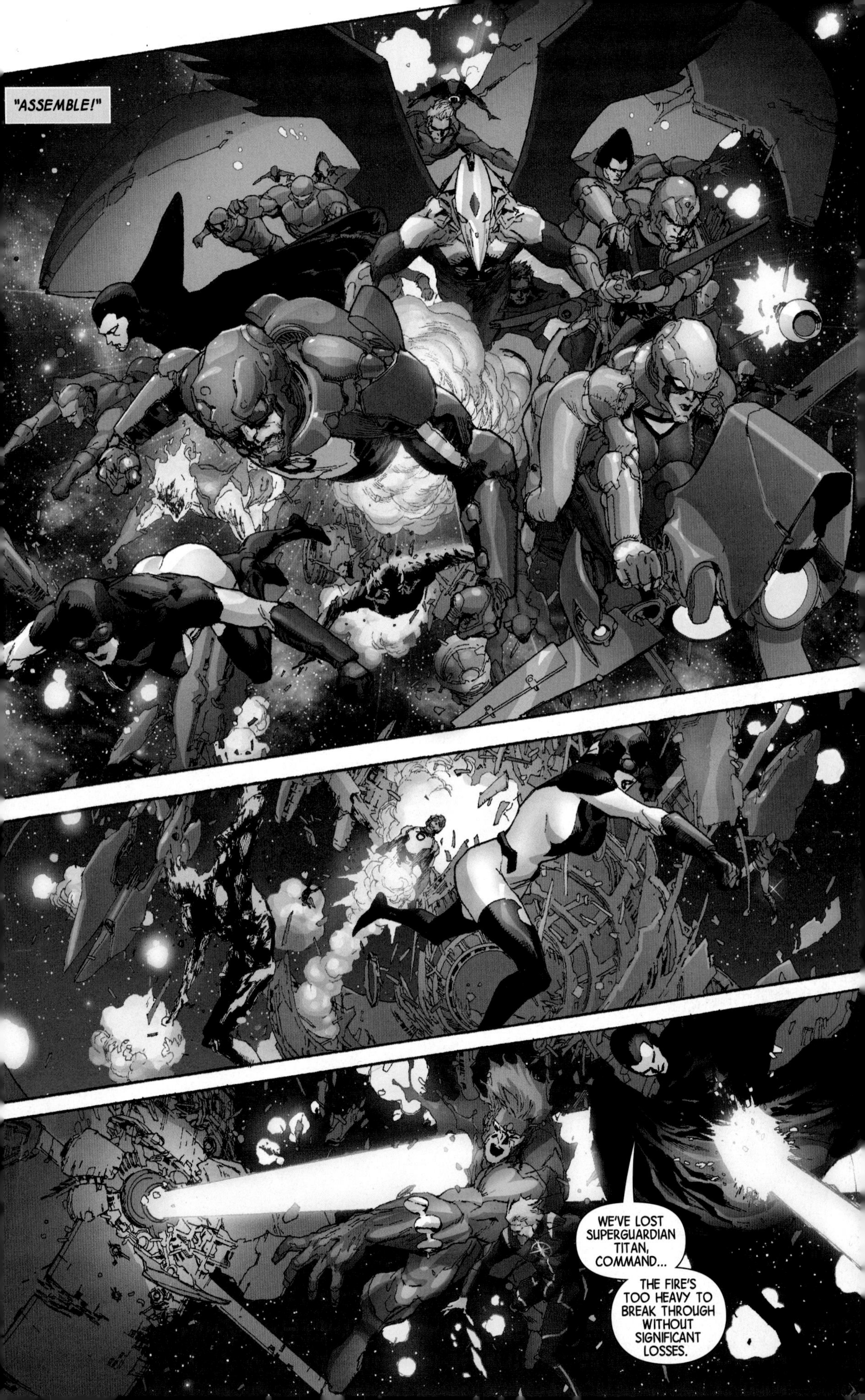
"ASSEMBLE!"
WE'VE LOST SUPERGUARDIAN TITAN, COMMAND...
THE FIRE'S TOO HEAVY TO BREAK THROUGH WITHOUT SIGNIFICANT LOSSES.

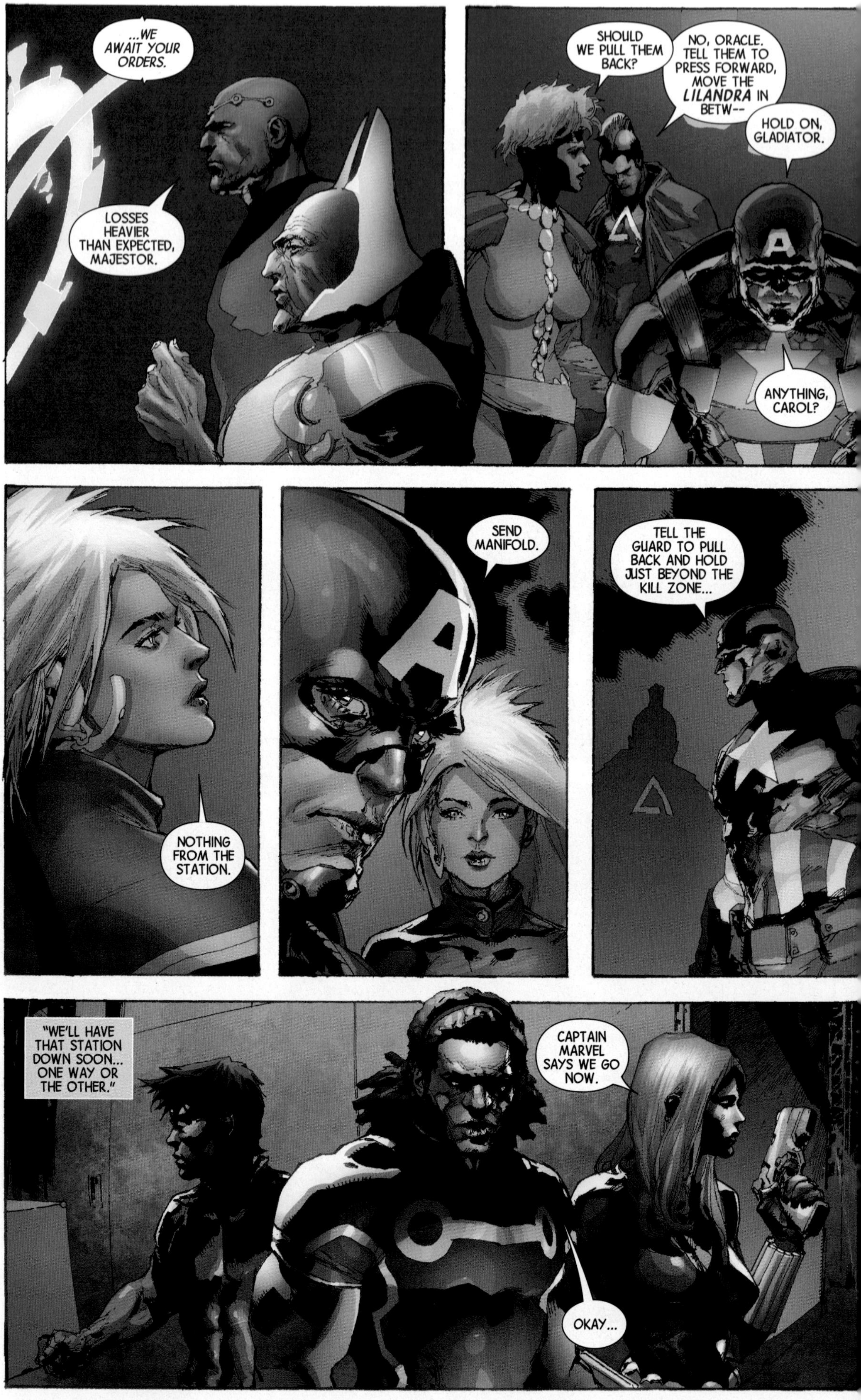
...WE AWAIT YOUR ORDERS.
LOSSES HEAVIER THAN EXPECTED, MAJESTOR.
SHOULD WE PULL THEM BACK?
NO, ORACLE. TELL THEM TO PRESS FORWARD, MOVE THE *LILANDRA* IN BETW--
HOLD ON, GLADIATOR.
ANYTHING, CAROL?
NOTHING FROM THE STATION.
SEND MANIFOLD.
TELL THE GUARD TO PULL BACK AND HOLD JUST BEYOND THE KILL ZONE...
"WE'LL HAVE THAT STATION DOWN SOON... ONE WAY OR THE OTHER."
CAPTAIN MARVEL SAYS WE GO NOW.
OKAY...

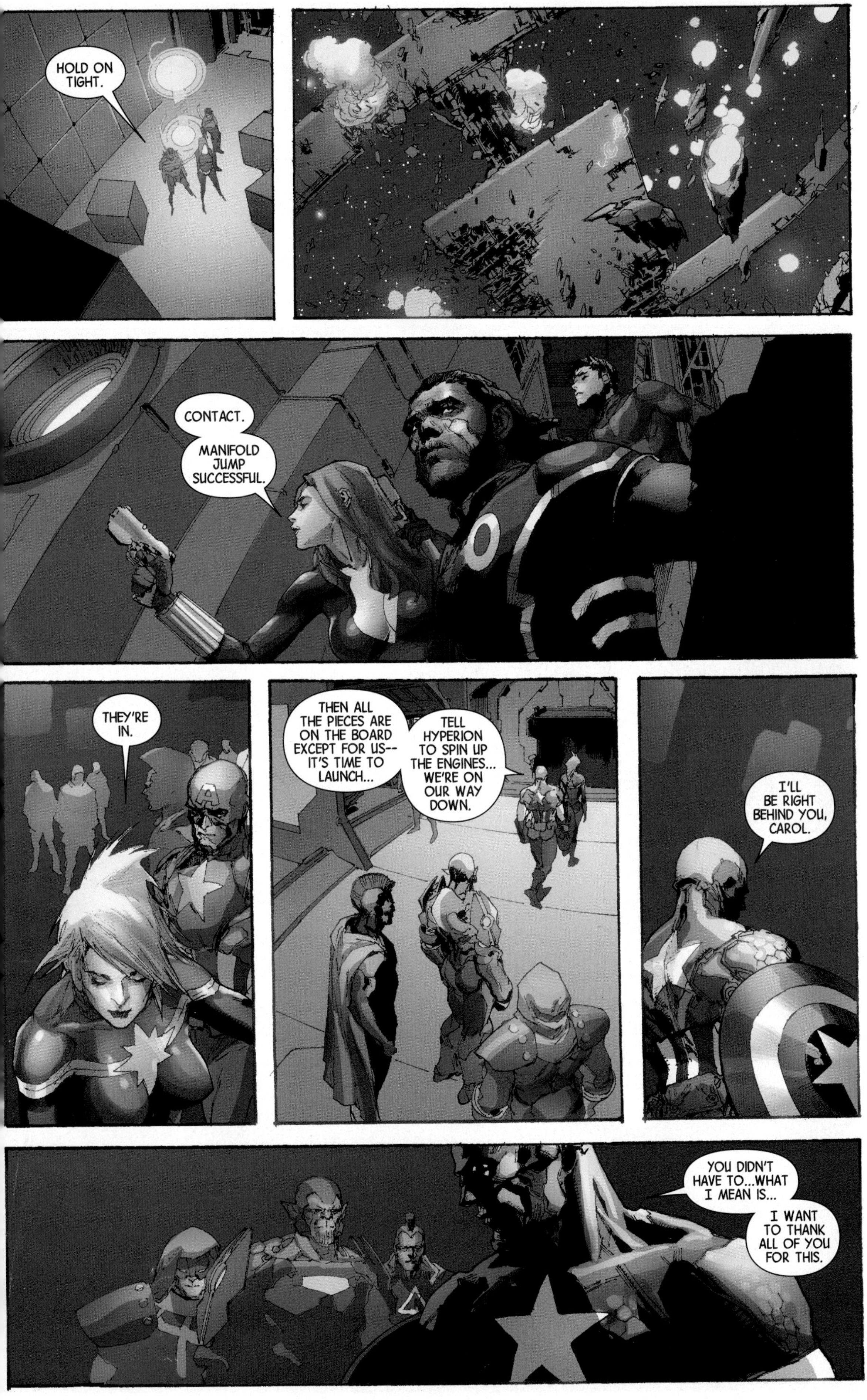
HOLD ON TIGHT.
CONTACT.
MANIFOLD JUMP SUCCESSFUL.
THEY'RE IN.
THEN ALL THE PIECES ARE ON THE BOARD EXCEPT FOR US-- IT'S TIME TO LAUNCH...
TELL HYPERION TO SPIN UP THE ENGINES... WE'RE ON OUR WAY DOWN.
I'LL BE RIGHT BEHIND YOU, CAROL.
YOU DIDN'T HAVE TO...WHAT I MEAN IS...
I WANT TO THANK ALL OF YOU FOR THIS.

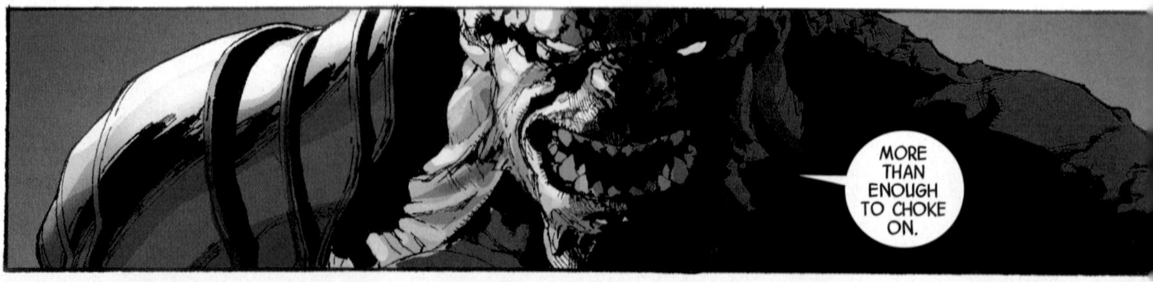
MORE THAN ENOUGH TO CHOKE ON.

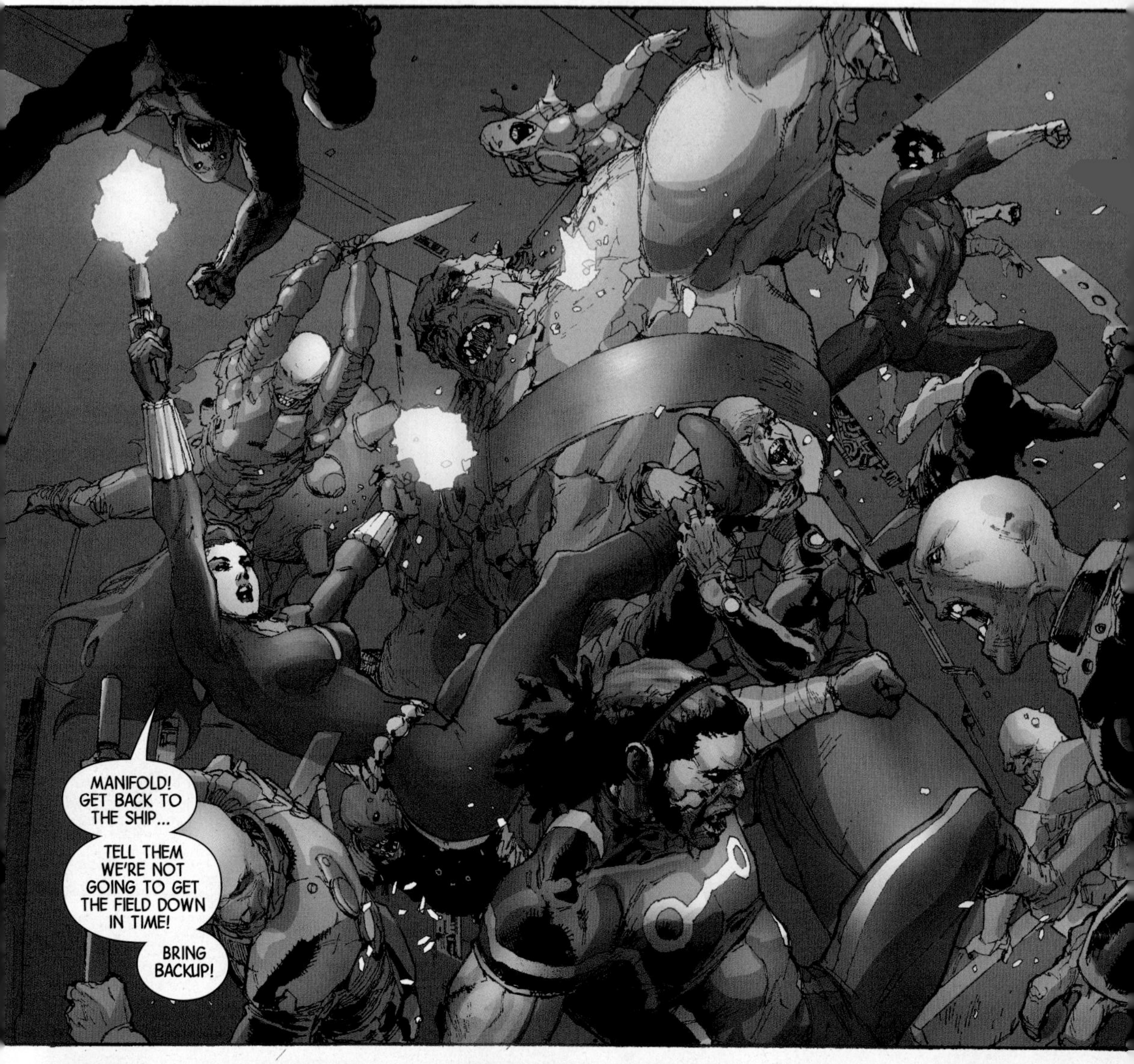
MANIFOLD! GET BACK TO THE SHIP...
TELL THEM WE'RE NOT GOING TO GET THE FIELD DOWN IN TIME!
BRING BACKUP!

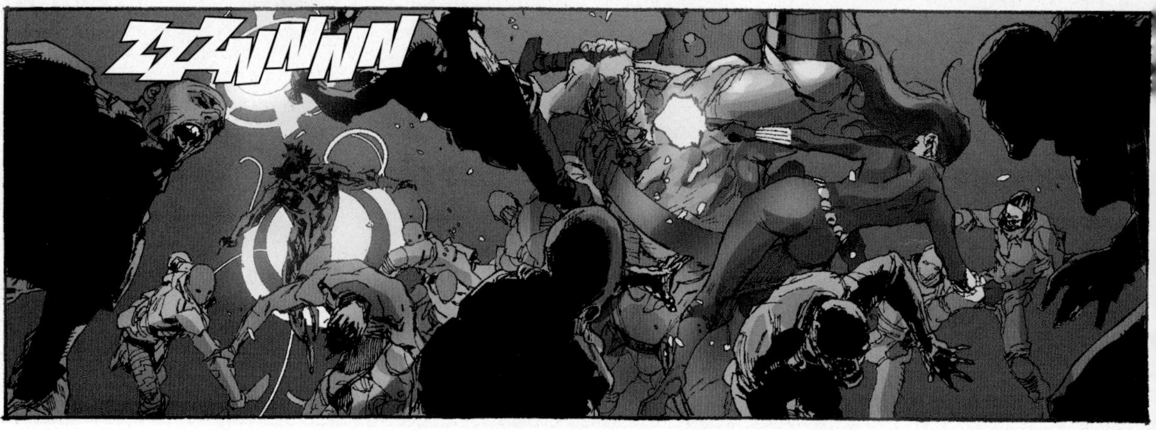
ZZZNNNNN

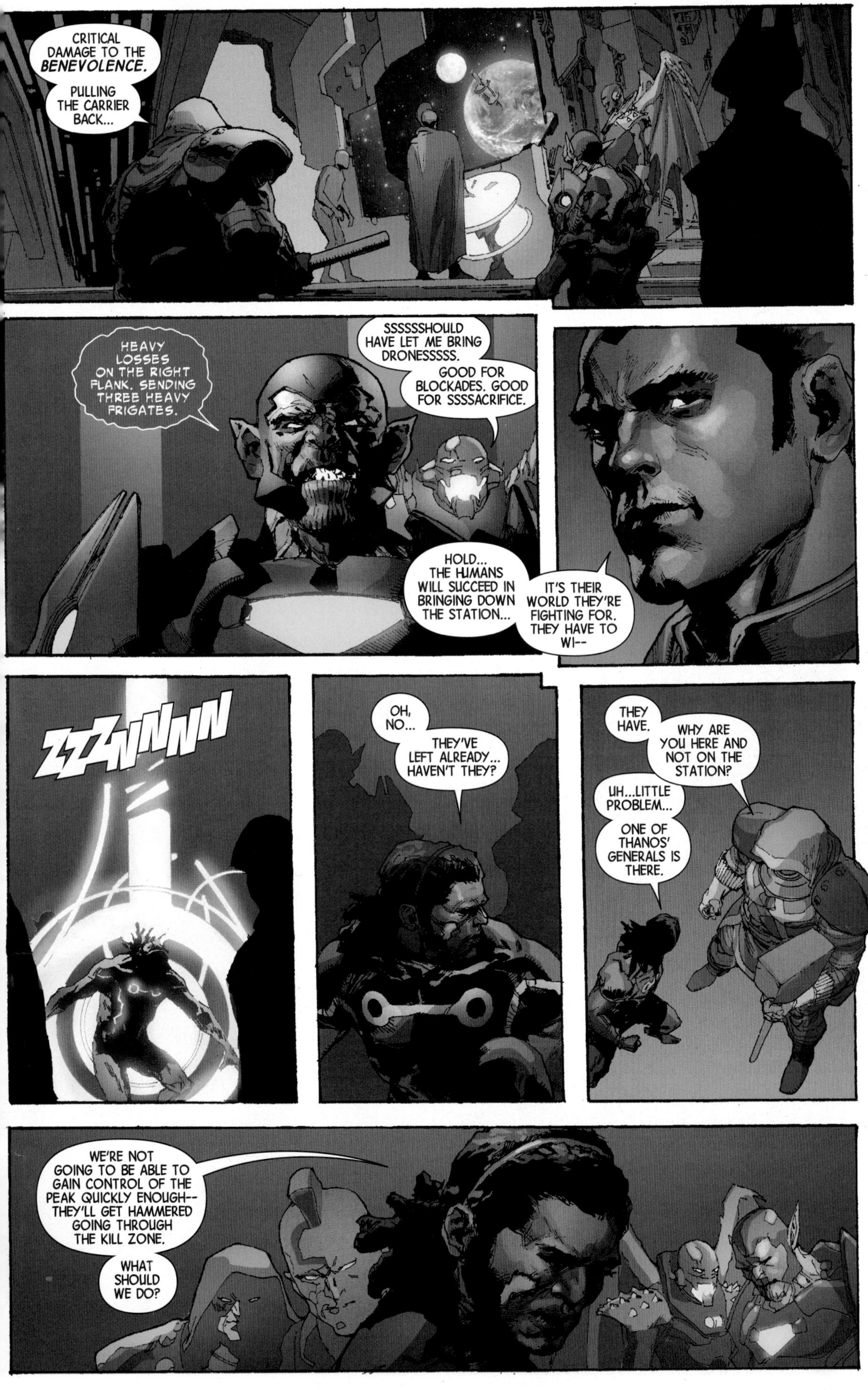
CRITICAL DAMAGE TO THE *BENEVOLENCE.*
PULLING THE CARRIER BACK...
HEAVY LOSSES ON THE RIGHT FLANK. SENDING THREE HEAVY FRIGATES.
SSSSSSHOULD HAVE LET ME BRING DRONESSSSS.
GOOD FOR BLOCKADES. GOOD FOR SSSSACRIFICE.
HOLD... THE HUMANS WILL SUCCEED IN BRINGING DOWN THE STATION...
IT'S THEIR WORLD THEY'RE FIGHTING FOR. THEY HAVE TO WI--
ZZZNNNNN
OH, NO...
THEY'VE LEFT ALREADY... HAVEN'T THEY?
THEY HAVE.
WHY ARE YOU HERE AND NOT ON THE STATION?
UH...LITTLE PROBLEM...
ONE OF THANOS' GENERALS IS THERE.
WE'RE NOT GOING TO BE ABLE TO GAIN CONTROL OF THE PEAK QUICKLY ENOUGH-- THEY'LL GET HAMMERED GOING THROUGH THE KILL ZONE.
WHAT SHOULD WE DO?

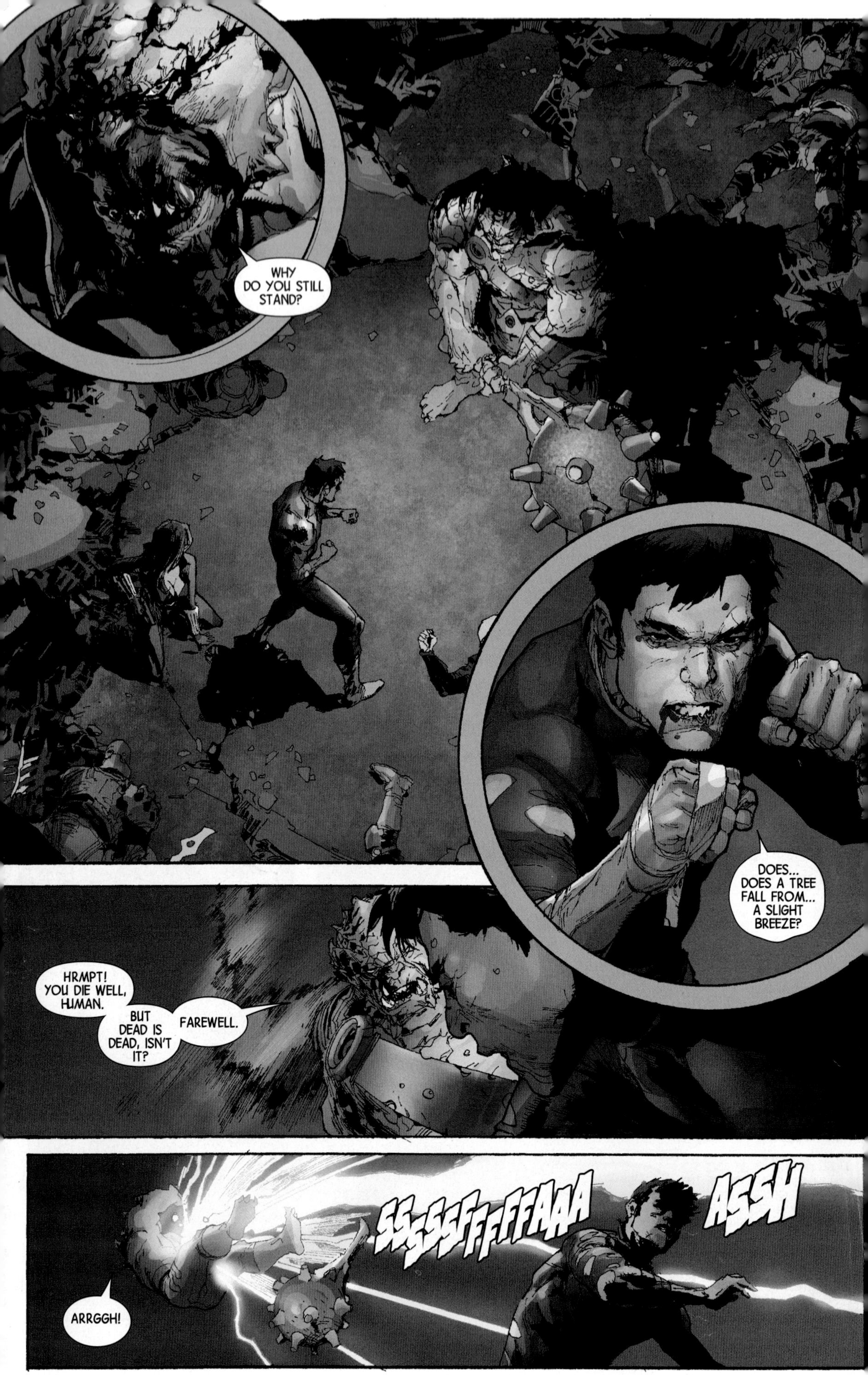
WHY DO YOU STILL STAND?
DOES... DOES A TREE FALL FROM... A SLIGHT BREEZE?
HRMPT! YOU DIE WELL, HUMAN.
BUT DEAD IS DEAD, ISN'T IT?
FAREWELL.
SSSSSFFFFFAAAASSH
ARRGGH!

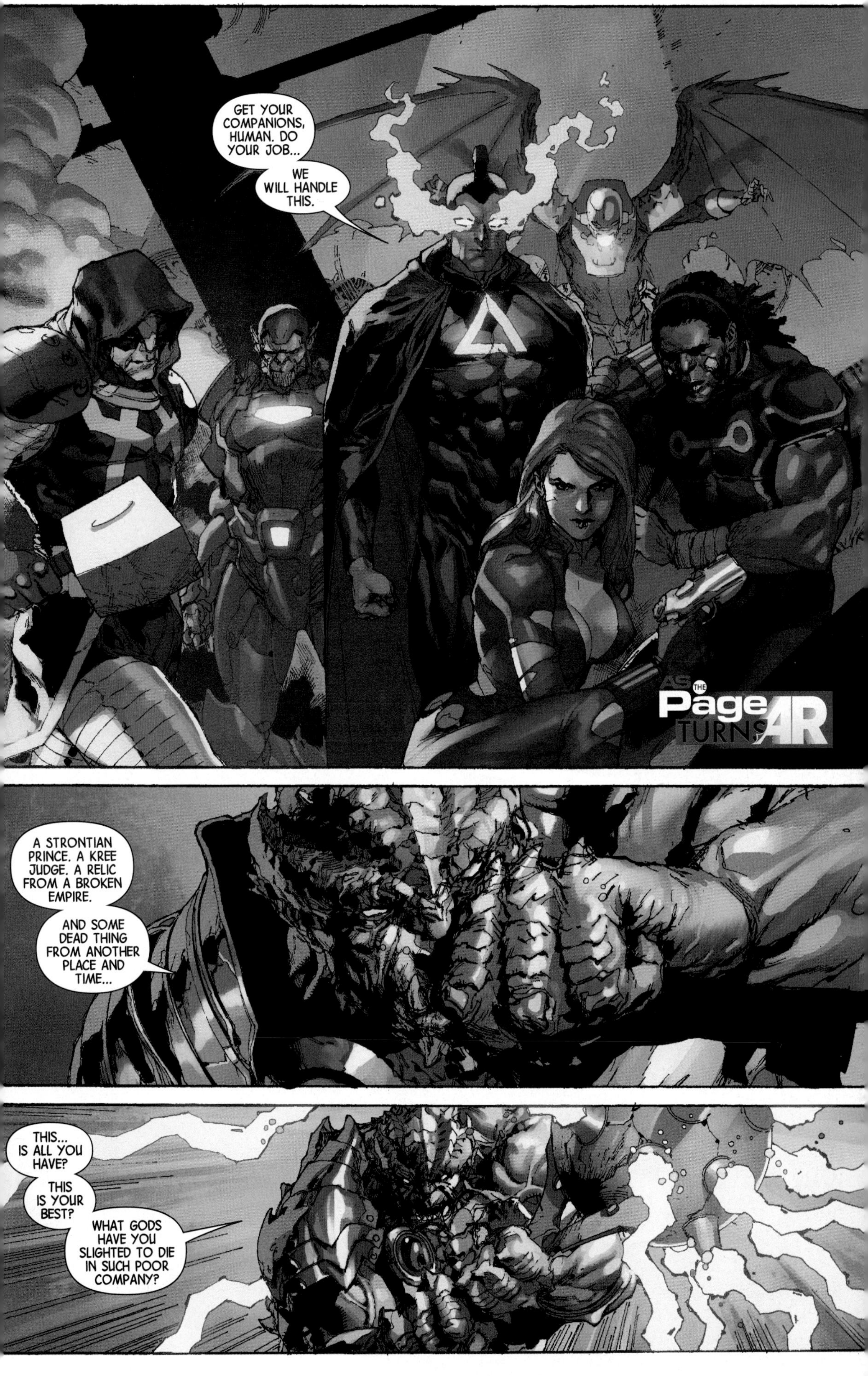

GET YOUR COMPANIONS, HUMAN. DO YOUR JOB...
WE WILL HANDLE THIS.
AS THE Page TURNS AR
A STRONTIAN PRINCE. A KREE JUDGE. A RELIC FROM A BROKEN EMPIRE.
AND SOME DEAD THING FROM ANOTHER PLACE AND TIME...
THIS... IS ALL YOU HAVE?
THIS IS YOUR BEST?
WHAT GODS HAVE YOU SLIGHTED TO DIE IN SUCH POOR COMPANY?

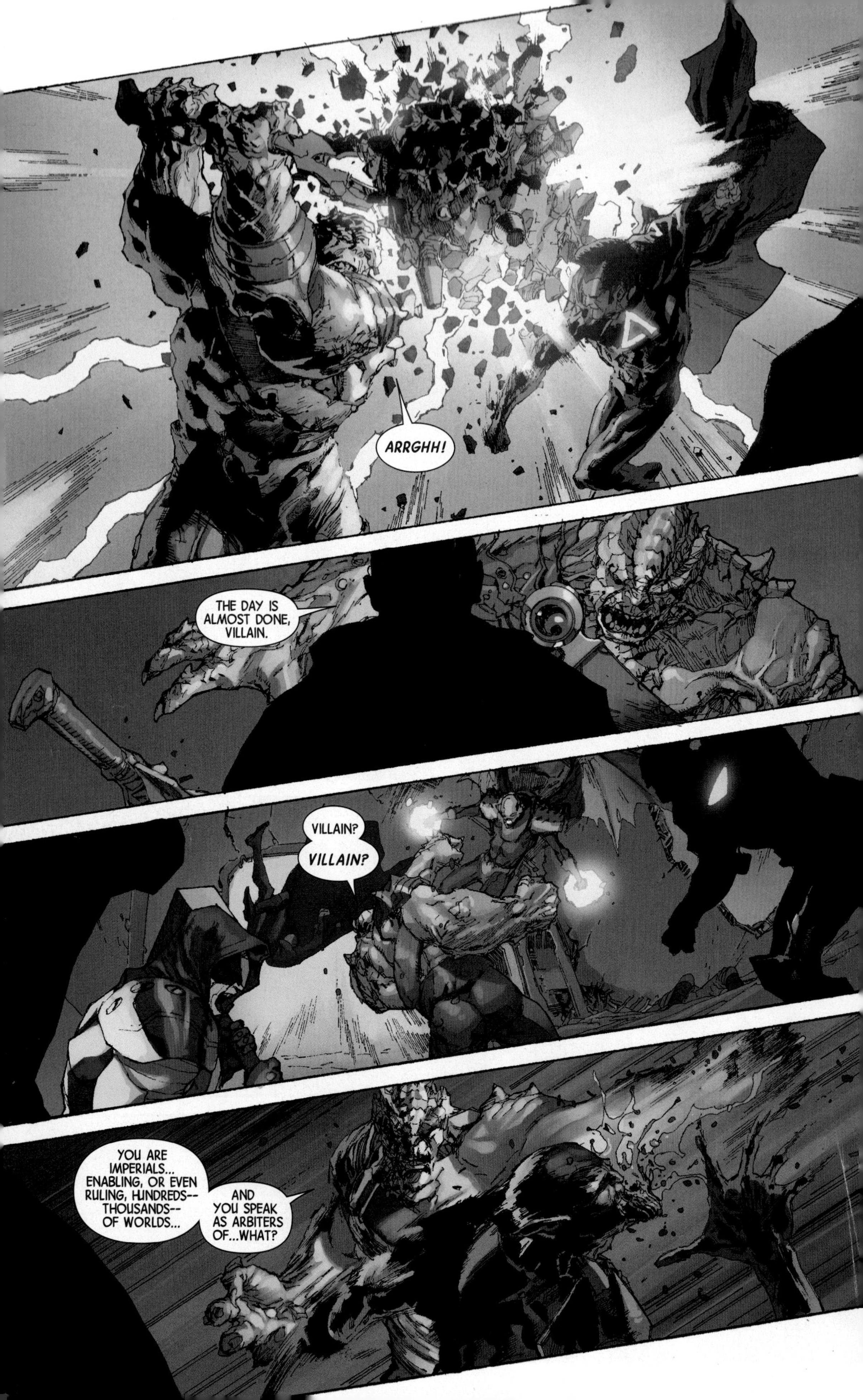
ARRGHH!
THE DAY IS ALMOST DONE, VILLAIN.
VILLAIN?
VILLAIN?
YOU ARE IMPERIALS... ENABLING, OR EVEN RULING, HUNDREDS-- THOUSANDS-- OF WORLDS...
AND YOU SPEAK AS ARBITERS OF...WHAT?

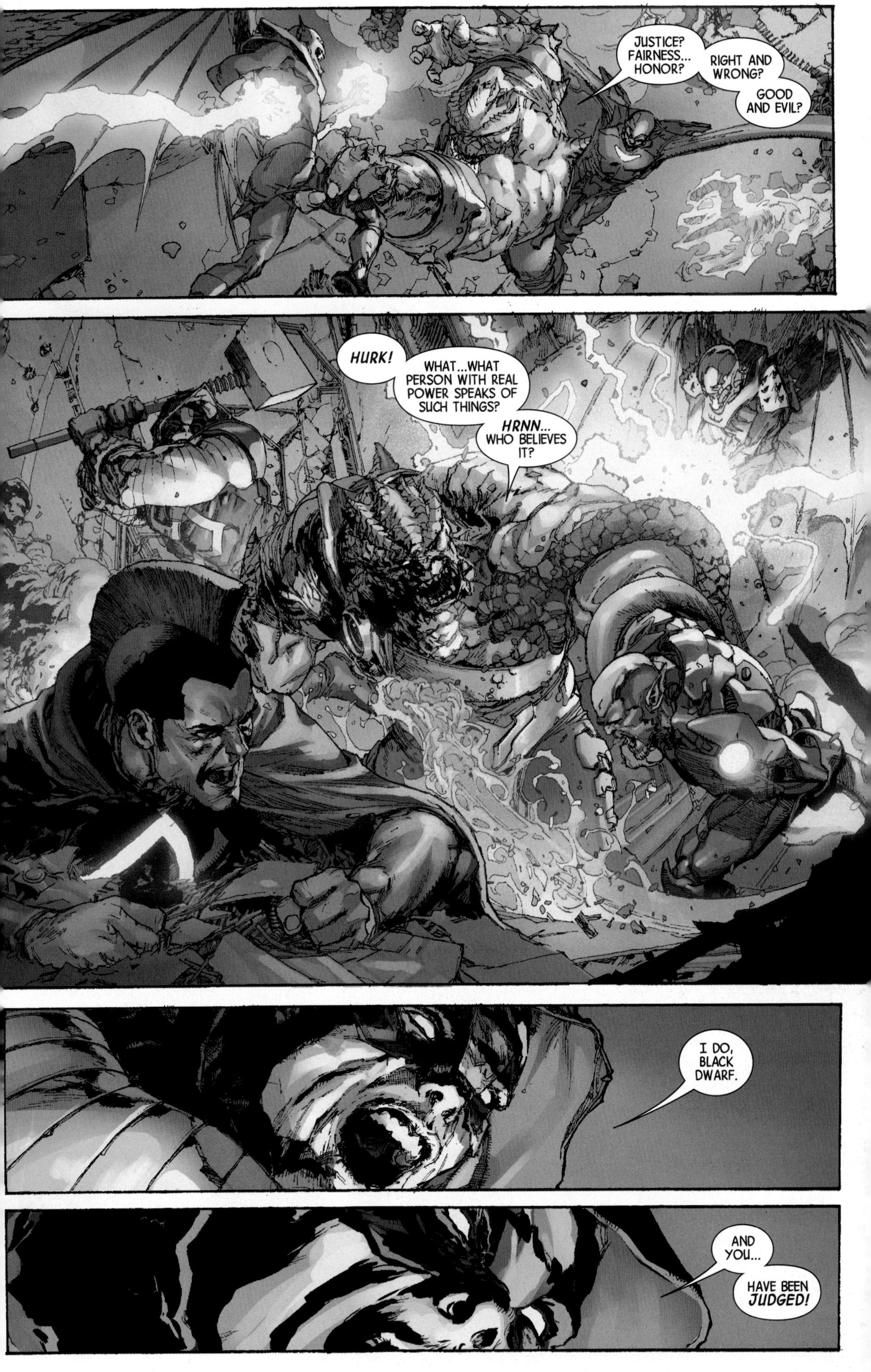
JUSTICE? FAIRNESS... HONOR?
RIGHT AND WRONG?
GOOD AND EVIL?
HURK!
WHAT...WHAT PERSON WITH REAL POWER SPEAKS OF SUCH THINGS?
HRNN... WHO BELIEVES IT?
I DO, BLACK DWARF.
AND YOU...
HAVE BEEN JUDGED!

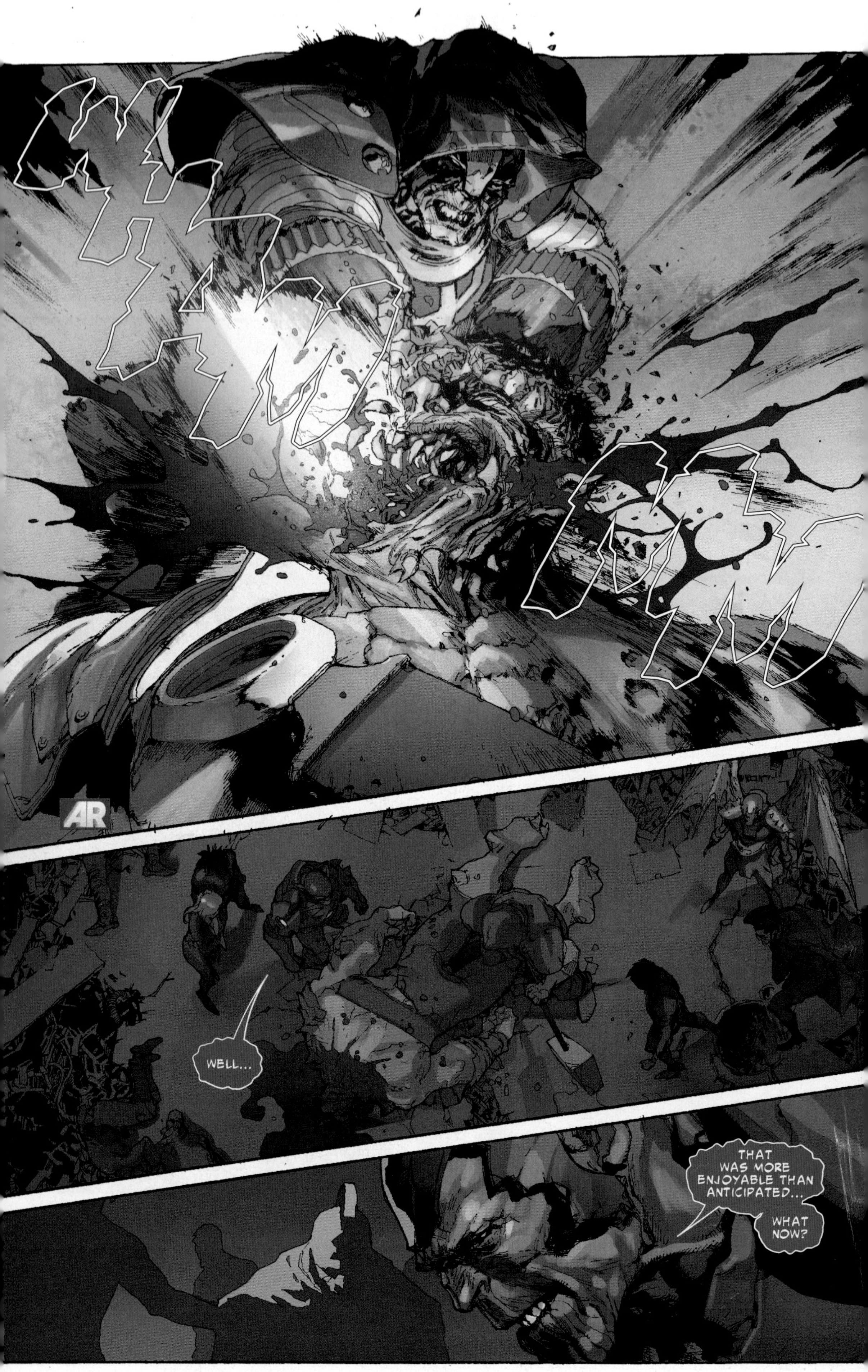
WELL...
THAT WAS MORE ENJOYABLE THAN ANTICIPATED...
WHAT NOW?

WE STILL HAVE THE PIRATE FLEET TO SEND RUNNING...

"SO THAT IS WHAT WE WILL DO...

"WHILE THE AVENGERS FIGHT FOR EARTH...

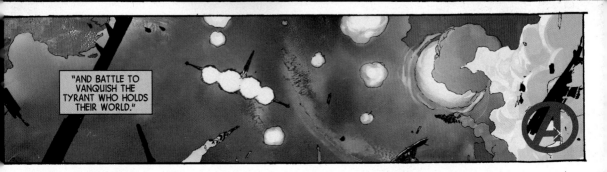

"AND BATTLE TO VANQUISH THE TYRANT WHO HOLDS THEIR WORLD."

#18

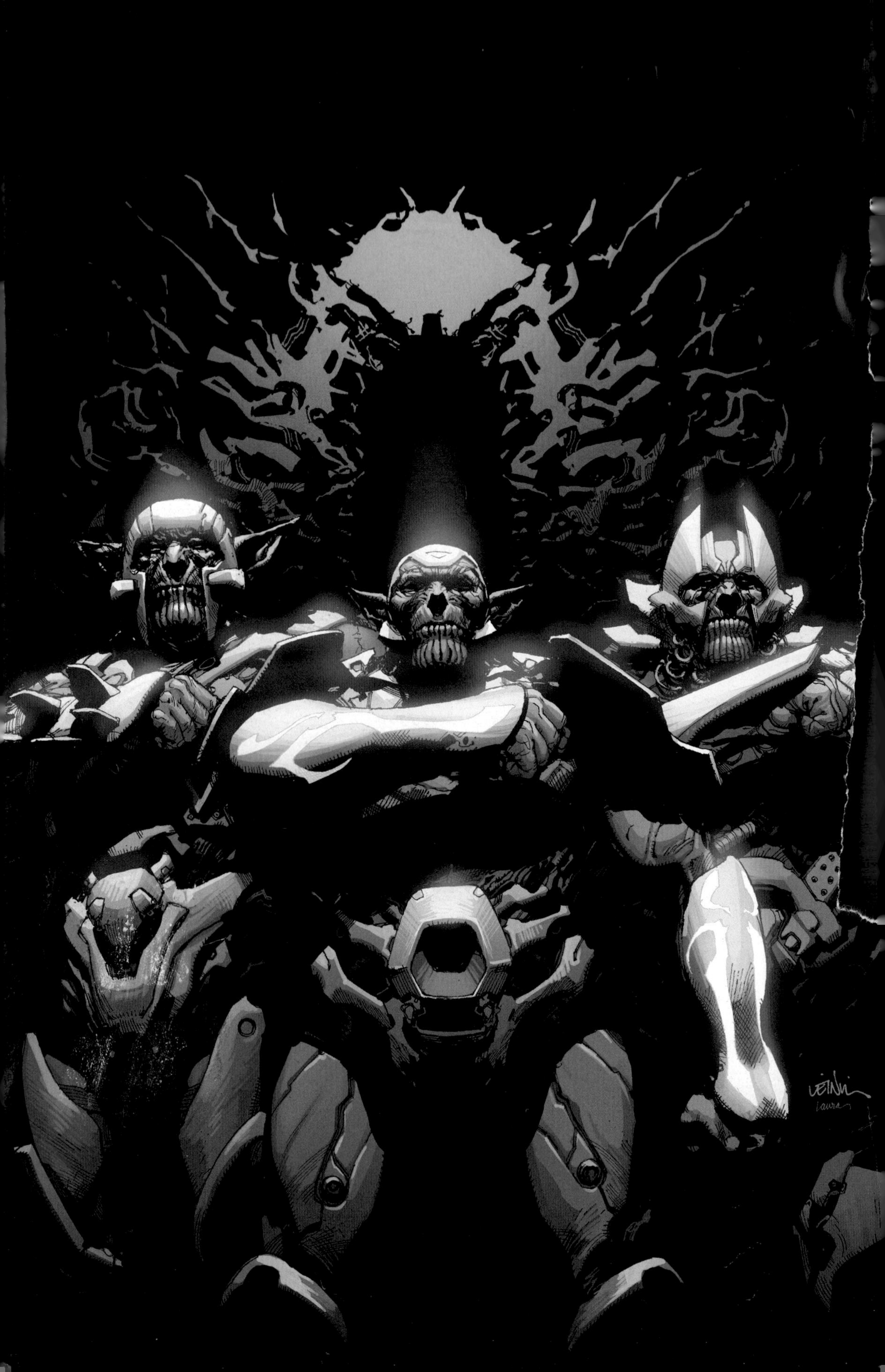

#19

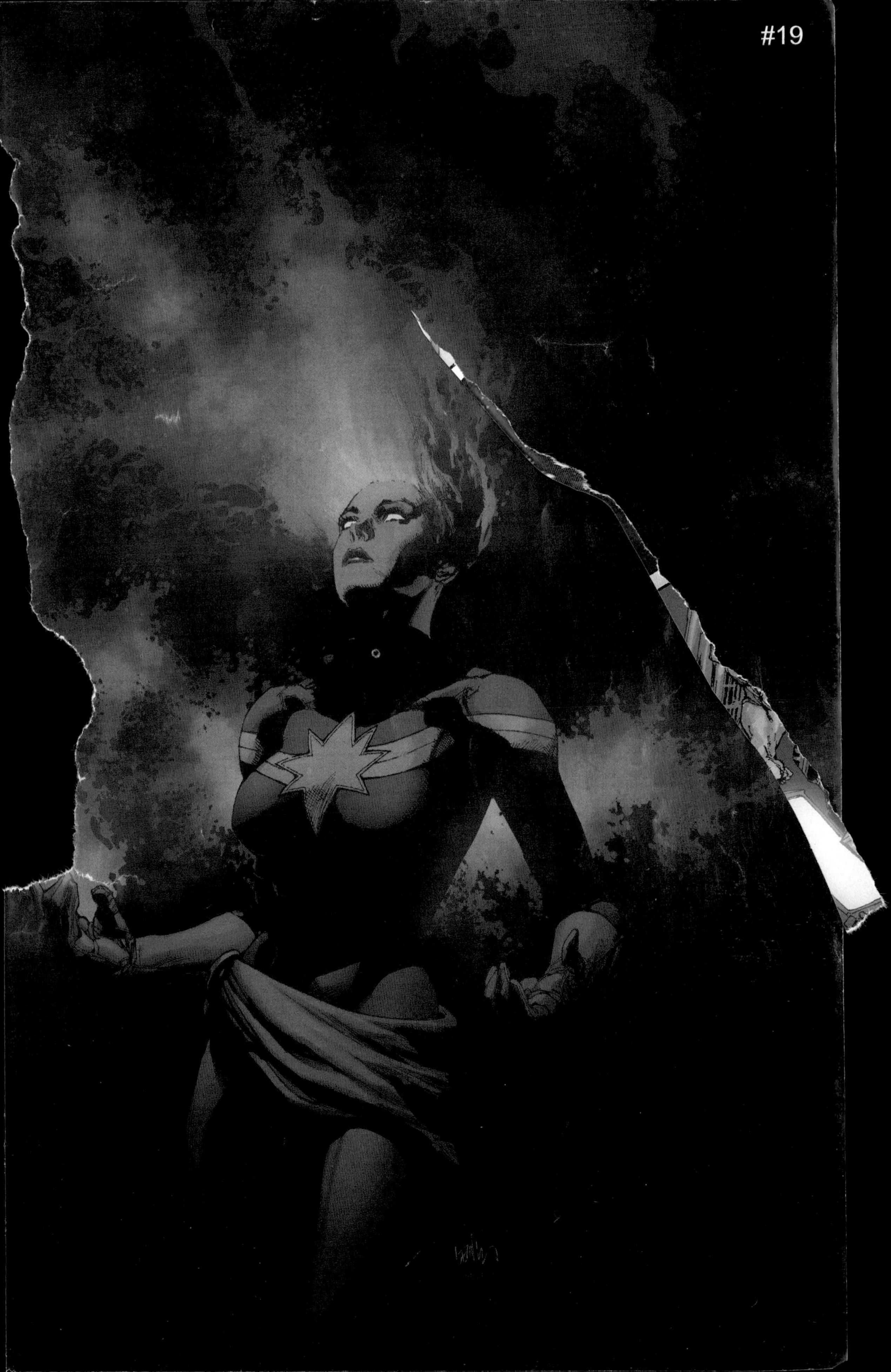

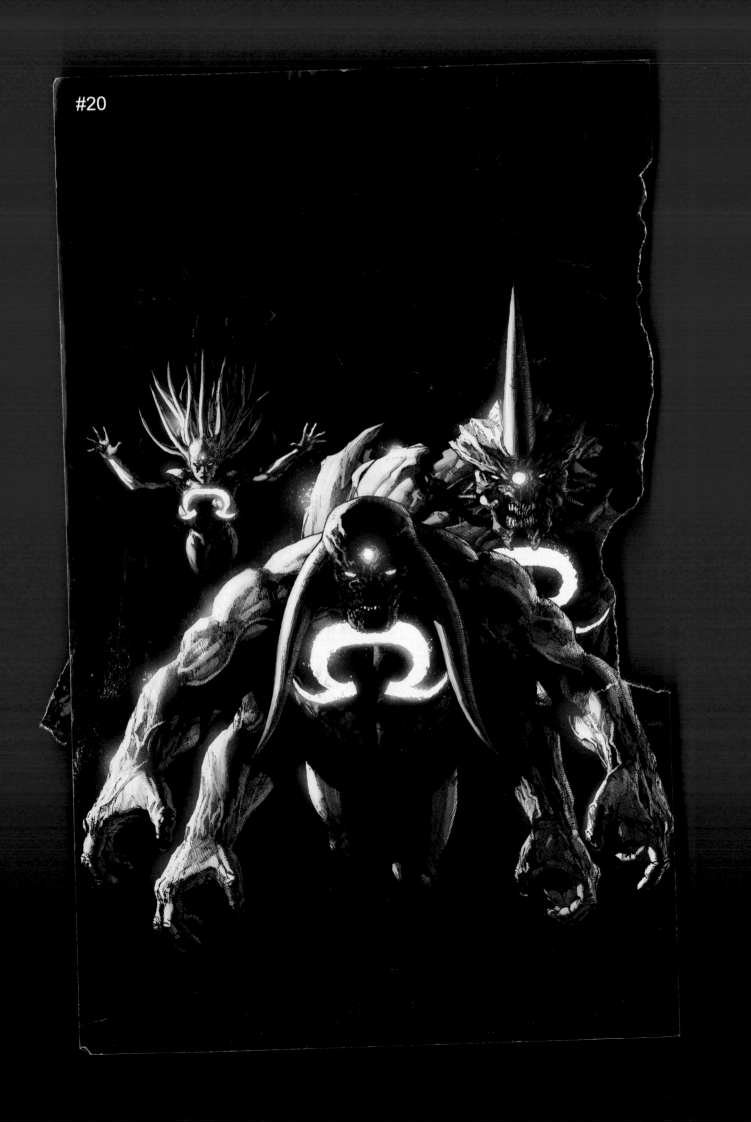

#21

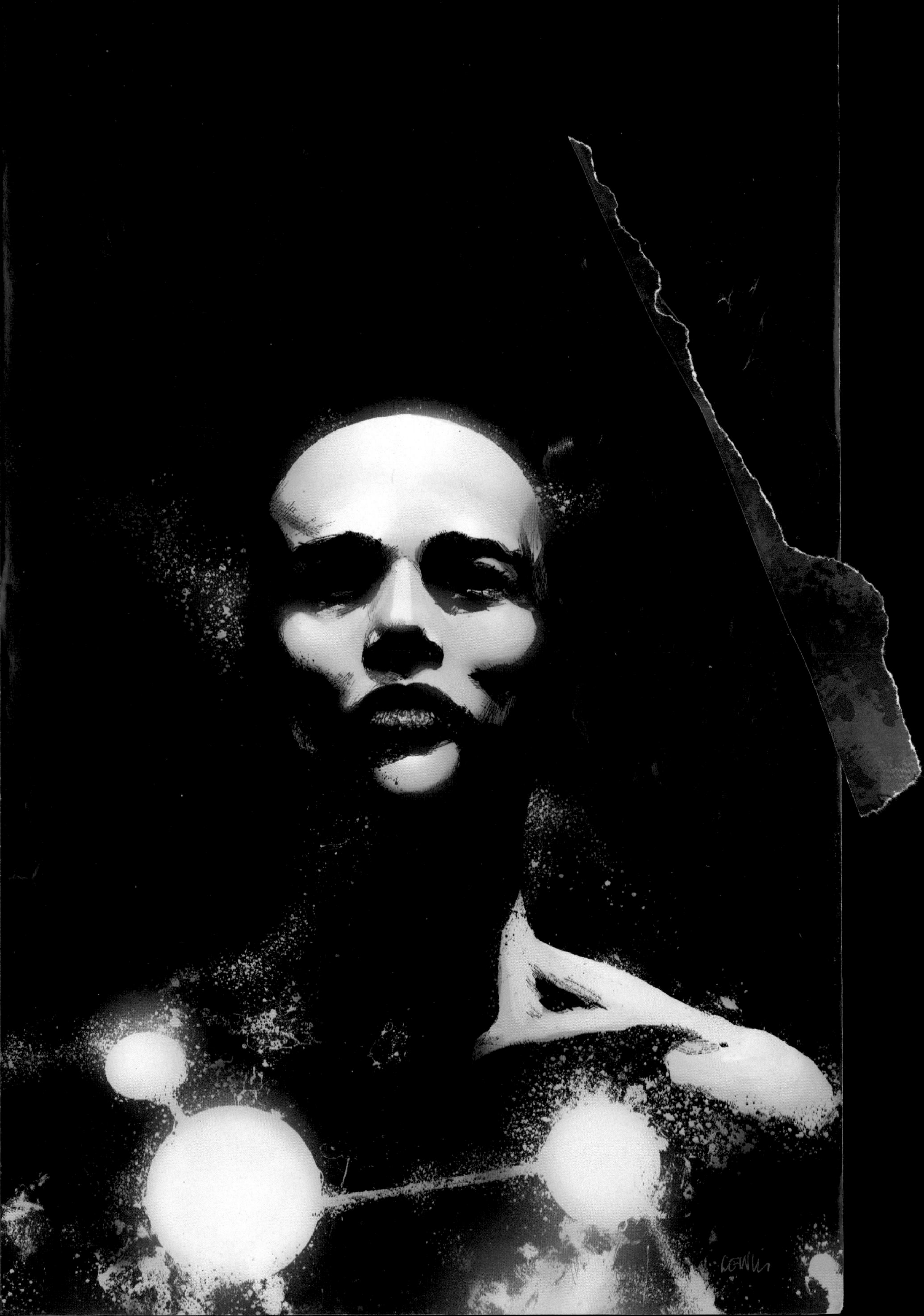

#22

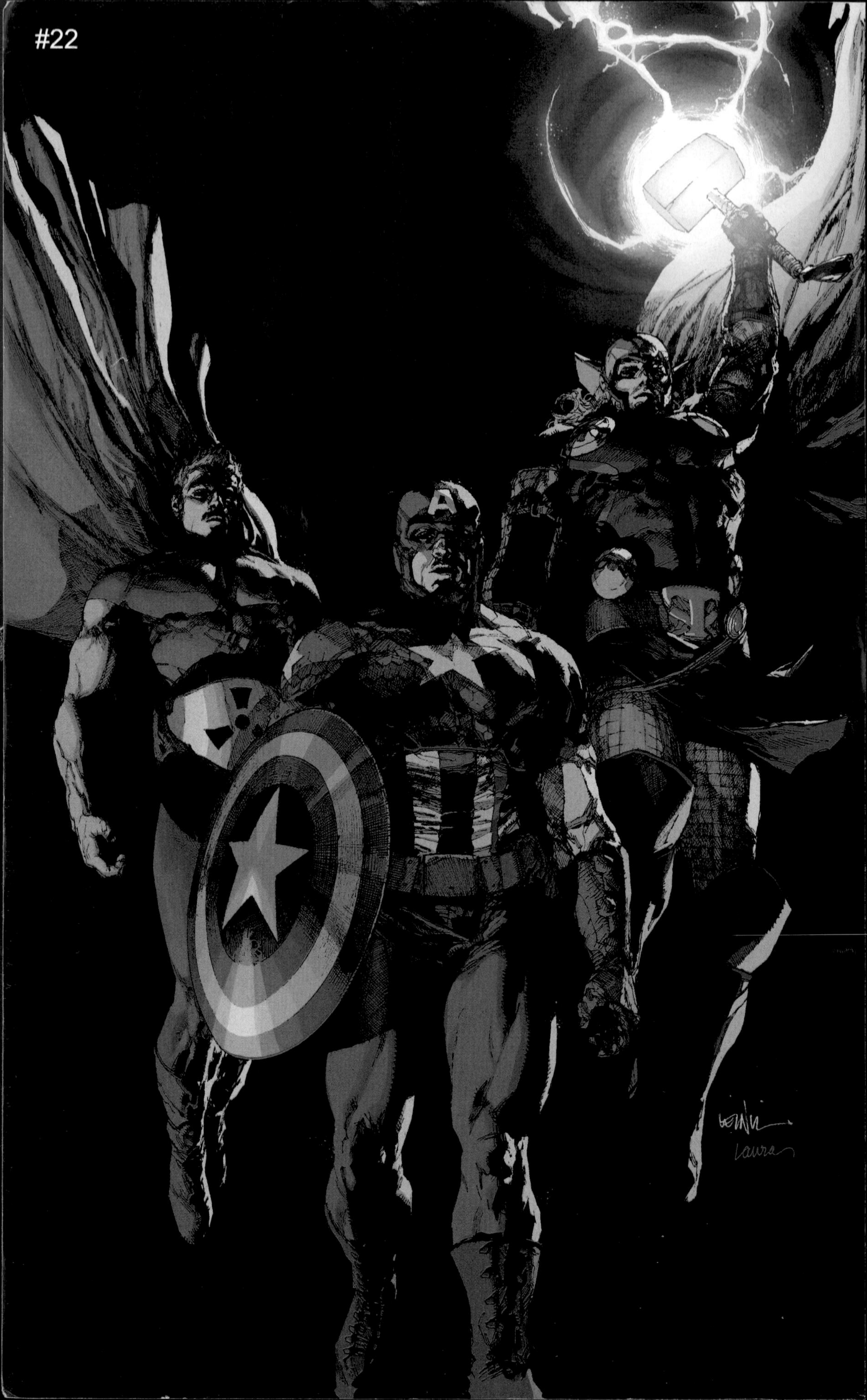

#23

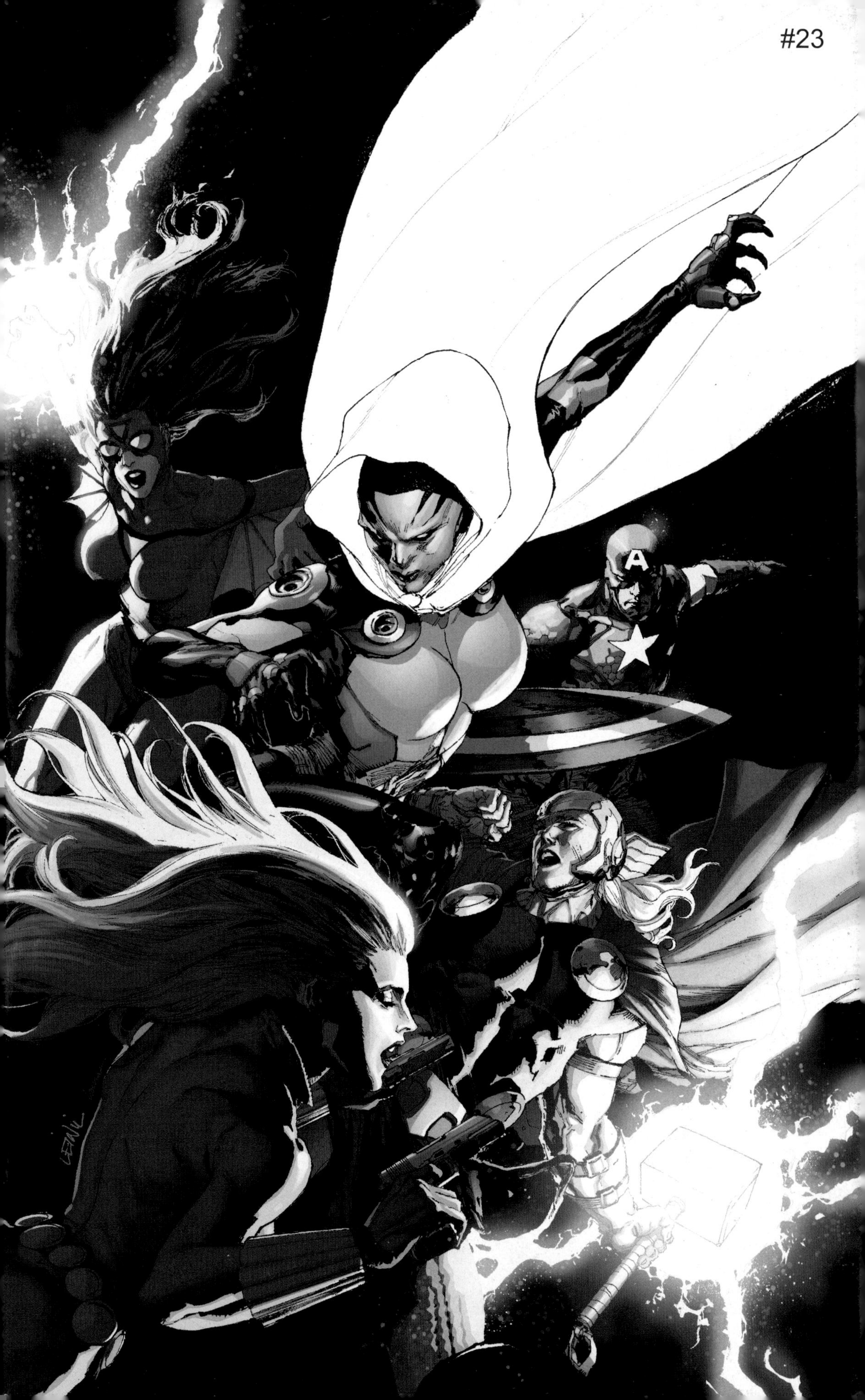

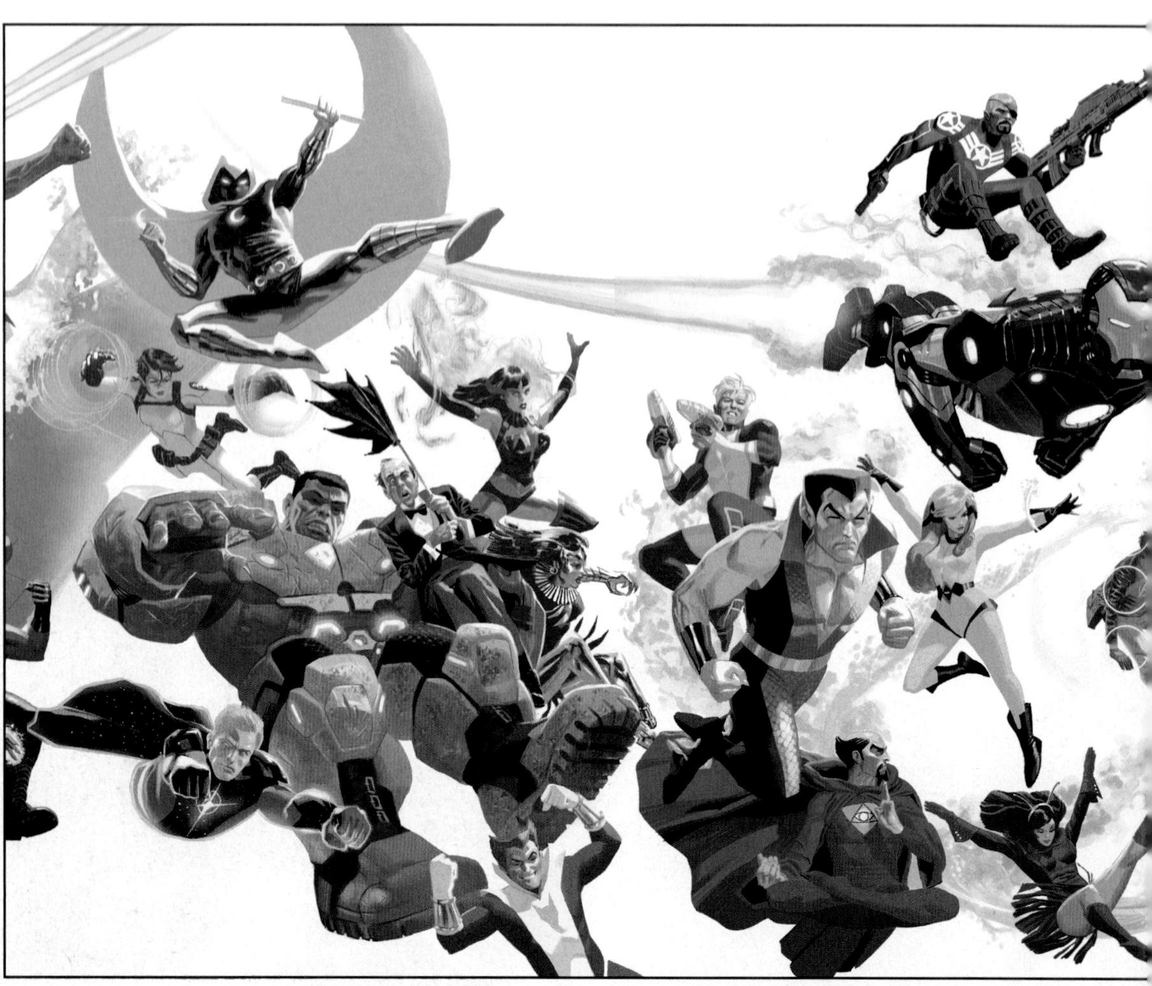

#18, #20 & #22-23 AVENGERS 50TH ANNIVERSARY VARIANTS:
DANIEL ACUÑA

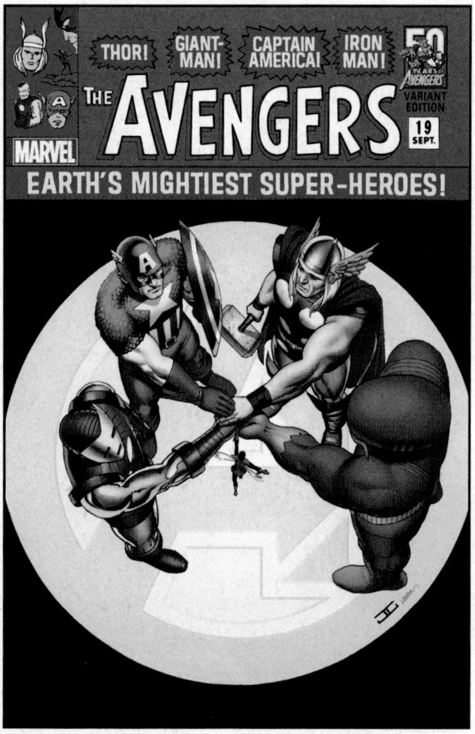
THOR!
GIANT-MAN!
CAPTAIN AMERICA!
IRON MAN!
THE AVENGERS
VARIANT EDITION
19 SEPT.
MARVEL
EARTH'S MIGHTIEST SUPER-HEROES!

#19 AVENGERS 50TH ANNIVERSARY VARIANT:
JOHN CASSADAY & LAURA MARTIN

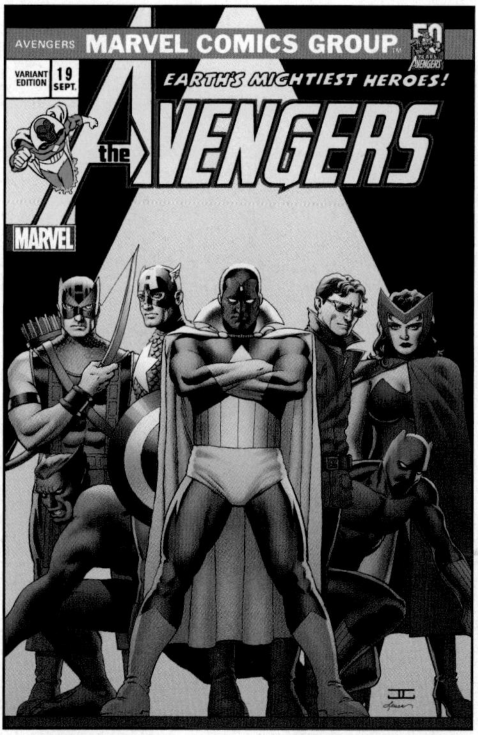
AVENGERS
MARVEL COMICS GROUP
VARIANT EDITION
19 SEPT.
EARTH'S MIGHTIEST HEROES!
the AVENGERS
MARVEL

#19 AVENGERS 50TH ANNIVERSARY VARIANT:
JOHN CASSADAY & LAURA MARTIN

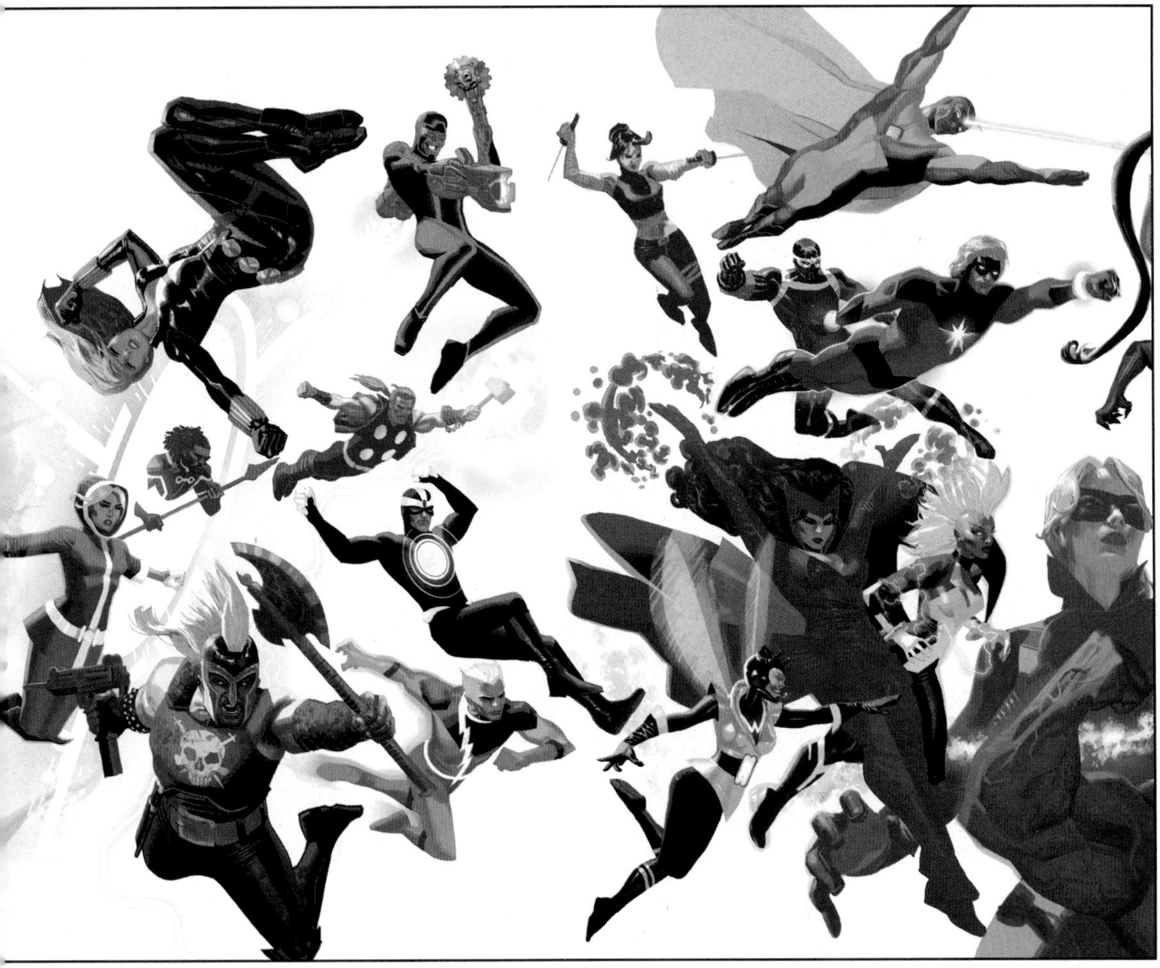

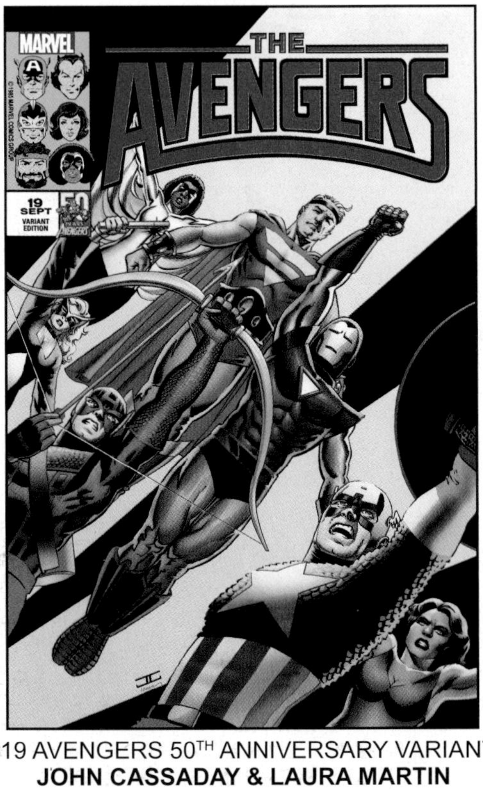
MARVEL
THE
AVENGERS
19
SEPT
VARIANT
EDITION

#19 AVENGERS 50TH ANNIVERSARY VARIANT:
JOHN CASSADAY & LAURA MARTIN

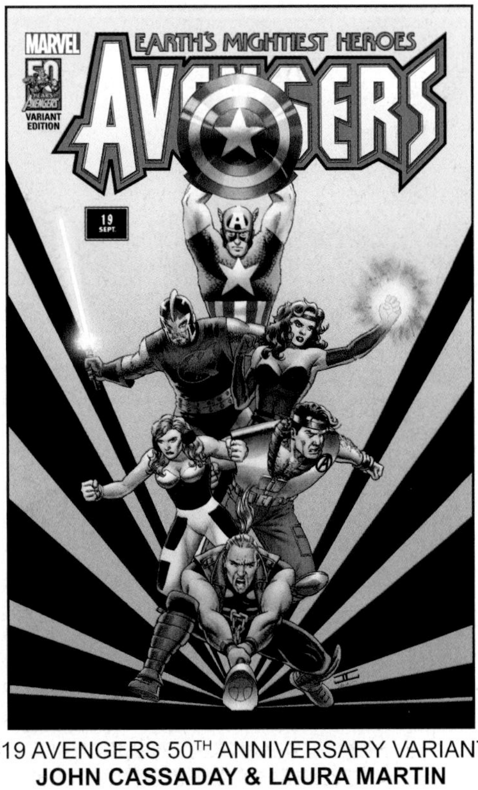
MARVEL
VARIANT
EDITION
EARTH'S MIGHTIEST HEROES
AVENGERS
19
SEPT.

#19 AVENGERS 50TH ANNIVERSARY VARIANT:
JOHN CASSADAY & LAURA MARTIN

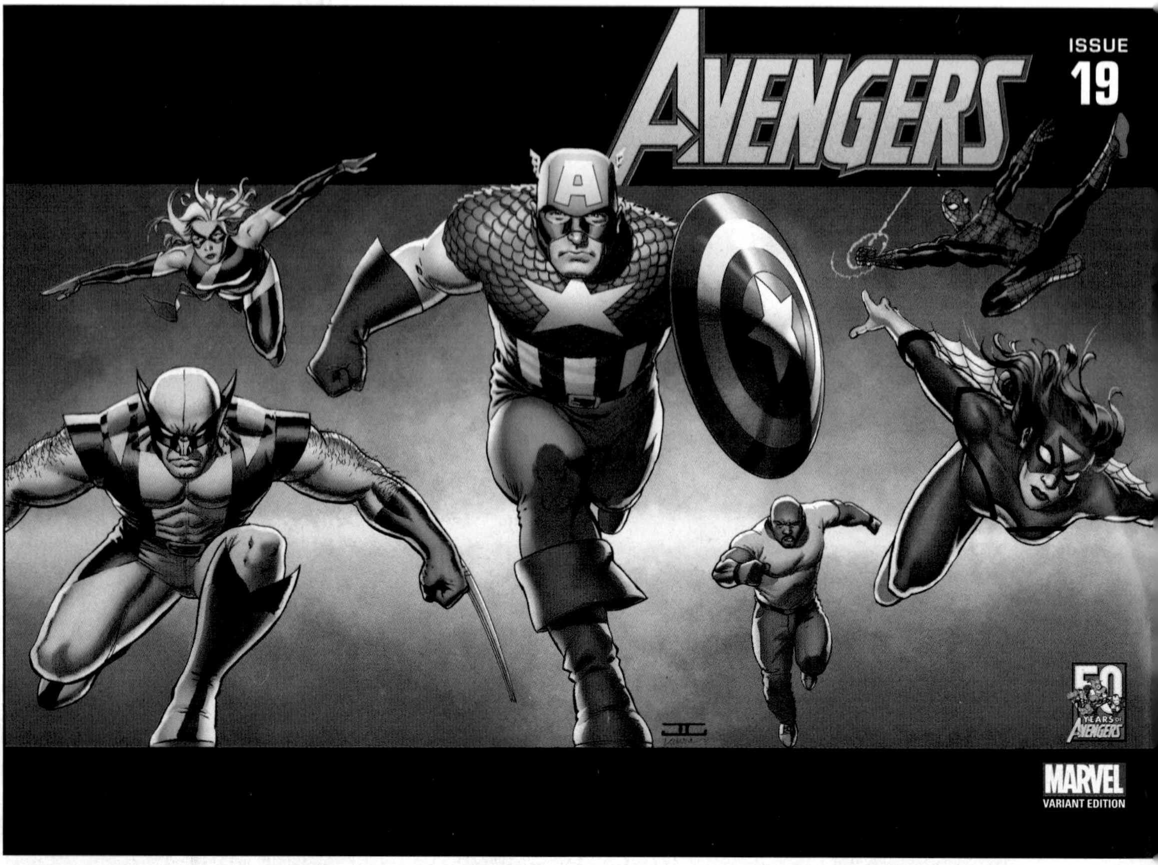
ISSUE
19
AVENGERS
50
YEARS OF
AVENGERS
MARVEL
VARIANT EDITION

#19 AVENGERS 50TH ANNIVERSARY VARIANT:
JOHN CASSADAY & LAURA MARTIN

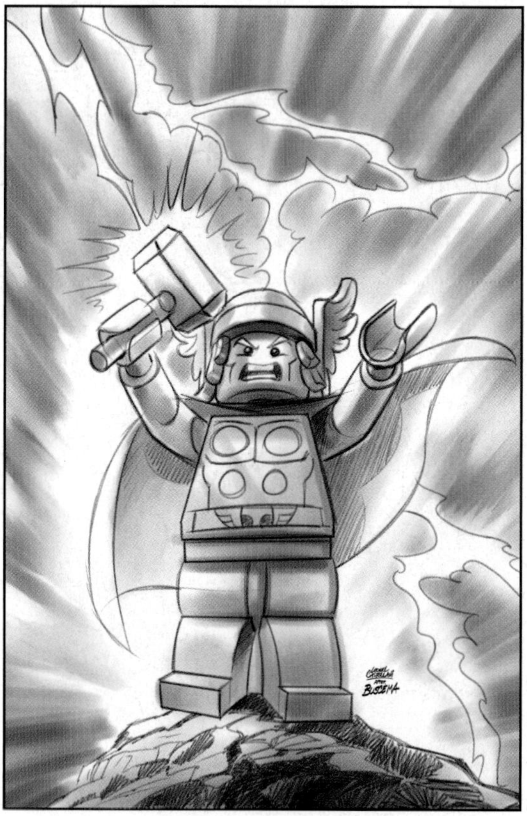

#21 LEGO SKETCH VARIANT:
LEONEL CASTELLANI

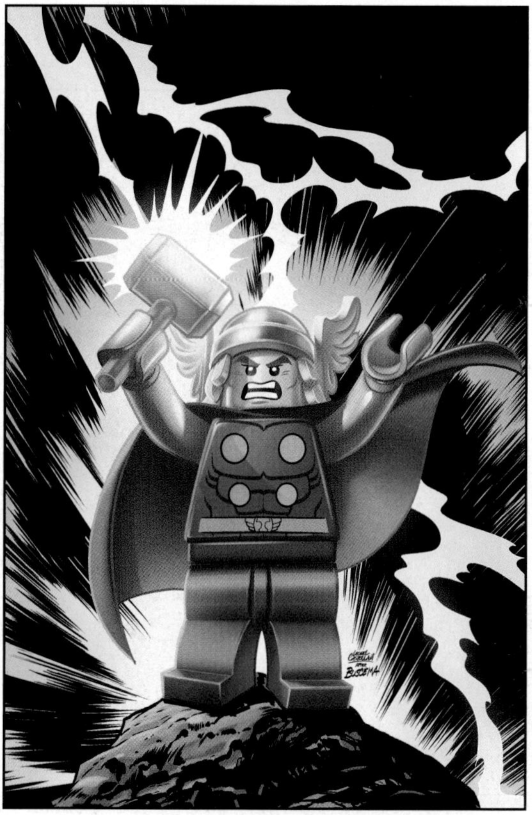

#21 LEGO VARIANT:
LEONEL CASTELLANI

MARVEL AUGMENTED REALITY (AR) ENHANCES AND CHANGES THE WAY YOU EXPERIENCE COMICS!

TO ACCESS THE FREE MARVEL AR CONTENT IN THIS BOOK*:

1. Locate the AR logo within the comic.
2. Go to Marvel.com/AR in your web browser.
3. Search by series title to find the corresponding AR.
4. Enjoy Marvel AR!

*All AR content that appears in this book has been archived and will be available only at Marvel.com/AR – no longer in the Marvel AR App. Content subject to change and availability.

AVENGERS

AR INDEX

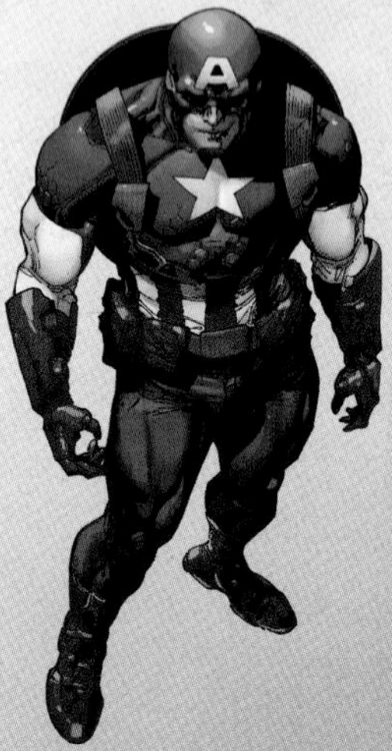

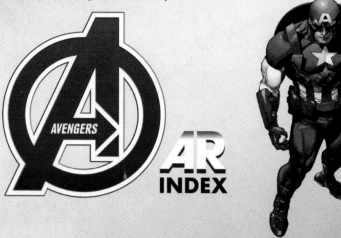